Cost Accounting Fundamentals

Essential Concepts and Examples

Fifth Edition

Steven M. Bragg

For more information about AccountingTools® products, visit our Web site at www.accountingtools.com.

ISBN-13: 978-1-938910-69-2

Printed in the United States of America

Table of Contents

Preface

Cost Accounting Fundamentals describes the key cost accounting concepts that most concern the practicing cost accountant, and illustrates them with numerous examples to improve comprehension. The book is designed for both professional accountants and students, since both can benefit from its detailed descriptions of inventory valuation methods, product pricing techniques, cost analysis methods, and more. *Cost Accounting Fundamentals* addresses five major cost accounting topics, which are:

- Part I – Job Overview. Chapters 1 and 2 describe the nature of cost accounting and the details of the cost accountant job description.
- Part II – Inventory Valuation. Chapters 3 through 9 describe the various methods used to value inventory, including job costing, process costing, standard costing, joint and by-product costing, and accounting for waste products.
- Part III – Product Pricing. Chapters 10 through 12 describe the contribution of cost accounting to product pricing, including a lengthy discussion of how much a product costs for pricing purposes, how target costing works, and the mechanics of transfer pricing.
- Part IV – Cost Analysis Methods. Chapters 13 through 16 address a number of analysis methods, including direct costing, activity-based costing, constraint analysis, and capital budgeting analysis.
- Part V – Other Topics. Chapters 17 through 19 cover several additional topics – how to collect cost-related information, the variability of costs under different circumstances, and the cost of quality.

Cost Accounting Fundamentals is designed to give you a complete grounding in the essentials of cost accounting. As such it may earn a place on your bookshelf as a reference tool for years to come.

Centennial, Colorado
February, 2016

About the Author

Steven Bragg, CPA, has been the chief financial officer or controller of four companies, as well as a consulting manager at Ernst & Young. He received a master's degree in finance from Bentley College, an MBA from Babson College, and a Bachelor's degree in Economics from the University of Maine. He has been a two-time president of the Colorado Mountain Club, and is an avid alpine skier, mountain biker, and certified master diver. Mr. Bragg resides in Centennial, Colorado. He has written the following books and courses:

Accountants' Guidebook	Fair Value Accounting
Accounting Changes and Error Corrections	Financial Analysis
Accounting Controls Guidebook	Financial Forecasting and Modeling
Accounting for Casinos and Gaming	Fixed Asset Accounting
Accounting for Derivatives and Hedges	Foreign Currency Accounting
Accounting for Earnings per Share	GAAP Guidebook
Accounting for Inventory	Hospitality Accounting
Accounting for Investments	Human Resources Guidebook
Accounting for Managers	IFRS Guidebook
Accounting for Stock-Based Compensation	Interpretation of Financial Statements
Accounting Procedures Guidebook	Inventory Management
Bookkeeping Guidebook	Investor Relations Guidebook
Budgeting	Lean Accounting Guidebook
Business Combinations and Consolidations	Mergers & Acquisitions
Business Insurance Fundamentals	New Controller Guidebook
Business Ratios	Nonprofit Accounting
Business Valuation	Payables Management
Capital Budgeting	Payroll Management
CFO Guidebook	Project Accounting
Closing the Books	Public Company Accounting
Coaching and Mentoring	Purchasing Guidebook
Constraint Management	Real Estate Accounting
Corporate Cash Management	Recruiting and Hiring
Corporate Finance	Revenue Recognition
Cost Accounting Fundamentals	The Soft Close
Cost Management Guidebook	The Statement of Cash Flows
Credit & Collection Guidebook	The Year-End Close
Developing and Managing Teams	Treasurer's Guidebook
Enterprise Risk Management	Working Capital Management

On-Line Resources by Steven Bragg

Steven maintains the accountingtools.com web site, which contains continuing professional education courses, the Accounting Best Practices podcast, and hundreds of articles on accounting subjects.

Cost Accounting Fundamentals is also available as a continuing professional education (CPE) course. You can purchase the course (and many other courses) and take an on-line exam at:

www.accountingtools.com/cpe

Chapter 1
Overview of Cost Accounting

Introduction

At its simplest, cost accounting is about calculating the cost of a product or service. However, this viewpoint does a disservice to the cost accountant, who can use a broad array of methods to provide a great deal of additional information to management. In many respects, cost accounting is the only truly value-added activity in the accounting department, because it yields many insights that management can use to pursue the most profitable products, streamline expensive operations, and reallocate resources.

This chapter focuses on the primary cost accounting activities, and how they can improve a company's tactical direction and profitability.

Financial Reporting

The cost accountant has an ongoing responsibility to calculate the cost of ending inventory. This calculation has a major impact on a company's gross margin (which is revenues less the cost of goods sold), and so draws the attention of auditors, who comb through the cost accountant's calculations to verify their accuracy. A small error in valuing the ending inventory can translate into a large change in a company's financial results, so this is likely the highest-profile activity in which a cost accountant engages.

Valuing inventory is not a simple calculation. It is the culmination of a complicated series of steps that involve having a high level of inventory record accuracy (which may require counting the inventory), correctly using an inventory layering method (see the Inventory Valuation chapter), accounting for any obsolete inventory, and adjusting inventory costs as necessary. There are a vast number of transactions that impact inventory valuation, so the cost accountant will likely spend a large amount of time investigating problems and updating recordation systems to improve the quality of information.

Early in a cost accountant's career, inventory valuation for financial reporting purposes is likely to be the central focus of his activities. Once he gains a working knowledge of how to deal with the intricacies of inventory valuation, he can move on to the other topics addressed in the remainder of this chapter.

Management Reporting

The cost accountant's financial reporting responsibilities do not end with valuing inventory for a company's financial statements. There are also an unending series of requests from management to provide information to them on many topics. Typical report requests are:

- *Analysis of capital expenditure proposals.* Department managers who want to spend large amounts on fixed assets usually provide documentation to management that supports their arguments. The cost accountant should review these proposals and comment on such factors as whether forecasts are reasonable, whether purchases will improve the company's bottleneck operation, and whether all costs likely to be incurred are actually included in the documentation. This analysis may not extend to making an approval recommendation, but the cost accountant should provide enough information to clarify the issue for management.

- *Cost center performance.* There are many cost centers in a company (such as the accounting department!), for which the cost accountant should report on the trend of expenses incurred, as well as their related output, so that management can view their levels of efficiency. This information may be used to outsource selected cost centers.

- *Cost trends for key commodities.* The profitability of some companies is heavily dependent upon the cost of the commodities that they incorporate into their products, especially if it is difficult to pass along cost increases to customers. The cost accountant should monitor these cost changes closely.

- *Customer performance.* It is easy to report on revenues by customer, but much more difficult (and insightful) to report on profits by customer. It is also useful to report on such additional factors as customer backlog, customer returns, discounts given, and outstanding accounts receivable.

- *Decision follow up.* This is a general category of report that applies to many types of analysis. Whenever management makes a decision, the cost accountant may be called upon to return to the decision at some point in the future to investigate whether the assumptions used to make the decision were accurate, and what circumstances caused changes in the original forecasts.

- *Metrics.* Management may want a trend-line report of those metrics that relate most closely to a company's critical success factors. It is not sufficient to simply present the information – the cost accountant should also investigate and provide explanations of why metrics have changed over time. Examples of commonly-used metrics are the return on assets, inventory turnover, and accounts receivable turnover.

- *Profitability by department.* These analyses tend to include a large amount of detail on all expense line items, and may include non-financial metrics, such as revenue or cost per employee, or transaction error rates pertaining to a specific department.

- *Profitability by job or project.* These reports generally do not include overhead costs, unless they can be reliably traced to specific jobs or projects. The cost accountant needs to have a good knowledge of what costs are truly relevant to determine what costs to include in these reports. Many jobs and projects have their own budgets, so these reports may include variances from their budgets, and why the variances occurred.

- *Profitability by product.* Reporting at the product level can be difficult, because such analyses should not include an overhead allocation in many instances, especially when management is deciding whether to drop a product. Instead, this analysis tends to focus on only those costs that vary directly with the presence or absence of a specific product.
- *Profitability by product line.* This is one of the best analyses, because it is usually possible to include a significant amount of overhead allocation; overhead costs are frequently incurred at the product line level, so overhead can be traced to a specific product line.

The advantage of internal reporting is that the cost accountant is not constrained by the dictates of generally accepted accounting principles or international financial reporting standards to present information in a certain format. Instead, it is quite allowable to add to or strip away information in accordance with the specific situation for which the cost accountant is creating a report. In many cases, it may be useful to use direct costing (see the Direct Costing chapter), which only includes information that will change as the result of a decision. Other possible reporting methods include job costing, process costing, standard costing, activity-based costing, and so on – in short, it is possible to select from a full palette of cost analysis methodologies.

In particular, the cost accountant will rarely have a need to use full absorption costing in a management report, since the inclusion of overhead costs that is required under full absorption costing is not only irrelevant to many situations, but may present misleading information. Absorption costing is a methodology under which all fixed and variable manufacturing costs are assigned to products, while all non-manufacturing costs are charged to expense in the current period.

EXAMPLE

Kelvin Corporation's president asks the cost accountant to create an analysis of whether the company should drop its oldest product line, which is a series of mercury-based glass thermometers that are primarily sold into the elementary school market for chemistry classes for an average price of $5.25 each. The cost accountant investigates and finds the following costs on a per-unit basis:

Cost Item	Total Cost	Relevant Cost
Direct materials	$2.25	$2.25
Direct labor	0.75	0.75
Variable overhead	1.00	1.00
Fixed overhead	1.50	--
Total	$5.50	$4.00

The company intends to shut down the entire production line for these glass thermometers, so the variable overhead element of the cost will be eliminated if the product line is stopped. However, the fixed overhead cost is related to the cost of the entire facility in which the company operates, and these costs will not go away if the company drops the product line. Thus, though the total cost of a thermometer is $5.50, the cost relevant to this product elimination decision is $4.00. The $4.00 cost is less than the price being charged to customers, so the company will fare better if it retains the product line and uses its gross margins to help pay for fixed overhead.

Note: A relevant cost is a cost that relates to a specific management decision, and which will change in the future as a result of that decision.

A key issue to remember when reviewing the preceding array of possible internal reports is that the cost accountant should have a strong ability to present information clearly. Too frequently, an otherwise perfectly competent cost accountant presents a dense spreadsheet to management, and points out that the answer to their query is buried deep in the spreadsheet. It takes considerable experience to create management reports that display key information prominently and persuasively.

Problem Resolution

If a company uses just-in-time manufacturing systems, management needs to know about production and inventory issues as soon as they occur, not at the end of the month (which is when most of the reports listed in the last section are released). Accordingly, the cost accountant may become deeply involved on the production floor and warehouse in tracking down the causes of problems, reporting them to management, and actively participating in their resolution.

This type of problem solving may not involve any written report at all – perhaps just a verbal discussion or a brief note. This is the type of cost accounting work that production managers deeply appreciate, and which is the hallmark of a fully-involved cost accountant.

Price Setting

The marketing department is responsible for setting prices, which should be based on supply and demand, rather than the cost of a product. Nonetheless, the cost accountant is closely involved in price setting for four reasons:

- *Incremental pricing.* There may be situations where the company receives an offer from a customer for a one-time deal to provide products at a reduced price. The cost accountant provides input into whether or not this will be a good deal for the company.
- *Cost-based pricing.* Many companies still base their prices on costs incurred, with a profit margin added. In these situations, the cost accountant likely controls a substantial recordkeeping system that accumulates direct costs and allocates overhead costs in detail.

- *Government contracts.* Many governments order items on a cost-plus basis, where the supplier is reimbursed for all costs incurred, plus a reasonable profit. This situation arises when the government orders completely unique items that suppliers are uncomfortable setting a price for (such as in military equipment contracting). In this situation, the cost accountant must learn the intricate government costing rules, create a system that can verifiably accumulate the correct costs, and properly allocate approved overhead costs. A government auditor may reject certain costs, in which case the cost accountant must also prepare a justification for why the company is applying for cost reimbursement. Government billing is a significant sub-discipline that can swallow up all of a cost accountant's time.
- *Lowest possible price.* The marketing manager does not want to inadvertently set a price below the company's cost to produce it, so the cost accountant supplies cost information pertinent to this decision.

Providing cost information for pricing decisions is a significant topic that is dealt with in much greater detail in the "Product Pricing: What Does This Cost?" chapter.

Cost Investigation

Thus far, we have focused on reports and analyses that other parties have asked the cost accountant to complete. The cost accountant also has an ongoing obligation to investigate costs throughout the company, to decide if those costs are reasonable, and to report back to management when he sees an opportunity to reduce costs. Here are some tools to use in the cost investigation role:

- *5S analysis.* Review the efficiency of the workplace. The name of this analysis is derived from Sorting through all items in the workplace to dispose of unneeded items, Straightening furniture and equipment to improve the process flow, Scrubbing the area, Systematizing the operation to ensure ongoing cleaning activities, and Standardizing the 5S system so that it is used in all company operations.
- *Fixed cost analysis.* Examine the option of expending more on various fixed costs in order to spend less on variable costs (such as when funds are invested in production line automation). In many cases, it makes more sense to avoid the high fixed cost option, which would otherwise increase the company's breakeven point and thereby make it more difficult to earn a profit if sales decline.
- *Parts consolidation.* Work with the engineering staff to reduce the variety of parts used in products. By designing the same components into multiple products, a company can achieve higher component purchasing volumes, which leads to higher volume discounts.
- *Spend analysis.* Work with the purchasing staff to summarize purchasing information by supplier and by commodity, and use the information to concentrate purchases with a small number of suppliers to achieve volume purchasing discounts.

- *Spend compliance.* Track the company's ability to purchase from just those suppliers with whom the company has engaged in volume discount arrangements, and issue reminders to anyone deviating from the established purchasing plan. Also, compare the contractual prices that suppliers have committed to charge the company to their actual billings, and apply for pricing reductions where necessary.
- *Waste analysis.* Identify various types of waste throughout the organization for elimination. This can include non-value-added activities, errors and defects that must be researched and repaired, any type of inventory, excess employee motion, the production of excessive quantities, the transport of materials over excessive distances, and excessive employee wait times.
- *Workforce cost analysis.* Determine which costs are directly traceable to individual employees, such as their wages, payroll taxes, benefits, stock grants, and so forth, and have this information available when management needs to conduct a workforce reduction. This may involve a further analysis of what services will be eliminated or reduced as a result of the reduction. It may also be necessary to review alternatives to a workforce reduction, such as delaying new hires, delaying pay raises, cutting pay, reducing the work week, and reducing staff through attrition.

The number of tools noted above makes it clear that the cost accountant works in a "target rich environment" that is a massive source of cost reduction opportunities. Cost reduction alone can easily be a full-time job, even in a smaller company. See the author's *Cost Management* book for more information.

The tools noted here can be used anywhere; it is perfectly acceptable to investigate costs in all departments, both in the production and administrative sides of a business.

Budget Formulation

The cost accountant is probably not responsible for creating the annual corporate budget, but he is certainly involved in supplying a large amount of the information used in the budget. The following information may be supplied or at least reviewed by the cost accountant:

- *Production budget.* Supply estimated materials, labor, and overhead costs. Also, comment on the validity of budgeted overtime, labor utilization, machine utilization, and efficiency.
- *Capacity planning.* If there is a capacity planning page in the budget, comment on whether the company has the capacity to achieve its budgeted goals.
- *Department budgets.* It may be necessary to derive estimated costs for any department, or to at least comment on the budgets proposed by department managers.

The cost accountant's level of involvement in the budgeting process is substantial, and is based on his knowledge of the inner workings of the company – the work capacity of each department, where costs are incurred, and when additional step costs may be required. A step cost is a fixed cost that does not change within a specific range of utilization levels. Once utilization shifts outside of that range, additional costs must be incurred (for increased utilization levels) or can be eliminated (for decreased utilization levels).

Constraint Analysis

The true level of profitability of the typical organization is driven by its bottleneck operation, which is also known as its constrained resource. The cost accountant should know exactly where this constrained resource is located, and have an excellent knowledge of how that resource can be maximized, such as through the positioning of an inventory buffer in front of it to ensure the smooth inflow of materials, using excess staffing on the equipment, or implementing a quick changeover study to create faster setups. This crucial topic is addressed further in the Constraint Analysis chapter.

Cost Accumulation Systems

An immensely important item that tends to be ignored is the type of system that a company uses to accumulate costs. This system is grounded on the types of analyses that are needed to properly steer a company into profitability.

EXAMPLE

Kelvin Corporation sells 50% of its electronic thermometers to a weather-oriented website that demands discount pricing, drop shipping services, free delivery to customers, and promotional discounts. It also pays late, at inconsistent intervals. Since this customer comprises such a large part of Kelvin's business, it is critical to determine the true cost of sales to it. Accordingly, Kelvin's cost accountant creates a cost accumulation system that tracks customer-specific costs for discounts, drop shipping, and freight. Since late payments vary, he elects to manually calculate the interest cost of these payments, and add it to the results of the cost accumulation system.

It is particularly important to have a robust cost accumulation system if a company does business with government entities, since they may require detailed cost information if they are paying under cost-plus arrangements.

Another cost accumulation issue is how to properly structure overhead allocation systems. Allocation of overhead is the process of assigning overhead costs to products or services based on some relevant measure of activity. Though overhead allocation is not relevant in many decision-making situations (see the Direct Costing chapter), it is still important in cost-plus reimbursement contracts and for financial reporting to have a justifiable reason for allocating overhead to a product or service.

Accordingly, the cost accountant needs to periodically verify which costs are defined as overhead, how they are being accumulated for allocation, and the basis upon which those allocations are calculated.

Summary

Much of the discussion in this chapter makes the cost accountant look like a glorified financial analyst who also happens to have a deep grounding in cost accounting. That impression is largely correct – the cost accountant is indeed the nearest thing to a financial analyst in many companies, since a multitude of analyses require a deep knowledge of cost data and how to manipulate it. The cost accountant then converts his findings into a report, along with an action recommendation.

Cost accounting is a considerably more interesting area than financial accounting. The cost accountant is involved in a broad range of daily decisions that impact the ongoing financial health of a corporation, whereas those accountants dealing with financial accounting are primarily concerned with producing financial statements in accordance with the rigid dictates of either generally accepted accounting principles or international financial reporting standards.

Chapter 2
The Cost Accountant Job Description

Introduction

This chapter covers the reporting relationships of the cost accountant, as well as the principal accountabilities of the position and the qualifications of someone who wants to be a cost accountant. The chapter is useful for developing a cost accountant job description for hiring purposes, as well as for properly defining the job for an existing cost accountant.

To Whom Does the Cost Accountant Report?

In a smaller company, the cost accountant reports directly to the controller. In a larger company, the cost accountant reports to either a cost accounting manager or an assistant controller.

What Are the Principal Accountabilities of the Cost Accountant?

The key tasks of the cost accountant are to accumulate cost information, aggregate this information for analysis purposes, and report on the results. These reports typically involve the analysis of the cost of goods sold to see if it is accurate, the identification of any unexpected costs, and the ability of the company to earn a profit at a variety of levels, such as by product, product line, and subsidiary. The principal accountabilities of the cost accountant are as follows:

- *Allocate overhead costs.* Both generally accepted accounting principles and international financial reporting standards require that overhead costs be applied to inventory, and the cost accountant should handle this task. He should create a standard procedure for overhead application, document the calculations for each reporting period, and ensure that the allocation is properly entered into the accounting records.
- *Capital budget requests.* If anyone requests that a large capital purchase be made, the cost accountant reviews the proposal for accuracy, and to see if its underlying assumptions make sense. If a company is large enough, this task may be shifted to a financial analyst.
- *Constraint analysis.* The cost accountant should know where the bottleneck operation is located within a company, how well it is utilized, and the amount of throughput (revenues minus variable expenses) that it processes. He should also be aware of any issues with the inventory buffer positioned in front of the bottleneck, and the ability of the system to keep the bottleneck fully supplied with raw materials. See the Constraint Analysis chapter for more information about bottlenecks and throughput.

- *Cost controls.* The cost accountant relies upon the accuracy of a large amount of information in order to conduct valid cost analyses, so he should ensure that sufficient controls are in place to keep data accuracy levels high. He also ensures that there are sufficient controls over the subsequent accumulation and reporting of cost information. This may involve testing collected data for accuracy, or having the internal audit staff conduct such tests.
- *Data collection systems.* The cost accountant needs access to a large amount of costing information, and so is responsible for designing and installing all necessary data collection systems.
- *Inventory counts.* The cost accountant is the person in the accounting department most closely associated with the valuation of inventory, so he either directly oversees physical inventory counts and cycle counts, or acts as a close advisor. Most commonly, the warehouse manager is directly responsible for inventory counts, while the cost accountant reviews and updates the physical count and cycle count procedures, investigates inventory record accuracy problems, and audits the inventory records. If the company is large enough to support its own internal audit staff, then the internal auditors will be responsible for auditing the inventory records.
- *Inventory error analysis.* If inventory counts uncover errors in the underlying inventory records, the cost accountant may be involved in determining why the errors occurred, and how to prevent them in the future. This task may instead be taken on by the warehouse manager.
- *Margin analysis.* The cost accountant conducts an ongoing review of the margins earned on all products, product lines, and company divisions. One goal of this review is to detect changes in profitability as soon as they occur, so that management can take action. Also, it is useful to delve into the primary components of the costs included in these calculations, to give management some insight into how it can make modifications to improve profit levels.
- *Obsolete inventory.* The cost accountant should periodically review the inventory, along with the materials review board (MRB), to determine which inventory items are obsolete, by how much they should be written down, and how best to disposition them. The MRB is responsible for periodically reviewing the inventory and deciding whether any items should be designated as obsolete and disposed of. The cost accountant is responsible for writing down the value of these items in the accounting records, and for documenting the reasoning for the amount of the write-down.
- *Standard costs.* If the company uses a standard costing system, the cost accountant monitors all changes to the standard costs (which can be done quite simply with a change log that automatically monitors all alterations to the item master file in the computer system). This is necessary in order to explain any sudden changes in the cost of goods sold that are caused by significant alterations in the standard costs. In order to maintain tight control over standard cost changes, the cost accountant can even be given sole access to the item master file, and personally updates this information.

- *Target costing*. Target costing involves the analysis of a proposed new product to determine in advance how much it should cost, and to monitor subsequent design work to see if the product can be produced for the target cost, while still generating a reasonable profit at a predetermined price point. If the cost accountant is asked to be part of a target costing team, he keeps track of estimated actual costs for product designs, and reports on the variances between target costs and estimated actual costs. This information is needed to make product design alterations, as well as to decide whether to stop projects that cannot meet their cost targets.
- *Validate the cost of goods sold*. The accounting software will create an initial cost of goods sold figure for each reporting period. Given the large number of transactions flowing through the cost of goods sold account, it is quite likely that there will be errors in this initial amount, so the cost accountant should conduct a detailed review, using both trend and margin analysis, to determine if the cost of goods sold is reasonable in relation to the amount of sales and the mix of products sold.
- *Variance analysis*. If there is a standard costing system in place, the cost accountant may be asked to create an analysis of variances from the standards, both for units consumed and prices paid. If there is no standard costing system, he conducts a horizontal analysis of the financial statements, and reports on the reasons for any unexpected spikes or dips in the trend lines. Historical analysis is the comparison of the trend line of historical financial information over a series of reporting periods. In a large company, horizontal analysis may instead be performed by a financial analyst. See the Standard Costing chapter for more information.
- *Other analyses*. The cost accountant will be called upon to complete a variety of special projects, usually involving the accumulation of costs for prospective products or projects, calculating breakeven points, or estimating profit levels for proposed products or special price points.

What Are the Qualifications of a Cost Accountant?

The cost accountant should have a Bachelor's degree in accounting, since he must deal with a number of technical accounting issues that call for an in-depth knowledge of accounting principles and methods. Further, he should possess significant experience with creating database reports and the manipulation of information with an electronic spreadsheet. If he is involved with a target costing project (see the Target Costing chapter), he should have prior experience working in a multi-department team.

The number of years' experience required depends upon the level of expertise that management wants in the position. If the company is a small one with low-complexity products, then someone with a single year of experience in cost accounting may be sufficient. However, a more complex environment that involves multiple locations, databases, product lines, and costing systems may call for five to ten years of intensive cost accounting experience.

There are a few skills that the cost accountant does *not* need. There is no particular need for management experience in most cases, nor does he have to be certified as a public accountant, management accountant, or internal auditor; there are no certifications that pertain specifically to the cost accountant position.

Who Does the Cost Accountant Supervise?

The cost accountant position is supposed to be that of a technical specialist, rather than a manager. Consequently, he does not supervise anyone. There are two possible exceptions:

- *Large accounting staff.* If a company is a large one that employs multiple cost accountants, then one cost accountant may manage the others; this is particularly common in a multi-location company, where there are cost accountants in many facilities, and someone should take on the task of not only coordinating their activities, but also of ensuring that they all calculate costs using the same cost accumulation models.
- *Clerical support.* Some costing projects call for the accumulation of a great deal of detailed information. If so, the cost accountant may temporarily supervise a clerical staff that collects this information and enters it into a database.

The cost accountant may also work with programmers during the installation of cost accounting software systems, or in the design of costing reports. However, this is not a supervisory role.

Summary

It is apparent from the preceding job description that the cost accounting position is an extremely specialized one that requires a considerable amount of training and experience. Besides a high skill level, the cost accountant needs significant interpersonal skills, for he will find himself regularly dealing with members of the warehouse staff, materials review board, programmers, target costing teams, and other members of the accounting department.

Chapter 3
Types of Costs

Introduction

When discussing cost accounting, there are many types of costs to be aware of. They are noted in passing as we address the various cost accounting topics in later chapters. In addition, this chapter is provided to concentrate in one place a more detailed discussion of those costs that the reader should understand. In the following sections, we present cost types in alphabetical order.

Actual Costs

Actual costing is the recordation of product costs based on the following factors:
- Actual cost of materials
- Actual cost of labor
- Actual overhead costs incurred, allocated using the actual quantity of the allocation base experienced during a reporting period

Thus, the key point in an actual costing system is that it only uses actual costs incurred and allocation bases experienced; it does not incorporate any budgeted amounts or standards.

A similar costing system is normal costing, where the key difference is the use of a budgeted amount of overhead. Actual costing will result in a greater fluctuation in overhead allocations, since it is based on short-term costs that can unexpectedly spike or dip in size. Normal costing results in less fluctuation in overhead allocations, since it is based on long-term expectations for overhead costs.

A company having relatively stable production volumes from month to month will have few problems with actual costing. However, one that experiences continual variation in its production volumes, and especially one that regularly faces questions from its investors may be better off using normal costing, since that method offers greater stability in reported costs.

Avoidable Costs

An avoidable cost is a cost that can be eliminated by not engaging in or no longer performing an activity. For example, if the decision is made to close a production line, then the cost of the building in which it is housed is now an avoidable cost, because it can be sold without harming the business.

Over the long term, all costs are avoidable. For example, a 30-year lease is avoidable if the decision-making period is more than 30 years. In the short term, legally-mandated or government-mandated costs, such as leases or environmental cleanup obligations, are not avoidable costs.

In general, a variable cost is considered to be an avoidable cost, while a fixed cost is not considered to be an avoidable cost. In the very short term, many costs are considered to be fixed and therefore unavoidable.

Committed Costs

A committed cost is an investment that a business entity has already made and cannot recover by any means, as well as obligations already made that the business cannot get out of. One should be aware of which costs are committed costs when reviewing company expenditures for possible cutbacks or asset sales.

For example, if a company buys a machine for $40,000 and also issues a purchase order to pay for a maintenance contract for $2,000 in each of the next three years, all $46,000 is a committed cost, because the company has already bought the machine, and has a legal obligation to pay for the maintenance. A multi-year property lease agreement is also a committed cost for the full term of the lease, since it is extremely difficult to terminate a lease agreement.

Conversion Costs

Conversion costs are those costs required to convert raw materials into finished goods that are ready for sale. The concept is used to derive the value of ending inventory, which is then reported in the financial statements. It can also be used to determine the incremental cost of creating a product, which could be useful for price setting purposes. Since conversion activities involve labor and manufacturing overhead, the calculation of conversion costs is:

$$\text{Conversion costs} = \text{Direct labor} + \text{Manufacturing overhead}$$

Thus, conversion costs are all manufacturing costs except for the cost of raw materials. Examples of costs that may be considered conversion costs are:
- Direct labor and related benefits
- Equipment depreciation
- Equipment maintenance
- Factory rent
- Factory supplies
- Factory insurance
- Machining
- Inspection
- Production utilities
- Production supervision
- Small tools charged to expense

As can be seen from this list, the bulk of all conversion costs are likely to be in the manufacturing overhead classification.

If a business incurs unusual conversion costs for a specific production run (such as reworking parts due to incorrect tolerances on the first pass), it may make sense to exclude these extra costs from the conversion cost calculation, on the grounds that the cost is not representative of day-to-day cost levels.

Deferred Costs

A deferred cost is a cost that a business has already incurred, but which will not be charged to expense until a later reporting period. In the meantime, it appears on the balance sheet as an asset. The reason for deferring recognition of the cost as an expense is that the organization has not yet consumed the item. Management may also defer recognition of a cost if it wishes to recognize the cost at the same time as related revenue is recognized, under the matching principle.

For example, if $1,000 is paid in February for March rent, it is a deferred cost in February, and so is initially recorded as a prepaid asset. Once March arrives, the asset is consumed, and the asset is changed into rent expense. Other examples of deferred costs are:

- Interest cost that is capitalized as part of a fixed asset
- The cost of a fixed asset that is charged to expense over time in the form of depreciation
- The cost of an intangible asset that is charged to expense over time as amortization
- Insurance paid in advance for coverage in future periods
- The costs incurred to register a debt issuance

A business should defer the costs of some expenditures when generally accepted accounting principles or international financial reporting standards require that they be included in the cost of a long-term asset, and then charged to expense over a long period of time. For example, the cost of interest may be included in the cost of a constructed asset, such as a building; the cost of the building is then charged to expense over many years in the form of depreciation. In this case, the cost of the interest is a deferred cost.

Differential Costs

Differential cost is the difference between the cost of two alternative decisions, or of a change in output levels. Here are two examples:

- *Example of alternative decisions.* Possible decisions are to run a fully automated operation that produces 100,000 widgets per year at a cost of $1,200,000, or to use direct labor to manually produce the same number of widgets for $1,400,000; the differential cost between the two alternatives is $200,000.

- *Example of change in output.* A work center can produce 10,000 widgets for $29,000 or 15,000 widgets for $40,000. The differential cost of the additional 5,000 widgets is $11,000.

In essence, one can line up the revenues and expenses from one decision next to similar information for the alternative decision, and the difference between all line items in the two columns is the differential cost.

A differential cost can be a variable cost, a fixed cost, or a mix of the two – there is no differentiation between these types of costs, since the emphasis is on the gross difference between the costs of the alternatives or change in output.

Since a differential cost is only used for management decision making, there is no accounting entry for it.

Direct Costs

A direct cost is traceable to a specific item, such as a product. For example, the cost of the materials used to create a product is a direct cost. There are very few direct costs. The cost of any consumable supplies directly used to manufacture a product can be considered a direct cost. However, production labor is frequently *not* a direct cost, because employees usually are not sent home if there is one less incremental item being produced; instead, they are paid for the duration of their work shifts, irrespective of the volume of production.

Other costs that are *not* direct costs include rent, production salaries, maintenance costs, insurance, depreciation, interest, and all types of utilities. Thus, when in doubt, assume that a cost is an indirect cost, rather than a direct cost.

For example, the materials used to produce an automobile are a direct cost, whereas the electrical cost of the metal stamping machine used to convert sheet metal into body panels for the automobile is not, because the machine must still (presumably) be powered up throughout the working day, irrespective of any changes in production volume.

Direct cost analysis can also be used outside the production department. For example, subtract the direct cost of goods sold to individual customers from the revenues generated by them, which yields the amount customers are contributing toward the company's coverage of overhead costs and profit. Based on this information, management may decide that some customers are unprofitable, and should be dropped.

However, there are a number of situations in which direct costing should not be used, and in which it will lead to incorrect behavior. Its single largest problem is that it completely ignores all indirect costs, which make up the bulk of all costs incurred by today's companies. This is a real problem when dealing with long-term costing and pricing decisions, since direct costing will likely yield results that do not achieve long-term profitability. For example, a direct costing system may calculate a minimum product price of $10.00 for a widget that is indeed higher than all *direct* costs, but which is lower than the additional *overhead* costs that are associated with the product line. If a company uses the $10.00 price for well into the future, the company will experience losses because overhead costs are not being covered by the price.

A direct cost is also known as a prime cost.

Discretionary Costs

A discretionary cost is a cost or capital expenditure that can be curtailed or even eliminated in the short term without having an immediate impact on short-term profitability.

Management may reduce discretionary costs when there are cash flow difficulties, or when it wants to present enhanced short-term earnings. However, a prolonged period of reduction in discretionary costs gradually reduces the quality of a company's product pipeline, reduces awareness by customers, increases machine downtime, and may also decrease product quality and increase employee turnover. Examples of discretionary costs are:

- Advertising
- Equipment maintenance
- Research and development

Expired Costs

An expired cost is a cost that has been recognized as an expense. This happens when an entity fully consumes or receives benefit from a cost. An expired cost may also be construed as the total loss in value of an asset.

For example, a company spends $10,000 to acquire product catalogs, which it records as a prepaid expense in January. It hands out the catalogs during a trade show in March, at which point it charges the $10,000 cost to marketing expense. The $10,000 becomes an expired cost in March.

Fixed Costs

A fixed cost is a cost that does not vary in the short term, irrespective of changes in production or sales levels. Examples of fixed costs are:

- Amortization
- Depreciation
- Insurance
- Interest expense
- Property taxes
- Rent

Over the long term, few (if any) costs are truly fixed. For example, a thirty-year lease can be eliminated after the thirtieth year, so the expense is actually variable if viewed over a 31-year time period.

Companies with a high proportion of fixed costs have a high breakeven point, above which they earn outsized profits. Companies with a low proportion of fixed costs have a low breakeven point, above which they earn more modest profits. Companies with high fixed costs have a greater incentive to engage in price wars to gain some additional incremental revenue, because they can recognize the bulk of these additional revenues as profit.

Historical Costs

Historical cost is the original cost of an asset, as recorded in an entity's accounting records. A historical cost can be easily proven by accessing the source purchase documents, but has the disadvantage of not necessarily representing the actual fair value of an asset, which is likely to diverge from its purchase cost over time.

Historical cost requires some adjustment over time. Depreciation expense is recorded for longer-term assets, thereby reducing their recorded value over their estimated useful lives. Also, if the value of an asset declines below its depreciation-adjusted cost, an impairment charge must be taken to bring the recorded cost of the asset down to its net realizable value.

The historical cost concept is clarified by the cost principle, which states that one should only record an asset, liability, or equity investment at its original acquisition cost.

Historical cost differs from a variety of other costs that can be assigned to an asset, such as its replacement cost (what would be paid to purchase the same asset now) or its inflation-adjusted cost (the original purchase price with cumulative upward adjustments for inflation since the purchase date).

Historical cost is still a central concept for recording assets, though fair value is replacing it for some types of assets, such as marketable investments.

Indirect Costs

Indirect costs are costs used by multiple activities, and which cannot therefore be assigned to specific products, services, geographical regions, customers, or other cost objects. Instead, indirect costs are needed to operate the business as a whole.

Indirect costs do not vary substantially within certain production volumes or other indicators of activities, and so are considered to be fixed costs. Examples of indirect costs are:

- Accounting and legal expenses
- Administrative salaries
- Office expenses
- Rent
- Telephone expenses
- Utilities

Irrelevant Costs

An irrelevant cost is a cost that will not change as the result of a management decision. However, the same cost may be relevant to a different management decision.

For example, the salary of an investor relations officer may be an irrelevant cost if a management decision relates to issuing a new product, since dealing with investors has nothing to do with that particular decision. However, if the board of directors is considering taking the company private, then it may no longer need an investor relations officer; in the latter case, the salary of the investor relations officer is highly relevant to the decision.

Non-cash items, such as depreciation and amortization, are frequently categorized as irrelevant costs for most types of decisions, since they do not impact cash flows.

Marginal Costs

Marginal cost is the cost of one additional unit of output. Marginal costing is used to determine the optimum production quantity for a company, where it costs the least amount to produce additional units. If a company operates within this "sweet spot," it can maximize its profits.

For example, a production line currently creates 10,000 widgets at a cost of $30,000, so that the average cost per unit is $3.00. However, if the production line creates 10,001 units, the total cost is $30,002, so that the marginal cost of the one additional unit is only $2. This is a common effect, because there is rarely any additional overhead cost associated with a single unit of output, resulting in a lower marginal cost.

In rare cases, step costs may take effect, so that the marginal cost is actually much higher than the average cost. To use the same example, what if the company must start up a new production line on a second shift in order to create unit number 10,001? If so, the marginal cost of this additional unit might be vastly higher than $2 - it may be thousands of dollars, because the company had to start up an extra production line in order to create that single unit.

A more common situation lying between the preceding two alternatives is when a production facility operating near capacity simply pays overtime to its employees for them to work somewhat longer to put out that one additional unit. If so, the marginal cost will increase to include the cost of overtime, but not to the extent caused by a step cost.

The marginal cost of customized goods tends to be quite high, whereas it is very low for highly standardized products that are manufactured in bulk.

Since marginal cost is only used for management decision making, there is no accounting entry for it.

Normal Costs

Normal costing is used to derive the cost of a product. It includes the following components:
- Actual cost of materials
- Actual cost of labor

- A standard overhead rate that is applied using the product's actual usage of whatever allocation base is being used (such as direct labor hours or machine time)

If there is a difference between the standard overhead cost and the actual overhead cost, one can either charge the difference to the cost of goods sold (for smaller variances) or prorate the difference between the cost of goods sold and inventory.

Normal costing is designed to yield product costs that do not contain the sudden cost spikes that can occur when actual overhead costs are used; instead, it uses a smoother long-term estimated overhead rate.

It is acceptable under generally accepted accounting principles and international financial reporting standards to use normal costing to derive the cost of a product.

Normal costing varies from standard costing, in that standard costing uses entirely predetermined costs for all aspects of a product, while normal costing uses actual costs for the materials and labor components.

Period Costs

A period cost is any cost that cannot be capitalized into inventory or fixed assets. Instead, a period cost is charged to expense in the period incurred. Examples of period costs are:

- Sales expenses
- Commissions
- General and administrative expenses
- Executive salaries
- Office rent
- Interest expense (that is not capitalized)

Items that are not period costs are:

- Costs included in inventory, such as direct labor, direct materials, and manufacturing overhead
- Costs included in fixed assets

Thus, if the entire use to which a cost can be put is consumed in the current accounting period (such as rent or utilities) it is probably a period cost, whereas if its use is linked to a product or is spread over multiple periods, it is probably not a period cost.

Replacement Costs

Replacement cost is the price that an entity would pay to replace an existing asset at current market prices with a similar asset. If the asset in question has been damaged, then the replacement cost relates to the pre-damaged condition of the asset.

The replacement cost of an asset may vary from the market value of that specific asset, since the asset that would actually replace it may have a different cost; the replacement asset only has to perform the same functions as the original asset - it does not have to be an exact copy of the original asset.

Semi-Fixed Costs

A semi-fixed cost is a cost that contains both fixed and variable elements. As a result, the minimum cost level that will be experienced will be greater than zero; once a certain activity level is surpassed, the cost will begin to increase beyond the base level, since the variable component of the cost has been triggered.

As an example of a semi-fixed cost, a company must pay a certain amount to maintain minimum operations for a production line, in the form of machinery depreciation, staffing, and facility rent. If the volume of production exceeds a certain amount, the company must hire additional staff or pay overtime, which is the variable component of the semi-fixed cost of the production line.

Another example of a semi-fixed cost is a salaried salesperson. This person earns a fixed amount of compensation (in the form of a salary), as well as a variable amount (in the form of a commission). In total, the cost of the salesperson is semi-fixed.

A third example is the monthly bill for a cell phone, where the recipient pays a fixed fee for phone usage, as well as a variable fee if the user exceeds a certain amount of data usage, calls, or text messages.

A cost that is classified as semi-fixed does not have to contain a certain proportion of fixed or variable costs to be classified as such. Instead, any material mix of the two cost types qualifies a cost as semi-fixed.

A semi-fixed cost may also be a step cost. That is, the cost remains the same until a certain activity threshold is exceeded, after which the cost increases. The same approach works in reverse, where the variable component of a cost will be eliminated when the activity level declines below a certain amount.

Step Costs

A step cost is a cost that does not change steadily, but rather at discrete points. A step cost is a fixed cost within certain boundaries, outside of which it will change.

For example, a facility cost will remain steady until additional floor space is constructed, at which point the cost will increase to a new and higher level as the entity incurs new costs to maintain the additional floor space, to heat and air condition it, and so forth.

As another example, a company can produce 10,000 widgets during one eight-hour shift. If the company receives additional customer orders for more widgets, it must add another shift, which requires the services of an additional shift supervisor. Thus, the cost of the shift supervisor is a step cost that occurs when the company reaches a production requirement of 10,001 widgets.

Step costing is extremely important to be aware of when a company is about to reach a new and higher activity level where it must incur a large incremental step cost. Conversely, it should be aware of step costs when the activity level declines, so that it can reduce costs in an appropriate manner to maintain profitability.

Sunk Costs

A sunk cost is a cost that an entity has incurred, and which it can no longer recover by any means. Sunk cost should not be considered when making the decision to continue investing in an ongoing project, since the cost cannot be recovered. However, many managers continue investing in projects because of the sheer size of the amounts already invested in the past. They do not want to "lose the investment" by curtailing a project that is proving to not be profitable, so they continue pouring more cash into it. Rationally, they should consider earlier investments to be sunk costs, and therefore exclude them from consideration when deciding whether to continue with further investments.

For example, ABC Company spends $50,000 on a marketing study to see if its new auburn widget will succeed in the marketplace. The study concludes that the widget will not be profitable. At this point, the $50,000 is a sunk cost. ABC should not continue with further investments in the widget project, despite its earlier investment.

Traceable Costs

A traceable cost is a cost for which there is a direct, cause-and-effect relationship with a process, product, customer, geographical area, or other cost object. Examples of traceable costs are:

Traceable Cost	Cost Object
Advertising	Product, product line, or company
Liability insurance	Company or subsidiary
Marketing manager	Product line
Rent	Product line
Warehouse cost	Geographical area

A traceable cost is important, because it is an overhead expense that can be reliably assigned to a cost object when constructing an income statement showing the financial results of that cost object.

Variable Costs

A variable cost is a cost that varies in relation to either production volume or services provided. If there is no production or no services are provided, there should be no variable costs. To calculate total variable costs, the formula is:

Total quantity of units produced × Variable cost per unit = Total variable cost

Direct materials are considered a variable cost. Direct labor may not be a variable cost if labor is not added to or subtracted from the production process as production volumes change. Most types of overhead are not considered a variable cost.

The sum total of all manufacturing overhead costs and variable costs is the total cost of products manufactured or services provided.

If a company has a large proportion of variable costs in its cost structure, most of its expenses will vary in direct proportion to revenues, so it can weather a business downturn better than a company that has a high proportion of fixed costs.

Summary

One of the key elements of cost accounting is to understand the incremental nature of costs, and how those costs relate to cost accounting decisions. Thus, it is essential to understand which costs are avoidable or have been committed, which costs are tied to a specific period of time, which ones are due to expire soon, and which costs will only be incurred when certain activity triggers are reached. We have noted all of these costs types in the preceding sections. Watch for them in the following chapters, and refer back to this chapter whenever there is a need to examine a more detailed explanation of the concepts involved.

Chapter 4
Inventory Valuation

Introduction

The cost accountant is responsible for calculating the value of inventory, which in turn drives a large part of the cost of goods sold – and *that* is usually the largest expense, and therefore the primary cause of a company's profits and losses. Thus, creating an accurate inventory valuation is critical. Unfortunately, as will be seen in this chapter, there are a number of complicated steps involved in creating such a valuation. The inventory valuation is comprised of:

1. *Inventory quantities.* The inventory quantities on hand at the end of the reporting period.
2. *Inventory cost.* The cost at which the inventory was acquired. There are multiple methods of inventory valuation, depending on the type of inventory involved.
3. *Overhead allocation.* The allocation of indirect costs to inventory.
4. *Inventory valuation.* Whether the value of the inventory has declined since it was purchased.

In this chapter, we address all four components of the inventory valuation process.

> **Related Podcast Episode:** Episode 66 of the Accounting Best Practices Podcast discusses obsolete inventory. It is available at: **accountingtools.com/podcasts** or **iTunes**

Valuation Step 1: The Quantity of Inventory on Hand

The following two sections describe the initial step in the valuation process, which is ensuring that correct inventory quantities are used. There are two alternative counting methods, which are the periodic inventory system and the perpetual system. The periodic inventory system requires a physical count of the inventory from time to time, whereas the perpetual system instead uses continual updating of the inventory records as each inventory transaction occurs.

An interesting method for estimating ending inventory is the gross profit method, which is also described in a separate section.

The Periodic Inventory System

The periodic inventory system only updates the ending inventory balance when a physical inventory count is conducted. Since physical inventory counts are time-consuming, few companies do them more than once a quarter or year. In the meantime, the inventory account continues to show the cost of the inventory that was recorded as of the last physical inventory count.

Under the periodic inventory system, all purchases made between physical inventory counts are recorded in a purchases account. When a physical inventory count is done, the balance in the purchases account is then shifted into the inventory account, which in turn is adjusted to match the cost of the ending inventory.

The calculation of the cost of goods sold under the periodic inventory system is:

Beginning inventory + Purchases = Cost of goods available for sale

Cost of goods available for sale – Ending inventory = Cost of goods sold

---

EXAMPLE

Mulligan Imports has beginning inventory of $100,000, has paid $170,000 for purchases, and its physical inventory count reveals an ending inventory cost of $80,000. The calculation of its cost of goods sold is:

$100,000 Beginning inventory + $170,000 Purchases - $80,000 Ending inventory

= $190,000 Cost of goods sold

The periodic inventory system is most useful for smaller businesses that maintain minimal amounts of inventory. For them, a physical inventory count is easy to complete, and they can estimate cost of goods sold figures for interim periods. However, there are also several problems with the system:

- It does not yield any information about the cost of goods sold or ending inventory balances during interim periods when there has been no physical inventory count.
- The cost of goods sold must be estimated during interim periods, which will likely result in a significant adjustment to the actual cost of goods whenever a physical inventory count is eventually completed.
- There is no way to adjust for obsolete inventory or scrap losses during interim periods, so there tends to be a significant (and expensive) adjustment for these issues when a physical inventory count is eventually completed.

A more up-to-date and accurate alternative to the periodic inventory system is the perpetual inventory system, which is described in the next section.

The Perpetual Inventory System

Under the perpetual inventory system, an entity continually updates its inventory records to account for additions to and subtractions from inventory for such activities as received inventory items, goods sold from stock, and items picked from inventory for use in the production process. Thus, a perpetual inventory system has the advantages of both providing up-to-date inventory balance information and requiring a reduced level of physical inventory counts. However, the calculated inventory levels derived by a perpetual inventory system may gradually diverge from actual inventory levels, due to unrecorded transactions or theft, so one should periodically compare book balances to actual on-hand quantities with cycle counting. Cycle counting is the process of counting a small proportion of the total inventory on a daily basis, and not only correcting any errors found, but also investigating the underlying reasons why the errors occurred. There are multiple methods used for selecting the inventory items to be counted each day for a cycle counting program. They are:

- *By location.* Simply work through the warehouse, section by section. This approach ensures that all inventory items will be counted, and is a simple way to coordinate the daily counts. Once the entire warehouse has been counted, start back at the beginning and do it again.
- *By usage.* The materials management department places a higher emphasis on the inventory record accuracy of those items used most frequently in the production process, since an unexpected shortage of one of these items could stop production. Consequently, high-usage items would be counted more frequently.
- *By criticality.* Some items must be on hand, or production cannot proceed. Also, these items may be extremely difficult to obtain, perhaps because suppliers require long lead times, or because the only supplier is selling goods on an allocation basis. In this situation, the very small number of critical items should be continually monitored, with all other goods receiving less cycle counting attention. A variation on this concept is to give counting priority to those items scheduled to go into production in the near future; under this approach, cycle counts should be scheduled earlier than the lead time required to replace a part, in case the counts reveal missing parts, and replacements must be ordered in time to meet the production schedule.
- *By valuation.* The accounting department is most concerned with the record accuracy of those inventory items having the largest aggregate cost, since an error here would impact reported profits. Consequently, high-valuation items would be counted more frequently.

Related Podcast Episode: Episode 192 of the Accounting Best Practices Podcast discusses cycle counting. It is available at: **accountingtools.com/podcasts** or **iTunes**

EXAMPLE

This example contains several journal entries used to account for transactions in a perpetual inventory system. Mulligan Imports records a purchase of $1,000 of golf clubs that are stored in inventory:

	Debit	Credit
Inventory	1,000	
Accounts payable		1,000

Mulligan records $250 of inbound freight cost associated with the delivery of golf clubs:

	Debit	Credit
Inventory	250	
Accounts payable		250

Mulligan records the sale of golf clubs from inventory for $2,000, for which the associated inventory cost is $1,200:

	Debit	Credit
Accounts receivable	2,000	
Revenue		2,000
Cost of goods sold	1,200	
Inventory		1,200

Mulligan records a downward inventory adjustment of $500, caused by inventory theft, and detected during a cycle count:

	Debit	Credit
Inventory shrinkage expense	500	
Inventory		500

The Gross Profit Method

The gross profit method can be used to estimate the amount of ending inventory. This is useful for interim periods between physical inventory counts, or when inventory was destroyed and there is a need to back into the ending inventory balance for the purpose of filing a claim for insurance reimbursement. Follow these steps to estimate ending inventory using the gross profit method:
1. Add together the cost of beginning inventory and the cost of purchases during the period to arrive at the cost of goods available for sale.

2. Multiply (1 - expected gross profit %) by sales during the period to arrive at the estimated cost of goods sold.
3. Subtract the estimated cost of goods sold (step #2) from the cost of goods available for sale (step #1) to arrive at the ending inventory.

The gross profit method is not an acceptable method for determining the year-end inventory balance, since it only estimates what the ending inventory balance may be. It is not sufficiently precise to be reliable for audited financial statements.

EXAMPLE

Mulligan Imports is calculating its month-end golf club inventory for March. Its beginning inventory was $175,000 and its purchases during the month were $225,000. Thus, its cost of goods available for sale are:

$$\$175,000 \text{ beginning inventory} + \$225,000 \text{ purchases}$$

$$= \$400,000 \text{ cost of goods available for sale}$$

Mulligan's gross margin percentage for all of the past 12 months was 35%, which is considered a reliable long-term margin. Its sales during March were $500,000. Thus, its estimated cost of goods sold is:

$$(1 - 35\%) \times \$500,000 = \$325,000 \text{ cost of goods sold}$$

By subtracting the estimated cost of goods sold from the cost of goods available for sale, Mulligan arrives at an estimated ending inventory balance of $75,000.

There are several issues with the gross profit method that make it unreliable as the sole method for determining the value of inventory, which are:

- *Applicability*. The calculation is most useful in retail situations where a company is simply buying and reselling merchandise. If a company is instead manufacturing goods, the components of inventory must also include labor and overhead, which make the gross profit method too simplistic to yield reliable results.
- *Historical basis*. The gross profit percentage is a key component of the calculation, but the percentage is based on a company's historical experience. If the current situation yields a different percentage (as may be caused by a special sale at reduced prices), the gross profit percentage used in the calculation will be incorrect.
- *Inventory losses*. The calculation assumes that the long-term rate of losses due to theft, obsolescence, and other causes is included in the historical gross profit percentage. If not, or if these losses have not previously been recognized, the calculation will likely result in an inaccurate estimated ending inventory (and probably one that is too high).

Valuation Step 2a: Inventory Costing (Typical Inventory)

Seven methods for calculating the cost of inventory are shown in the following sections. Of the methods presented, only the first in, first out method and the weighted average method have gained worldwide recognition. The last in, first out method and its variations cannot realistically be justified based on the actual flow of inventory, and is only used in the United States under the sanction of the Internal Revenue Service; it is specifically banned under international financial reporting standards. Standard costing is an acceptable alternative to cost layering, as long as any associated variances are properly accounted for. Finally, the retail inventory method should be used only to derive an approximation of the ending inventory cost, and so should be used only in interim reporting periods when a company does not intend to issue any financial results to outside parties.

The First In, First Out Method

The first in, first out (FIFO) method of inventory valuation operates under the assumption that the first goods purchased are also the first goods sold. In most companies, this accounting assumption closely matches the actual flow of goods, and so is considered the most theoretically correct inventory valuation method.

Under the FIFO method, the earliest goods purchased are the first ones removed from the inventory account. This results in the remaining items in inventory being accounted for at the most recently incurred costs, so that the inventory asset recorded on the balance sheet contains costs quite close to the most recent costs that could be obtained in the marketplace. Conversely, this method also results in older historical costs being matched against current revenues and recorded in the cost of goods sold, so the gross margin does not necessarily reflect a proper matching of revenues and costs.

EXAMPLE

Mulligan Imports decides to use the FIFO method for the month of January. During that month, it records the following transactions:

	Quantity Change	Actual Unit Cost	Actual Total Cost
Beginning inventory (Layer 1)	+100	$210	$21,000
Sale	-75		
Purchase (Layer 2)	+150	280	42,000
Sale	-100		
Purchase (Layer 3)	+50	300	15,000
Ending inventory	= 125		

The cost of goods sold in units is calculated as:

100 Beginning inventory + 200 Purchased – 125 Ending inventory = 175 Units

Mulligan's cost accountant uses the information in the preceding table to calculate the cost of goods sold for January, as well as the cost of the inventory balance as of the end of January.

	Units	Unit Cost	Total Cost
Cost of goods sold			
FIFO layer 1	100	$210	$21,000
FIFO layer 2	75	280	21,000
Total cost of goods sold	175		$42,000
Ending inventory			
FIFO layer 2	75	280	$21,000
FIFO layer 3	50	300	15,000
Total ending inventory	125		$36,000

Thus, the first FIFO layer, which was the beginning inventory layer, is completely used up during the month, as well as half of Layer 2, leaving half of Layer 2 and all of Layer 3 to be the sole components of the ending inventory.

Note that the $42,000 cost of goods sold and $36,000 ending inventory equals the $78,000 combined total of beginning inventory and purchases during the month.

The Last In, First Out Method

The last in, first out (LIFO) method operates under the assumption that the last item of inventory purchased is the first one sold. Picture a store shelf where a clerk adds items from the front, and customers also take their selections from the front; the remaining items of inventory that are located further from the front of the shelf are rarely picked, and so remain on the shelf – that is a LIFO scenario.

The trouble with LIFO is that it is rarely encountered in practice. If a company were to use the process flow embodied by LIFO, a significant part of its inventory would be very old, and likely obsolete. Nonetheless, a company does not actually have to experience the LIFO process flow in order to use the method to calculate its inventory valuation.

The reason why companies use LIFO is the assumption that the cost of inventory increases over time, which is a reasonable assumption in times of inflating prices. If LIFO were to be used in such a situation, the cost of the most recently acquired inventory will always be higher than the cost of earlier purchases, so the ending inventory balance will be valued at earlier costs, while the most recent costs appear in the cost of goods sold. By shifting high-cost inventory into the cost of goods sold, a company can reduce its reported level of profitability, and thereby defer its recognition of income taxes. Since income tax deferral is the only justification for LIFO in most situations, it is banned under international financial reporting standards (though it is still allowed in the United States under the approval of the Internal Revenue Service).

EXAMPLE

Mulligan Imports decides to use the LIFO method for the month of March. The following table shows the various purchasing transactions for the company's Golf Elite clubs. The quantity purchased on March 1 actually reflects the inventory beginning balance.

Date Purchased	Quantity Purchased	Cost per Unit	Units Sold	Cost of Layer 1	Cost of Layer 2	Total Cost
March 1	150	$210	95	(55 × $210)		$11,550
March 7	100	235	110	(45 × $210)		9,450
March 11	200	250	180	(45 × $210)	(20 × $250)	14,450
March 17	125	240	125	(45 × $210)	(20 × $250)	14,450
March 25	80	260	120	(25 × $210)		5,250

The following bullet points describe the transactions noted in the preceding table:
- *March 1.* Mulligan has a beginning inventory balance of 150 units, and sells 95 of these units between March 1 and March 7. This leaves one inventory layer of 55 units at a cost of $210 each.
- *March 7.* Mulligan buys 100 additional units on March 7, and sells 110 units between March 7 and March 11. Under LIFO, we assume that the latest purchase was sold first, so there is still just one inventory layer, which has now been reduced to 45 units.
- *March 11.* Mulligan buys 200 additional units on March 11, and sells 180 units between March 11 and March 17, which creates a new inventory layer that is comprised of 20 units at a cost of $250. This new layer appears in the table in the "Cost of Layer 2" column.
- *March 17.* Mulligan buys 125 additional units on March 17, and sells 125 units between March 17 and March 25, so there is no change in the inventory layers.
- *March 25.* Mulligan buys 80 additional units on March 25, and sells 120 units between March 25 and the end of the month. Sales exceed purchases during this period, so the second inventory layer is eliminated, as well as part of the first layer. The result is an ending inventory balance of $5,250, which is derived from 25 units of ending inventory, multiplied by the $210 cost in the first layer that existed at the beginning of the month.

Before implementing the LIFO system, consider the following points:
- *Consistent usage.* The Internal Revenue Service states that a company using LIFO for its tax reporting must also use LIFO for its financial reporting.

Thus, a company wanting to defer tax recognition through early expense recognition must show those same low profit numbers to the users of its financial statements.

- *Layering*. Since the LIFO system is intended to use the most recent layers of inventory, earlier layers may never be accessed, which can result in an administrative problem if there are many layers to document.
- *Profit fluctuations*. If early layers contain inventory costs that depart substantially from current market prices, a company could experience sharp changes in its profitability if those layers are ever used.

In summary, LIFO is only useful for deferring income tax payments in periods of cost inflation. It does not reflect the actual flow of inventory in most situations, and may even yield unusual financial results that differ markedly from reality.

The Dollar-Value LIFO Method

A variation on the LIFO concept is to calculate a conversion price index that is based on a comparison of the year-end inventory to the base year cost. In essence, the dollar-value LIFO method is designed to aggregate cost information for large amounts of inventory, so that individual cost layers do not need to be compiled for each item of inventory. Instead, layers are compiled for pools of inventory items.

The key concept in the dollar-value LIFO system is the conversion price index. To calculate the index, follow these steps:

1. Calculate the extended cost of the ending inventory at base year prices.
2. Calculate the extended cost of the ending inventory at the most recent prices.
3. Divide the total extended cost at the most recent prices by the total extended cost at base year prices.

These calculations yield an index that represents the change in prices since the base year. The calculation should be derived and retained for each year in which a business uses the LIFO method. Once the index is available, follow these additional steps to determine the cost of the LIFO cost layer in each successive period:

1. Determine any incremental increases in units of inventory in the next reporting period.
2. Calculate the extended cost of these incremental units at base year prices.
3. Multiply the extended amount by the conversion price index. This yields the cost of the LIFO layer for the next reporting period.

The concept is illustrated in the following example:

EXAMPLE

Entwhistle Electric has had the same cell phone battery version in stock for the past four years. The company uses the dollar-value LIFO method. Entwhistle's inventory database contains the following quantity and pricing information for the battery:

Year	Year-end Quantity	Year-end Price	Extended Price
1	1,000	$15.00	$15,000
2	2,500	16.50	41,250
3	2,200	17.25	39,750
4	3,500	18.10	63,350

The first year is designated as the base year for purposes of creating the index in later years. The current price index for Year 2 is calculated as follows:

Year	Year-end Quantity	Base Year Cost	Year 2 Cost	Extended Base Year Cost	Extended Year 2 Cost	Index
2	2,500	$15.00	$16.50	$37,500	$41,250	110%

In Year 2, the incremental amount of cell phone batteries added to stock is 1,500 units. To arrive at the cost of the Year 2 LIFO layer, Entwhistle's controller multiplies the 1,500 units by the base year cost of $15.00 and again by the 110% index to arrive at a layer cost of $24,750. In total, at the end of Year 2, Entwhistle has a base layer cost of $15,000 and a Year 2 layer cost of $24,750, for a total inventory valuation of $39,750.

In Year 3, there is a decline in the ending inventory unit count, so there is no new layer to calculate. Instead, the controller assumes that the units sold off are from the most recent inventory layer, which is the Year 2 layer. To calculate the year-end inventory valuation, we multiply the presumed residual balance of 1,200 units from the Year 2 layer by the $15.00 base year cost, and again by the 110% index, to arrive at a revised layer cost of $19,800. When combined with the $15,000 cost of the base layer, Entwhistle now has an ending inventory valuation of $34,800.

In Year 4, the inventory level has increased, which calls for the calculation of a new index. The calculation for the Year 4 current price index is:

Year	Year-end Quantity	Base Year Cost	Year 4 Cost	Extended Base Year Cost	Extended Year 4 Cost	Index
4	3,500	$15.00	$18.10	$52,500	$63,350	121%

There is an incremental increase in Year 4 from Year 3 of 1,300 units. The controller multiplies this amount by the $15.00 base year cost and again by the 121% current cost index to arrive at a cost for this new inventory layer of $23,595.

After four years of inventory accumulation under the dollar-value LIFO method, the ending inventory is comprised of the following LIFO inventory layers:

Layer Identification	Layer Price Index	Layer Valuation
Base layer	--	$15,000
Year 2 layer	110%	19,800
Year 4 layer	121%	23,595
	Total	$58,395

Tip: The method can be used to create separate indexes for a number of different pools of inventory. However, since doing so increases the labor associated with calculating and applying conversion price indices, it is better to minimize the number of inventory pools employed.

The dollar-value method is not commonly used to derive inventory valuations, for the following reasons:

- *Calculation volume.* A large number of calculations are required to determine the differences in pricing through the indicated periods.
- *Base year issue.* Under IRS regulations, a base year cost must be located for each new inventory item added to stock, which can require considerable research. Only if such information is impossible to locate can the current cost also be considered the base year cost.

The Link-Chain Method

The main problem with the dollar-value LIFO method is that a base year cost must be compiled for each inventory item, which can be difficult or impossible to do. In situations where there is a high level of turnover in the types of inventory kept in stock, tax regulations allow for the alternative use of the link-chain method. This method eliminates the use of a base year cost, instead using a price index whose baseline is the immediately preceding year. Since each successive pricing index is compiled from the index in the immediately preceding year, there is said to be a link between the years being used, hence the name of this method.

The calculation steps for this method closely follow those just noted for the dollar-value LIFO method. The calculation flow is illustrated in the following example:

EXAMPLE

The controller of Entwhistle Electric is frustrated with the amount of work associated with tying current period costs back to base year costs under the dollar-value LIFO method, and so is experimenting with what would be required if the company were to instead use the link-chain method. He begins with the same information noted in the last example, which is replicated here, along with beginning-of-year information:

Year	Year-end Quantity	Year-end Price	Extended Ending Price	Beginning Price	Extended Beginning Price
1	1,000	$15.00	$15,000	$--	$--
2	2,500	16.50	41,250	15.00	37,500
3	2,200	17.25	39,750	16.50	36,300
4	3,500	18.10	63,350	17.25	60,375

Year 1 is considered the base year, so there is no index associated with it. The price index for Year 2 is 110%, which is the extended ending price of $41,250 divided by the extended beginning price of $37,500. Thus far, there is no difference between the outcome of this method and the dollar-value LIFO method.

The valuation of the Year 2 inventory layer is then derived by dividing the $41,250 ending extended price by the 110% price index, which yields an extended base year cost of $37,500. The base year layer of $15,000 is subtracted from this amount to yield a Year 2 LIFO layer at the base year cost of $22,500. This amount is then multiplied by the price index to bring its cost back to the Year 2 pricing level, which is $24,750. At the end of Year 2, the LIFO layering situation is as follows:

Layer Identification	Cumulative Price Index	Layer Valuation	Base Year Valuation
Base layer	--	$15,000	$15,000
Year 2 layer	110%	24,750	22,500
	Total	$39,750	$37,500

In Year 3, the price index is calculated as the extended price based on the year-end price, divided by the extended price based on the beginning-of-year price, which is 109.5%. To arrive at the cumulative price index, the original price index of 110% is multiplied by the next-year price index of 109.5% to arrive at 120.5% (calculated as 110% × 1.095).

To determine the base year cost of the Year 3 ending inventory, the Year 3 ending inventory price of $39,750 is divided by the cumulative price index of 120.5% to arrive at $32,988. Since this amount is less than the ending valuation for Year 2, there is no new LIFO layer to record. Instead, the base year layer of $15,000 is subtracted from the $32,988 Year 3 year-end figure to arrive at the $17,988 base year cost of the remaining Year 2 layer. This base year cost is then multiplied by the Year 2 price index of 110% to determine the revised Year

2 inventory valuation of $19,787. At the end of Year 3, the LIFO layering situation is as follows:

Layer Identification	Cumulative Price Index	Layer Valuation	Base Year Valuation
Base layer	--	$15,000	$15,000
Year 2 layer	110.0%	19,787	17,988
Year 3 layer	120.5%	--	--
Total		$34,787	$32,988

In Year 4, the price index is calculated as the extended price based on the year-end price, divided by the extended price based on the beginning-of-year price, which is 104.9%. The cumulative index is derived by multiplying the preceding cumulative price index of 120.5% by the next-year price index of 104.9% to arrive at 126.4% (calculated as 120.5% × 1.049).

To determine the base year cost of the Year 4 ending inventory, the Year 4 ending inventory price of $63,350 is divided by the cumulative price index of 126.4% to arrive at $50,119. This amount is then netted against the existing base year valuation of $32,988 to determine the base year valuation of the LIFO layer associated with Year 4, which is $17,131. The last step is to multiply the base year valuation of this newest layer by the cumulative price index of 126.4% to determine the current year valuation of the Year 4 layer, which is $21,654. At the end of Year 4, the LIFO layering situation is as follows:

Layer Identification	Cumulative Price Index	Layer Valuation	Base Year Valuation
Base layer	--	$15,000	$15,000
Year 2 layer	110.0%	19,787	17,988
Year 3 layer	120.5%	--	--
Year 4 layer	126.4%	21,654	17,131
Total		$56,441	$50,119

Tip: The tax regulations allow a company to derive a link-chain index based on a subset of the total inventory. This subset must include those inventory items whose values collectively comprise at least half of the total inventory valuation.

A comparison of the calculation steps involved in the determination of the dollar-value LIFO and link-chain methods will reveal that many of the steps are the same or similar. The primary difference between the two methods is that knowledge of the base year cost is not needed under the link-chain method to determine the price index in later reporting periods.

The Weighted Average Method

When using the weighted average method, divide the cost of goods available for sale by the number of units available for sale, which yields the weighted-average cost per unit. In this calculation, the cost of goods available for sale is the sum of beginning inventory and net purchases. This weighted-average figure is then used to assign a cost to both ending inventory and the cost of goods sold.

The singular advantage of the weighted average method is the complete absence of any inventory layers, which avoids the recordkeeping problems that would be encountered with either the FIFO or LIFO methods that were described earlier.

EXAMPLE

Mulligan Imports elects to use the weighted-average method for the month of May. During that month, it records the following transactions:

	Quantity Change	Actual Unit Cost	Actual Total Cost
Beginning inventory	+150	$220	$33,000
Sale	-125		
Purchase	+200	270	54,000
Sale	-150		
Purchase	+100	290	29,000
Ending inventory	=175		

The actual total cost of all purchased or beginning inventory units in the preceding table is $116,000 ($33,000 + $54,000 + $29,000). The total of all purchased or beginning inventory units is 450 (150 beginning inventory + 300 purchased). The weighted average cost per unit is therefore $257.78 ($116,000 ÷ 450 units).

The ending inventory valuation is $45,112 (175 units × $257.78 weighted average cost), while the cost of goods sold valuation is $70,890 (275 units × $257.78 weighted average cost). The sum of these two amounts (less a rounding error) equals the $116,000 total actual cost of all purchases and beginning inventory.

In the preceding example, if Mulligan used a perpetual inventory system to record its inventory transactions, it would have to recompute the weighted average after every purchase. The following table uses the same information in the preceding example to show the recomputations:

	Units on Hand	Purchases	Cost of Sales	Inventory Total Cost	Inventory Moving Average Unit Cost
Beginning inventory	150	$ --	$ --	$33,000	$220.00
Sale (125 units @ $220.00)	25	--	27,500	5,500	220.00
Purchase (200 units @ $270.00)	225	54,000	--	59,500	264.44
Sale (150 units @ $264.44)	75	--	39,666	19,834	264.44
Purchase (100 units @ $290.00)	175	29,000	--	48,834	279.05
Total			$67,166		

Note that the cost of goods sold of $67,166 and the ending inventory balance of $48,834 equal $116,000, which matches the total of the costs in the original example. Thus, the totals are the same, but the moving weighted average calculation results in slight differences in the apportionment of costs between the cost of goods sold and ending inventory.

Standard Costing

The preceding methods (FIFO, LIFO, and weighted average) have all operated under the assumption that some sort of cost layering is used, even if that layering results in nothing more than a single weighted-average layer. The standard costing methodology arrives at inventory valuation from an entirely different direction, which is to set a standard cost for each item and then value those items at the standard cost – not the actual cost at which the items were purchased.

Standard costing is clearly more efficient than any cost layering system, simply because there are no layers to keep track of. However, its primary failing is that the resulting inventory valuation may not equate to the actual cost. The difference is handled through several types of variance calculations, which may be charged to the cost of goods sold (if minor) or allocated between inventory and the cost of goods sold (if material).

Standard costing is a substantial subject, and so is dealt with separately in the Standard Costing chapter. That chapter describes how to create standards, which specific journal entries to use, how to calculate all of the variances associated with the methodology, and how to report these variances to management.

The Retail Inventory Method

The retail inventory method is sometimes used by retailers that resell merchandise to estimate their ending inventory balances. This method is based on the relationship between the cost of merchandise and its retail price. To calculate the cost of ending inventory using the retail inventory method, follow these steps:

1. Calculate the cost-to-retail percentage, for which the formula is (Cost ÷ Retail price).

2. Calculate the cost of goods available for sale, for which the formula (Cost of beginning inventory + Cost of purchases).
3. Calculate the cost of sales during the period, for which the formula is ales × cost-to-retail percentage).
4. Calculate ending inventory, for which the formula is (Cost of gds available for sale - Cost of sales during the period).

EXAMPLE

Mulligan Imports sells golf clubs for an average of $200, and which cost it $140. This is a cost-to-retail percentage of 70%. Mulligan's beginning inventory has a cost of $1,000,000, it paid $1,800,000 for purchases during the month, and it had sales of $2,400,000. The calculation of its ending inventory is:

Beginning inventory	$1,000,000	(at cost)
Purchases	+ 1,800,000	(at cost)
Goods available for sale	= 2,800,000	
Sales	-1,680,000	(sales of $2,400,000 × 70%)
Ending inventory	= $1,120,000	

The retail inventory method is a quick and easy way to determine an approximate ending inventory balance. However, there are also several issues with it:

- The retail inventory method is only an estimate. Do not rely upon it too heavily to yield results that will compare with those of a physical inventory count.
- The retail inventory method only works when there is a consistent mark-up across all products sold. If not, the actual ending inventory cost may vary wildly from what was derived using this method.
- The method assumes that the historical basis for the mark-up percentage continues into the current period. If the mark-up was different (as may be caused by an after-holidays sale), the results of the calculation will be incorrect.

Valuation Step 2b: Inventory Costing (Special Situations)

Thus far, the inventory costing methods presented have all been based on the assumption that there is an inventory comprised of a variety of different items. But what if production is based on customized products instead? The solution is a job costing system, which is presented below. Another scenario is when a company produces large quantities of exactly the same product – if so, process costing may be the best way to assign a cost to it. And finally, what if some products are split off from a common production process, so that it is not possible to determine their separate costs during the early stages of manufacturing? The solution is to use by-produce and joint product costing. All of these methods are described briefly in the following sections; because they are so specialized, there is also a separate chapter containing additional information about each one.

Jc Costing

A job costing system is useful when a business is producing customized products or services. In these situations, it is necessary to compile costs for each specific product. To do so, create a separate job number for each job, and compile cost information for each one, which involves the accumulation of costs related to materials, labor, and overhead. There is no inventory layering in job costing – instead, simply assign each cost to a job as it is incurred. When the job is completed, charge the contents of the job file to the cost of goods sold, and close down the job.

Job costing is a substantial topic, and so is covered separately in the Job Costing chapter. That chapter gives an overview of job costing, which journal entries to use, how to track job costs, and which controls to implement for a job costing system.

Process Costing

A process costing system is used when an entity manufactures large quantities of the same product. In this scenario, there is no point in tracking costs on an individual unit basis, since all of the units are the same. Instead, it is much more efficient to track costs for the entire production process (hence the name), and divide by the number of units produced to determine unit costs.

There are several calculation options for process costing, which are addressed in the Process Costing chapter. The weighted average method is the most commonly used, though variations are available that incorporate standard costs or the first in, first out cost flow model. The chapter also includes the journal entries to use in a process costing environment.

By-Product and Joint Product Costing

There are manufacturing processes where a number of products can be derived from a single set of production steps. If so, a method is needed to allocate the cost of production to the various products that are created. We address a variety of allocation options in the Joint and By-Product Costing chapter. When reviewing the chapter, please note that *all* of the options presented are merely allocations – there is no justifiable basis for accurately assigning joint costs to products. A joint cost is a cost which benefits more than one product, and for which it may not be possible to separate its contribution to each product.

Valuation Step 3: Overhead Allocation

The preceding valuation step was concerned with charging the direct costs of production (those costs that can be clearly associated with products) to inventory, but what about overhead expenses? In many businesses, the cost of overhead is substantially greater than direct costs, so the cost accountant must expend considerable attention on the proper method of allocating overhead to inventory.

There are two types of overhead, which are administrative overhead and manufacturing overhead. *Administrative overhead* includes those costs not involved in the development or production of goods or services, such as the costs of front office administration and sales; this is essentially all overhead that is not included in manufacturing overhead. *Manufacturing overhead* is all of the costs that a factory incurs, other than direct costs.

Allocate the costs of manufacturing overhead to any inventory items that are classified as work-in-process or finished goods. Overhead is not allocated to raw materials inventory, since the operations giving rise to overhead costs only impact work-in-process and finished goods inventory.

The following items are usually included in manufacturing overhead:

Depreciation of factory equipment	Quality control and inspection
Factory administration expenses	Rent, facility and equipment
Indirect labor and production supervisory wages	Repair expenses
Indirect materials and supplies	Rework labor, scrap and spoilage
Maintenance, factory and production equipment	Taxes related to production assets
Officer salaries related to production	Uncapitalized tools and equipment
Production employees' benefits	Utilities

The typical procedure for allocating overhead is to accumulate all manufacturing overhead costs into one or more cost pools (which are groups of similar costs), and then use an activity measure to apportion the overhead costs in the cost pools to inventory. Thus, the overhead allocation formula is:

Cost pool ÷ Total activity measure = Overhead allocation per unit

EXAMPLE

Mulligan Imports has a small production line for an in-house line of golf clubs. During April, it incurs costs for the following items:

Cost Type	Amount
Building rent	$65,000
Building utilities	12,000
Factory equipment depreciation	8,000
Production equipment maintenance	7,000
Total	$92,000

All of these items are classified as manufacturing overhead, so Mulligan creates the following journal entry to shift these costs into an overhead cost pool:

Inventory Valuation

	Debit	Credit
Overhead cost pool	92,000	
Depreciation expense		8,000
Maintenance expense		7,000
Rent expense		65,000
Utilities expense		12,000

Overhead costs can be allocated by any reasonable measure, as long as it is consistently applied across reporting periods. Common bases of allocation are direct labor hours charged against a product, or the amount of machine hours used during the production of a product. The amount of allocation charged per unit is known as the *overhead rate*.

The overhead rate can be expressed as a proportion, if both the numerator and denominator are in dollars. For example, ABC Company has total indirect costs of $100,000 and it decides to use the cost of its direct labor as the allocation measure. ABC incurs $50,000 of direct labor costs, so the overhead rate is calculated as:

$$\frac{\$100,000 \text{ Indirect costs}}{\$50,000 \text{ Direct labor}}$$

The result is an overhead rate of 2.0.

Alternatively, if the denominator is not in dollars, then the overhead rate is expressed as a cost per allocation unit. For example, ABC Company decides to change its allocation measure to hours of machine time used. ABC has 10,000 hours of machine time usage, so the overhead rate is now calculated as:

$$\frac{\$100,000 \text{ Indirect costs}}{10,000 \text{ Machine hours}}$$

The result is an overhead rate of $10.00 per machine hour.

EXAMPLE

Mulligan Imports has a small golf shaft production line, which manufactures a titanium shaft and an aluminum shaft. Considerable machining is required for both shafts, so Mulligan concludes that it should allocate overhead to these products based on the total hours of machine time used. In May, production of the titanium shaft requires 5,400 hours of machine time, while the aluminum shaft needs 2,600 hours. Thus, 67.5% of the overhead cost pool is allocated to the titanium shafts and 32.5% to the aluminum shafts.

In May, Mulligan accumulates $100,000 of costs in its overhead cost pool, and allocates it between the two product lines with the following journal entry:

	Debit	Credit
Finished goods – Titanium shafts	67,500	
Finished goods – Aluminum shafts	32,500	
Overhead cost pool		100,000

This entry clears out the balance in the overhead cost pool, readying it to accumulate overhead costs in the next reporting period.

If the basis of allocation does not appear correct for certain types of overhead costs, it may make more sense to split the overhead into two or more overhead cost pools, and allocate each cost pool using a different basis of allocation. For example, if warehouse costs are more appropriately allocated based on the square footage consumed by various products, then store warehouse costs in a warehouse overhead cost pool, and allocate these costs based on square footage used.

Thus far, we have assumed that only actual overhead costs incurred are allocated. However, it is also possible to set up a standard overhead rate that one can continue to use for multiple reporting periods, based on long-term expectations regarding how much overhead will be incurred and how many units will be produced. If the difference between actual overhead costs incurred and overhead allocated is small, charge the difference to the cost of goods sold. If the amount is material, allocate the difference to both the cost of goods sold and inventory.

EXAMPLE

Mulligan Imports incurs overhead of $93,000, which it stores in an overhead cost pool. Mulligan uses a standard overhead rate of $20 per unit, which approximates its long-term experience with the relationship between overhead costs and production volumes. In September, it produces 4,500 golf club shafts, to which it allocates $90,000 (allocation rate of $20 × 4,500 units). This leaves a difference between overhead incurred and overhead absorbed of $3,000. Given the small size of the variance, Mulligan charges the $3,000 difference to the cost of goods sold, thereby clearing out the overhead cost pool.

The example mentions the concept of overhead absorbed. This is manufacturing overhead that has been applied to products or other cost objects. Overhead is *overabsorbed* when the amount allocated to a product or other cost object is higher than the actual amount of overhead, while the amount is *underabsorbed* when the amount allocated is lower than the actual amount of overhead.

A key issue is that overhead allocation is not a precisely-defined science – there is plenty of latitude in how to allocate overhead. The amount of allowable diversity in practice can result in slipshod accounting, so be sure to use a standardized and well-documented method to allocate overhead using the same calculation in every reporting period. This allows for great consistency, which auditors appreciate when they validate the supporting calculations.

Valuation Step 4: Inventory Valuation

Many cost accountants may complete the preceding steps to create an inventory valuation, and go no further. However, there are two situations worth reviewing on a regular basis, which are to reduce the recorded cost of inventory under either the lower of cost or market rule, or to account for obsolete inventory. The next two sections address these issues. Of the two, the one to be most careful of is obsolete inventory, which nearly always is present in any inventory that has been in existence for more than a few years.

The Lower of Cost or Market Rule

The lower of cost or market rule (LCM) is required by generally accepted accounting principles, and essentially states that the cost of inventory is recorded at whichever cost is lower – the original cost or its current market price (hence the name of the rule). More specifically, the rule mandates that the recognized cost of an inventory item should be reduced to a level that does not exceed its replacement cost as derived in an open market. This replacement cost is subject to the following two conditions:

- The recognized cost cannot be greater than the likely selling price minus costs of disposal (known as net realizable value).
- The recognized cost cannot be lower than the net realizable value minus a normal profit percentage.

This situation typically arises when inventory has deteriorated, or has become obsolete, or market prices have declined. The following example illustrates the concept.

EXAMPLE

Mulligan Imports resells five major brands of golf clubs, which are noted in the following table. At the end of its reporting year, Mulligan calculates the upper and lower price boundaries of the LCM rule for each of the products, as noted in the table:

Product	Selling Price	-	Completion/ Selling Cost	=	Upper Price Boundary	-	Normal Profit	=	Lower Price Boundary
Free Swing	$250		$25		$225		$75		$150
Golf Elite	190		19		171		57		114
Hi-Flight	150		15		135		45		90
Iridescent	1,000		100		900		300		600
Titanium	700		70		630		210		420

The normal profit associated with these products is a 30% margin on the original selling price.

The information in the preceding table for the upper and lower price boundaries is then included in the following table, which completes the LCM calculation:

Product	Upper Price Boundary	Lower Price Boundary	Existing Recognized Cost	Replacement Cost*	Market Value**	Lower of Cost or Market
Free Swing	$225	$150	$140	$260	$225	$140
Golf Elite	171	114	180	175	171	171
Hi-Flight	135	90	125	110	110	110
Iridescent	900	600	850	550	600	600
Titanium	630	420	450	390	420	420

* The cost at which the item could be acquired on the open market
** The replacement cost, as limited by the upper and lower pricing boundaries

The LCM decisions noted in the last table are explained as follows:
- *Free Swing clubs.* It would cost Mulligan $260 to replace these clubs, which is above the upper price boundary of $225. This means the market value for the purposes of this calculation is $225. Since the market price is higher than the existing recognized cost, the LCM decision is to leave the recognized cost at $140 each.
- *Golf Elite clubs.* The replacement cost of these clubs has declined to a level below the existing recognized cost, so the LCM decision is to revise the recognized cost to $171. This amount is a small reduction from the unadjusted replacement cost of $175 to the upper price boundary of $171.

- *Hi-Flight clubs.* The replacement cost is less than the recognized cost, and is between the price boundaries. Consequently, there is no need to revise the replacement cost. The LCM decision is to revise the recognized cost to $110.
- *Iridescent clubs.* The replacement cost of these clubs is below the existing recognized cost, but is below the lower price boundary. Thus, the LCM decision is to set the market price at the lower price boundary, which will be the revised cost of the clubs.
- *Titanium clubs.* The replacement cost is much less than the existing recognized cost, but also well below the lower price boundary. The LCM decision is therefore to set the market price at the lower price boundary, which is also the new product cost.

A variation on the LCM rule simplifies matters somewhat, but only if a business is *not* using the last in, first out method or the retail method. The variation states that the measurement can be restricted to just the lower of cost and net realizable value.

> **Related Podcast Episode:** Episode 200 of the Accounting Best Practices Podcast discusses the revised lower of cost or market rule. It is available at: **accounting-tools.com/podcasts** or **iTunes**

If the amount of a write-down caused by the LCM analysis is minor, charge the expense to the cost of goods sold, since there is no reason to separately track the information. If the loss is material, track it in a separate account (especially if such losses are recurring), such as "Loss on LCM adjustment." A sample journal entry for a large adjustment is:

	Debit	Credit
Loss on LCM adjustment	147,000	
Finished goods inventory		147,000

Additional factors to consider when applying the LCM rule are:
- *Analysis by category.* The LCM rule is normally applied to a specific inventory item, but it can be applied to entire inventory categories. In the latter case, an LCM adjustment can be avoided if there is a balance within an inventory category of items having market below cost and in excess of cost.
- *Hedges.* If inventory is being hedged by a fair value hedge, add the effects of the hedge to the cost of the inventory, which frequently eliminates the need for an LCM adjustment.
- *Last in, first out layer recovery.* A write-down to the lower of cost or market can be avoided in an interim period if there is substantial evidence that inventory amounts will be restored by year end, thereby avoiding recognition of an earlier inventory layer.

- *Raw materials.* Do not write down the cost of raw materials if the finished goods in which they are used are expected to sell either at or above their costs.
- *Recovery.* A write-down to the lower of cost or market can be avoided if there is substantial evidence that market prices will increase before the inventory is sold.
- *Sales incentives.* If there are unexpired sales incentives that will result in a loss on the sale of a specific item, this is a strong indicator that there may be an LCM problem with that item.

Tip: When there is an LCM adjustment, it must be taken at once – the expense cannot be recognized over multiple reporting periods.

Obsolete Inventory Accounting

What should the accountant do if there is obsolete inventory on hand? Determine the most likely disposition of the obsolete items, subtract the amount of this projected amount from the book value of the obsolete items, and set aside the difference as a reserve. As the company later disposes of the items, or the estimated amounts to be received from disposition change, adjust the reserve account to reflect these events.

EXAMPLE

Mulligan Imports has $100,000 of excess golf clubs that it cannot sell. However, it believes there is a market for the clubs through a reseller in China, but only at a sale price of $20,000. Accordingly, the Mulligan cost accountant recognizes a reserve of $80,000 with the following journal entry:

	Debit	Credit
Cost of goods sold	80,000	
Reserve for obsolete inventory		80,000

After finalizing the arrangement with the Chinese reseller, the actual sale price is only $19,000, so the cost accountant completes the transaction with the following entry, recognizing an additional $1,000 of expense:

	Debit	Credit
Reserve for obsolete inventory	80,000	
Cost of goods sold	1,000	
Inventory		81,000

The example makes inventory obsolescence accounting look simple enough, but it is not. The issues are:

- *Timing*. One can improperly alter a company's reported financial results by altering the timing of the actual dispositions. As an example, if a supervisor knows that he can receive a higher-than-estimated price on the disposition of obsolete inventory, he can either accelerate or delay the sale in order to shift gains into whichever reporting period needs the extra profit.
- *Expense recognition*. Management may be reluctant to suddenly drop a large expense reserve into the financial statements, preferring instead to recognize small incremental amounts which make inventory obsolescence appear to be a minor problem. Since generally accepted accounting principles mandate immediate recognition of any obsolescence as soon as it is detected, the cost accountant may have a struggle forcing immediate recognition through the objections of management.
- *Timely reviews*. Inventory obsolescence is likely to be a minor issue as long as management reviews inventory on a regular basis, so that the incremental amount of obsolescence detected is small in any given period. However, if management does not conduct a review for a long time, this allows obsolete inventory to build up to quite impressive proportions, along with an equally impressive amount of expense recognition. To avoid this issue, conduct frequent obsolescence reviews, and maintain a reserve based on historical or expected obsolescence, even if the specific inventory items have not yet been identified. Also, encourage the warehouse manager to make full use of the reserve, which he should treat as an opportunity to eliminate ancient items from stock.
- *Management resistance*. Senior managers may not believe the cost accountant when he presents them with a massive write down, and so will reject any attempt to recognize an obsolescence reserve. If so, hire outside consultants who will independently review the inventory and present their own obsolescence report to management. This second opinion may bring sufficient professional weight to bear that management will grudgingly allow the creation of a reserve.

EXAMPLE

Mulligan Imports sets aside an obsolescence reserve of $25,000 for obsolete drivers. However, in January the purchasing manager knows that the resale price for obsolete drivers has plummeted, so the real reserve should be closer to $35,000, which would call for the immediate recognition of an additional $10,000 of expense. However, since this would result in an overall reported loss in Mulligan's financial results in January, he waits until April, when Mulligan has a very profitable month, and completes the sale at that time, thereby delaying the additional obsolescence loss until the point of sale.

At the time of the sale, the cost accountant realizes what has happened and takes the matter to the controller, who elects not to bring up the issue with management. The cost accountant, knowing that he can no longer trust the purchasing manager to give him correct inventory valuation information, takes a job with a different company.

Summary

This chapter has described the four steps involved in creating an accurate inventory valuation. All four are fraught with problems. There are a multitude of ways in which to incorrectly arrive at the quantity of units in stock, and a similar number of ways in which to arrive at an incorrect product cost. Further, given the large amount of costs in overhead, even a small change in the overhead allocation methodology can result in a startling change in reported profit levels. And finally, many companies do not spend sufficient time reviewing inventory obsolescence issues, so that their inventories should be valued lower than the cost at which they are actually reported. Given this potential morass of issues, it is no surprise that inventory valuation causes the most problems for cost accountants out of all their responsibilities, and is an area in which they spend a substantial proportion of their time.

Chapter 5
Job Costing

Introduction

Job costing is the system for compiling costs that are associated with a specific job or project. It is one of the most heavily used methods for tracking costs. In this chapter, we give an overview of job costing, and also discuss the specific accounting transactions and controls associated with it.

Overview of Job Costing

Job costing is used to accumulate costs at a small-unit level. For example, job costing is appropriate for deriving the cost of constructing a custom machine, designing a software program, or building a small batch of products. Job costing involves the following accounting activities:

- *Materials*. It accumulates the cost of components and then assigns these costs to a product or project once the components are used.
- *Labor*. Employees charge their time to specific jobs, which are then assigned to the jobs based on the labor cost of the employees.
- *Overhead*. It accumulates overhead costs in cost pools, and then allocates these costs to jobs.

Job costing is an excellent tool for tracing specific costs to individual jobs and examining them to see if the costs can later be reduced.

EXAMPLE

Twill Machinery has just completed job number 1003, which is for a custom-designed milling machine ordered by a long-term customer. The costs assigned to the job include an allocation of $12,000 for 200 hours of rework on burrs discovered in numerous places on the metal edges of the machine. Further investigation reveals that the burrs were caused by improper metal stamping when the component parts were originally created.

Since the customer is likely to order additional versions of the same machine, management assigns a task group to investigate and correct the metal stamping process. Twill would probably not have found this problem if the job costing system had not highlighted it.

Job costing results in discrete "buckets" of information about each job that the cost accountant can review to see if it really should be assigned to that job. If there are many jobs currently in progress, there is a strong chance that costs will be incorrectly assigned, but the very nature of the job costing system makes it highly auditable.

If a job is expected to run for a long period of time, the cost accountant can periodically compare the costs accumulated in the bucket for that job to its budget, and give management advance warning if costs appear to be running ahead of projections. This gives management time to either get costs under control over the remainder of the project, or possibly to approach the customer about a billing increase to cover some or all of the cost overrun.

Job costing demands a considerable amount of costing precision if costs are to be reimbursed by customers (as is the case in a cost-plus contract, where the customer pays all costs incurred, plus a profit). In such cases, the cost accountant must carefully review the costs assigned to each job before releasing it to the billing staff, which creates a customer invoice. This can cause long hours for the cost accountant at the end of a job, since the company controller will want to issue an invoice as soon as possible.

When Not to Use Job Costing

As just noted, job costing is the ideal solution for discrete manufacturing situations where costs can be clearly associated with specific products or projects. There are also a number of situations where job costing is not the best alternative. Here are some examples:

- *High data entry cost.* If it is extremely difficult to collect information for the job costing system, the compiled information may be more expensive than the cost of the product. Usually, it is possible to obtain some of the required information at a lower cost, but the cost accountant must decide whether to pursue incremental improvements in costing information at a higher marginal cost.
- *High proportion of allocated costs.* In many production environments, the overhead cost is so high that it exceeds the amount of those costs directly traceable to a job. If the basis of overhead allocation is arbitrary, then does it make sense to allocate costs to jobs at all? An alternative may be to only accumulate costs that have a proven relationship to a job, and to leave all other costs in a general overhead cost pool.
- *Low cost per unit.* If a product has a minimal per-unit cost, as is the case for a downloaded electronic product, there is no point in collecting what little cost information may be available.
- *Process environment.* If a company is building vast quantities of the same product, such as in a ball bearing plant or an oil refinery, there is no way to collect information for a specific unit of production.

Accounting for Direct Materials in Job Costing

In a job costing environment, materials to be used on a product or project first enter the facility and are stored in the warehouse, after which they are picked from stock and issued to a specific job. If spoilage or scrap is created, then normal amounts are charged to an overhead cost pool for later allocation, while abnormal amounts are charged directly to the cost of goods sold. Once work is completed on a job, the cost of the entire job is shifted from work-in-process inventory to finished goods inventory. Then, once the goods are sold, the cost of the asset is removed from the inventory account and shifted into the cost of goods sold, while the company also records a sale transaction. The following example shows how to account for these direct material movements.

EXAMPLE

Twill Machinery orders $10,000 of sheet metal, which arrives and is stored in the warehouse. Twill records this transaction with the following entry:

	Debit	Credit
Raw materials inventory	10,000	
Accounts payable		10,000

Twill's production scheduling staff creates job number 1200, which is designated to accumulate the costs associated with a laying press for an antique book bindery. The production scheduling staff authorizes the issuance of a pick list to the warehouse, which is used to pick items from stock for the construction of job 1200. The pick list includes the following items:

Item	Cost
Sheet metal	$1,500
Hardboard platen	450
Press bed	280
Adjustment wheel	150
Total cost	$2,380

Twill uses the following entry to record the transfer of raw materials to work-in-process for job 1200. Note that only a portion of the sheet metal is moved to work-in-process; the rest of the purchased amount remains in the warehouse, to be used on some other job.

	Debit	Credit
Work-in-process (Job 1200)	2,380	
Raw materials inventory		2,380

During production of the laying press, Twill experiences $300 of abnormal scrap, which it charges directly to the cost of goods sold (not to Job 1200), on the grounds that it must recognize the expense at once. The entry is:

	Debit	Credit
Cost of goods sold	300	
Work-in-process (Job 1200)		300

At the end of the month, $5,000 of normal scrap costs have accumulated in the waste overhead cost pool, which accumulates the costs of normal scrap and spoilage (see the Waste Accounting chapter). The cost accountant determines that 10% of this amount, or $500, should be allocated to Job 1200. The entry is:

	Debit	Credit
Work-in-process (Job 1200)	500	
Waste cost pool		500

Twill completes work on the laying press and shifts all related material costs to the finished goods inventory account. The entry is:

	Debit	Credit
Finished goods (Job 1200)	2,580	
Work-in-process (Job 1200)		2,580

Please note that these entries do not yet include labor costs or an allocation for manufacturing overhead; these topics are addressed in the following sections.

Accounting for Labor in Job Costing

In a job costing environment, labor may be charged directly to individual jobs, if the labor is directly traceable to those jobs. All other manufacturing-related labor is recorded in an overhead cost pool and is then allocated to the various open jobs. The first type of labor is called direct labor, and the second type is known as indirect labor. When a job is completed, it is then shifted into a finished goods inventory account. Then, once the goods are sold, the cost of the asset is removed from the inventory account and shifted into the cost of goods sold, while the company also records a sale transaction. The following example shows how to account for these labor transactions.

EXAMPLE

This is a continuation of the preceding example, where Twill Machinery is building a laying press for an antique book bindery. Twill pays its employees at the end of each month, and records the following payroll entry for its production department:

	Debit	Credit
Work-in-process (Job 1200)	8,000	
Work-in-process (Job 1201)	16,000	
Work-in-process (Job 1202)	41,000	
Overhead cost pool	35,000	
Wages payable		100,000

At the end of the month, Twill allocates the indirect labor in the overhead cost pool to the various open jobs. Of the $35,000 of labor in the overhead cost pool, Twill allocates $4,000 to Job 1200 with the following entry:

	Debit	Credit
Work-in-process (Job 1200)	4,000	
Overhead cost pool		4,000

Twill completes work on the laying press and shifts all related labor costs to the finished goods inventory account. The entry is:

	Debit	Credit
Finished goods (Job 1200)	12,000	
Work-in-process (Job 1200)		12,000

This final entry comes from the $8,000 of direct labor that was initially charged against Job 1200, and the $4,000 of indirect labor that was allocated to it.

Accounting for Actual Overhead Costs in Job Costing

In a job costing environment, non-direct costs are accumulated into one or more overhead cost pools, from which costs are allocated to open jobs based upon some measure of cost usage. The key issues when applying overhead are to consistently charge the same types of costs to overhead in all reporting periods, and to consistently apply these costs to jobs. Otherwise, it can be extremely difficult for the cost accountant to explain why overhead cost allocations vary from one month to the next.

EXAMPLE

This is a continuation of the preceding example, where Twill Machinery is building a laying press for an antique book bindery. During the most recent reporting period, Twill incurred the following costs, all of which it records in an overhead cost pool:

Expense Type	Amount
Production facility rent	$60,000
Equipment repair costs	15,000
Building repair costs	9,000
Production supplies	3,000
Total	$87,000

Twill allocates overhead costs to jobs based on their use of production equipment. Job 1200 accounted for 12% of total equipment usage during the month, so Twill allocates 12% of the $87,000 in the cost pool to Job 1200 with the following entry:

	Debit	Credit
Work-in-process (Job 1200)	10,440	
Overhead cost pool		10,440

Twill completes work on the laying press and shifts all related overhead costs to the finished goods inventory account. The entry is:

	Debit	Credit
Finished goods (Job 1200)	10,440	
Work-in-process (Job 1200)		10,440

Accounting for Standard Overhead Costs in Job Costing

The accumulation of actual costs into overhead pools and their allocation to jobs, as noted in the preceding section, can be a time-consuming process that interferes with closing the books on a reporting period. To speed up the process, an alternative is to allocate standard costs that are based on historical costs. These standard costs will never be exactly the same as actual costs, but can be easily calculated and allocated.

The overhead allocation process for standard costs is to use historical cost information to arrive at a standard rate per unit of activity, and then allocate this standard amount to jobs based on their units of activity. One can then subtract the total amount allocated from the overhead cost pool (which contains actual overhead costs), and dispose of any remaining amount in the overhead cost pool. Use any of the following methods to dispose of the remaining amount:

- *Charge to cost of goods sold.* Charge the entire variance to the cost of goods sold. This is the simplest method.

- *Allocate the variance.* Allocate the variance to the accounts for finished goods, work-in-process, and cost of goods sold, based on the ending balances in these accounts. This approach is slightly more time-consuming, but is the most theoretically correct method under generally accepted accounting principles.
- *Charge to jobs.* Allocate the variance to those jobs that were open during the reporting period. This approach is the most time-consuming. It essentially reverts a company back to an actual costing system, since the results of this method will approximate those created under an actual cost allocation system.

The allocation of an overhead cost pool is by definition inherently inaccurate, since the underlying costs cannot be directly associated with a job. Consequently, it is best to use the simplest of the above methods to dispose of any residual amounts in the overhead cost pool.

EXAMPLE

Twill Manufacturing decides to revise its cost allocation method to the standard costing system. In the past three months, the company incurred the following amounts of manufacturing overhead:

Month 1	$71,000
Month 2	82,000
Month 3	87,000
Average monthly overhead	$80,000

The manufacturing facility usually experiences 2,000 hours of machine usage per month, so Twill adopts a standard overhead allocation rate of $40 per hour of machine usage, which it derives as follows:

$80,000 Average monthly overhead ÷ 2,000 Hours of machine usage = $40/hour allocation rate

During the most recent month, Job 1200 incurred $10,440 of actual overhead costs (see the preceding example). In that month, it used 240 hours of machine time, which at a standard application rate of $40/hour, results in an overhead allocation of $9,600. Thus, the use of a standard overhead rate that is based on an historical average amount of costs incurred results in an $840 reduction in the amount of overhead charged to Job 1200.

In Month 3, the standard $40/hour rate is charged to 2,000 hours of machine time used, for a total allocation of $80,000. This leaves $7,000 of actual overhead costs remaining in the overhead cost pool (since $87,000 of actual overhead costs were incurred in Month 3). Rather than go through the effort of allocating this residual to any accounts or jobs, the cost accountant elects to charge it directly to the cost of goods sold with the following entry:

	Debit	Credit
Cost of goods sold	7,000	
Overhead cost pool		7,000

The net effect of this adjustment is that Twill records $7,000 more expense in the current month than might otherwise have been the case. If it had instead elected to use the allocation of actual overhead costs, the costs would have remained in the inventory account as an asset until the jobs were billed to customers.

The Importance of Closing a Job

A job is the same as an account – it is a bucket in which transactions are recorded. Once all work on a specific job is complete, close the associated job. By doing so, people can be kept from inadvertently (or deliberately) charging additional expenses to it. More particularly, the monthly overhead cost allocation may result in overhead being charged to *all* open jobs, even if there has been no activity in some of those accounts in months. Further, closing a job keeps anyone from deliberately shifting both billings and expenses in and out of the related account; this activity is used to alter the reported profitability levels of specific jobs.

It may be several weeks or a month after a job is complete, before a job can be closed. Before that time, late supplier invoices may arrive that should be charged against the job. However, once a job has been closed, it should not be reopened without documented approval from senior management. Otherwise, the cost accountant is continually dealing with minor account adjustments for many months into the future.

The Role of the Subsidiary Ledger in Job Costing

The preceding sections should make it clear that a job costing system causes quite a large number of accounting transactions. If a company has many jobs, this can result in a veritable blizzard of transactions, which can create a recordkeeping problem. There are three ways to record accounting transactions at the job level, which are:

- *In a spreadsheet.* The most primitive way to record job-level transactions is to treat the primary accounting software as though there are no jobs, and instead record the job-specific information on a separate spreadsheet for each job. Under this approach, all transactions are still recorded in the accounting system under the corporate chart of accounts, but jobs are not identified. Using a spreadsheet greatly increases the risk that information stored in the spreadsheet will not match the information in the general ledger, but also eliminates the need for separate job-level accounts in the accounting software. This method is acceptable if there are few jobs that do not involve a large number of transactions.
- *In the general ledger.* A more advanced method is to create a new account in the general ledger for each job. This approach centralizes all information

in a single database, but also clutters up the general ledger with a large number of additional accounts and transactions. This method is acceptable if there are few jobs having low-to-moderate amounts of transactions.

- *In subsidiary ledgers.* The cleanest method is to record job-related transactions in a subsidiary ledger. Under this approach, create a unique account for each job in a subsidiary ledger, and roll up summary totals from the subsidiary ledger to the general ledger at the end of each month. This keeps a great deal of clutter out of the general ledger, though it does mean that the subsidiary ledger must be accessed to research the details of transactions – the information will not be available in the general ledger. This method is nearly mandatory when there are many jobs and large transaction volumes.

There is an obvious progression in the record keeping methods presented here. A small operation can usually get by with spreadsheet-based records until it begins to have problems reconciling the information in the spreadsheets with the accounting system. It then moves to recordkeeping in the general ledger until the number of accounts and transactions makes the general ledger too complex, and then finally shifts to subsidiary ledgers to handle more high-volume situations.

Job Costing Controls

The volume and flow of transactions in a job costing environment give rise to several problems that require the imposition of controls. The key problem areas are:

- *Abnormal variance treatment.* The default journal entry in job costing for any type of abnormal variance is to charge it to the cost of goods sold. This approach means that expense recognition tends to be accelerated into the current period. A profit-minded manager (perhaps one with a bonus riding on the outcome) may put pressure on the cost accountant to find a way to not treat these variances as abnormal, and thereby shift their recognition into a future period. The best control is to have an outside entity, such as the internal audit department, periodically investigate how these variances are recorded.
- *Allocation methodology.* A manager may adopt whichever cost allocation methodology tends to shift overhead costs toward those jobs that are still open, and away from those about to be closed, thereby deferring expense recognition. This technique only works reliably when the allocation method constantly changes to whichever one yields the best results, so a prime indicator of this problem is a history of constantly altering the allocation method. Another control is to require senior management approval of any change in allocation methodology.
- *Cost shifting.* Managers may shift costs among a variety of open jobs in order to defer their recognition for as long as possible. This is a particular problem for old jobs that remain open despite minimal activity, since no one is overseeing them. The best controls are to promptly close jobs as soon as

they are completed, and to have the internal audit department periodically review the contents of the job accounts.

- *Designate direct labor as indirect labor.* It is possible to defer the recognition of labor expenses by reclassifying direct labor as indirect labor and thereby moving it into an overhead cost pool. By doing so, some portion of this cost is apportioned to jobs that may not be charged to expense until a later time period. A good control is to lock in a direct labor or indirect labor designation for every person in the payroll, and track any designation changes over time.
- *Period expense treatment.* A manager may attempt to record a current-period expense in an overhead cost pool, thereby deferring recognition of some portion of the expense until a later period. A current-period expense is one that is directly associated with the passage of time, rather than the production of inventory items, such as administrative expenses. A reasonable control is to conduct periodic reviews of the sources from which costs are pulled into the overhead cost pool. An indicator of a problem is a spike or increasing trend in the amount of this pool.
- *Variance recordation.* A manager may attempt to report excessively high profits by incorrectly charging negative job cost variances to an inventory account, rather than to the cost of goods sold, which defers recognition to a later period. A possible control is for the internal audit staff to trace how these variances are calculated, and where they are recorded.

The primary reason for many of the preceding controls is that managers twist the results of the job costing system to defer expense recognition. Since managers are the ones most likely to be at fault, the only good control is to have an outside entity – such as the internal audit department – examine the results of the job costing system. Any other controls probably fall under the authority of the managers who are misusing the system, and so are useless.

Summary

Job costing is one of the most common cost accumulation systems in existence, since it is ideally suited to giving accurate information about the cost of a specific product or project. However, it is a time-consuming system that requires a large amount of data entry, control points, and error checking. Consequently, only use it if there is a real need for such a large amount of detailed cost information. If not, there are simpler cost accumulation systems described elsewhere in this book that will yield a sufficient amount of less-accurate information – and that may be enough for management's reporting needs.

Chapter 6
Process Costing

Introduction

Process costing is a costing system used in situations where large quantities of the same item are manufactured. In these situations, it is much too inefficient to track the cost of each individual product. Instead, accumulate the cost of a large number of units produced, and allocate the entire cost over all units produced. Thus, every unit created has exactly the same cost as every other unit produced.

In this chapter, we give an overview of process costing, how it is calculated, discuss situations where it should (and should not) be used, and also address how it can be integrated into a hybrid accounting system.

Overview of Process Costing

Job costing is generally the preferred method for deriving a product's cost. However, there are many situations where the volume of production is so high that there is no way to track the cost of each individual product in a cost-effective manner. Also, it may be impossible to differentiate the costs associated with individual products. If either situation is the case, the usual solution is to use process costing. The classic example of a process costing situation is oil refining, where the cost of any individual gallon of fuel cannot be differentiated from another one.

In process costing, there are three methods available for generating a cost per unit. They are:

- *Weighted average costing.* Averages all costs from multiple periods and assigns them to units. This method is most applicable to simple costing environments, and where there are few cost changes from period to period. It is the simplest calculation method.
- *Standard costing.* Assign standard costs to production units and treat variances from actual costs separately. This method is used when a company has a standard costing system in operation.
- *First in, first out (FIFO) costing.* Assigns costs to production units based on the periods in which costs are incurred. This method produces the highest degree of accuracy, and is also the most complex to calculate. The FIFO method is most useful where costs vary substantially from period to period, so that management can see product cost trends.

There is no last in, first out (LIFO) costing method used in process costing, since the underlying assumption of process costing is that the first unit produced is, in fact, the first unit used, which is the FIFO concept. Thus, the LIFO concept is invalid in a true process costing environment.

The typical manner in which costs flow in process costing is that direct material costs are added at the beginning of the process, while all other costs (both direct labor and overhead) are gradually added over the course of the production process. For example, in a food processing operation, the direct material (such as a cow) is added at the beginning of the operation, and then various rendering operations gradually convert the direct material into finished products (such as steaks).

The Weighted Average Method

The weighted average method is the simplest way to calculate process costs. To calculate the weighted average cost of a production unit, begin by deriving the number of units of production, which assumes that direct materials are added at the beginning of the process. This calculation is shown in the "Production Units" section of the following example, where 500 units are completed in the reporting period, and 200 units are still in production. We assume that direct materials were added to all 700 units, but that additional conversion costs were only fully applied to the 500 completed units. In the example, we assume that the 200 units still in process are only 30% complete, so we multiply the 200 units in process by the 30% conversion estimate to arrive at an adjusted 60 production units for the purposes of applying conversion costs. This means that there are 560 production units to which conversion costs can be applied.

EXAMPLE

	Direct Materials	Conversion Costs	Totals
Step 1: Production Units			
Completed units	500	500	
Units in process*	200	60	
Production unit totals	700	560	
Step 2: Cost per Unit			
Beginning cost in WIP	$4,000	$2,000	$6,000
Costs in current period	30,000	15,000	45,000
Total costs	$34,000	$17,000	$51,000
Cost per unit**	$48.571	$30.357	
Step 3: Allocate Costs			
Completed units cost	$24,286	$15,179	$39,465
Ending WIP units cost	9,714	1,821	11,535
Total costs	$34,000	$17,000	$51,000

* 30% complete at month-end
** Based on production unit totals listed above

The second step in using the weighted average method is to calculate the cost per production unit, which appears in the "Cost per Unit" section in the preceding example. The calculation steps are:

1. Enter the beginning direct materials costs for any beginning work-in-process items in the Direct Materials column, in the "Beginning cost in WIP" row. Work-in-process inventory is inventory that has been partially converted through the production process, but for which additional work must be completed before it can be recorded as finished goods inventory.
2. Enter the beginning conversion costs for any beginning work-in-process items in the Conversion Costs column, in the "Beginning cost in WIP" row.
3. Enter all current period direct materials costs in the Direct Materials column, in the "Costs in current period" row.
4. Enter all current period conversion costs in the Conversion Costs column, in the "Costs in current period" row.
5. Total all costs in the Direct Materials column and the Conversion Costs column, and enter the total in the "Total costs" row for each column, respectively.
6. Divide the total costs in the Direct Material column by the production unit totals listed in the same column, and enter the cost per unit in the "Cost per unit" row for that column.
7. Divide the total costs in the Conversion Costs column by the production unit totals listed in the same column, and enter the cost per unit in the "Cost per unit" row for that column.

The final step in using the weighted average method is to calculate total costs to assign to the work-in-process and finished goods inventory accounts. The following calculations appear in the Allocate Costs section in the preceding example:

1. Multiply the number of completed units in the Direct Materials column (500 in the example) by the cost per unit ($48.571 in the example), and enter the total in the Direct Materials column, in the "Completed units cost" row.
2. Multiply the number of completed units in the Conversion Costs column (500 in the example) by the cost per unit ($30.357 in the example), and enter the total in the Conversion Costs column, in the "Completed units cost" row.
3. Multiply the number of units in process in the Direct Materials column (200 in the example) by the cost per unit ($48.571 in the example), and enter the total in the Direct Materials column, in the "Ending WIP units cost" row.
4. Multiply the number of units in process in the Conversion Costs column (60 in the example) by the cost per unit ($30.357 in the example), and enter the total in the Conversion Costs column, in the "Ending WIP units cost" row.

In essence, these calculations create a reduced number of units in process, based on the presumed percentage of completion, which results in a reduced allocation of conversion costs to ending work-in-process units. In contrast, direct materials are allocated to the full number of work-in-process units, because the assumption is that direct materials are added at the *beginning* of the production process.

A great deal of the effort in these calculations is directed at creating different allocations for direct costs and conversion costs. If we did not differentiate between the two types of costs, and instead assumed that *all* costs are assigned at the beginning of the production process, then the amount allocated to the work-in-process account will increase, while the amount allocated to finished goods will decline. This shift in costs can have an impact on reported profits if a large part of the finished goods are sold by the end of the reporting period, since the costs that would normally be recorded as finished goods are not charged to the cost of goods sold, but are instead recorded as a work-in-process asset, and deferred from recognition until a later reporting period.

The Standard Costing Method

If a company uses a standard costing system (see the Standard Costing chapter), the cost accountant is accustomed to working with predetermined costs and then calculating variances from those standards. It is possible to alter the basic process costing model to accommodate standard costs.

In the following example, we use the same general format as was just outlined for the weighted average method, with the following modifications:

- *Cost per unit.* In Step 2 in the example, we have replaced actual costs with a single standard cost for direct materials, and a single standard cost for conversion costs. These standard costs are derived by the company, and are generally close to the actual costs used in the weighted average method.
- *Allocate costs.* In Step 3 in the example, we have multiplied the production units by the standard costs noted in Step 2, rather than the actual costs that would have been used in the weighted average method.
- *Variance analysis.* The final portion of the example contains a new Step 4, which contains a compilation of the actual costs incurred during the period (taken from Step 3 of the preceding example), from which the standard costs calculated in Step 3 of this example are subtracted to derive variances. These variances are then charged to the cost of goods sold in the current period.

EXAMPLE

	Direct Materials	Conversion Costs	Totals
Step 1: Production Units			
Completed units	500	500	
Units in process*	200	60	
Production unit totals	700	560	
Step 2: Cost per Unit			
Standard cost per unit**	$48.500	$30.000	
Step 3: Allocate Costs			
Completed units cost	$24,250	$15,000	$39,250
Ending WIP units cost	9,700	1,800	11,500
Total costs	$33,950	$16,800	$50,750
Step 4: Variance Analysis			
Actual cost totals:			
Beginning cost in WIP	$4,000	$2,000	$6,000
Costs in current period	30,000	15,000	45,000
Total actual costs	$34,000	$17,000	$51,000
Total standard costs	$33,950	$16,800	$50,750
Cost variance	$50	$200	$250

* 30% complete at month-end
** Based on standard costs

The standard costing variation on the process costing model is slightly more difficult to derive than the weighted average model, since it adds standard costs and a variance calculation to the basic model. Still, it is not an especially difficult calculation.

The First In, First Out Method

The first in, first out (FIFO) method is more complicated than the weighted average or standard costing methods, so do not use it unless the increased accuracy of its results is of importance to management's decision making. Generally, only use the FIFO method when there are significant cost fluctuations between consecutive reporting periods that will result in notable differences in cost allocations in each of the periods.

The key change in the FIFO calculation from the weighted average method revolves around the segregation of the work-in-process costs that had been recorded in the preceding period. The key calculation steps, using the same example from the weighted average method section, are:

1. *Separate beginning work-in-process*. In Step 1 of the example, segregate the units in beginning work-in-process from the other production units. There should be no allocation of direct materials to these units, since that allocation would have been done in a prior period. Also, the conversion factor for the beginning work-in-process units may very well differ from the conversion factor used for the ending units in process. The following example shows a conversion factor for the beginning work-in-process of 50%, and of 30% for the ending work-in-process. The result is a lower unit total in the Direct Materials column, since the FIFO method only lists units here if additional costs are to be added to the units. There is also a lower unit total in the Conversion Costs column, because the 200 beginning work-in-process units are only 50% complete, and are therefore listed as 100 units.

2. *Calculate cost per unit*. In Step 2 of the example, we no longer include the cost of beginning work-in-process, since that is dealt with in the following step. Instead, we only calculate the cost per unit for costs incurred in the current period.

3. *Allocate costs*. In Step 3 of the example, we have created a cost layer for the beginning work-in-process called the "Beginning WIP cost," which establishes a separate cost layer for beginning inventory. We then follow the usual calculation steps, excluding the beginning work-in-process cost, which are:

   a. Multiply the 100 beginning WIP units in the Conversion Costs column by the $32.609 conversion cost per unit to derive the $3,261 of conversion costs added to beginning work-in-process.

   b. Multiply the 300 completed units in the Direct Materials column by the $60.000 direct materials cost per unit to derive the $18,000 of direct materials costs added to the new completed units.

   c. Multiply the 300 completed units in the Conversion Costs column by the $32.609 conversion cost per unit to derive the $9,783 of conversion costs added to the new completed units.

   d. Multiply the 200 ending WIP units in the Direct Materials column by the $60.000 direct materials cost per unit to derive the $12,000 of direct materials costs added to the ending work-in-process units.

   e. Multiply the 60 ending WIP units in the Conversion Costs column by the $32.609 conversion cost per unit to derive the $1,956 of conversion costs added to the ending work-in-process units.

EXAMPLE

	Direct Materials	Conversion Costs	Totals
Step 1: Production Units			
Beginning WIP units*	--	100	
Completed units	300	300	
Ending WIP units**	200	60	
Production unit totals	500	460	
Step 2: Cost per Unit			
Costs in current period	$30,000	$15,000	$45,000
Cost per unit***	$60.000	$32.609	
Step 3: Allocate Costs			
Beginning WIP cost	$4,000	$2,000	$6,000
Costs added to beginning WIP	--	3,261	3,261
Costs added to new completed units	18,000	9,783	27,783
Costs added to ending WIP	12,000	1,956	13,956
Total costs	$34,000	$17,000	$51,000

* 50% complete at the beginning of the month
** 30% complete at the end of the month
*** Based on production unit totals listed above

The end result is an allocation of the same amount of costs used in the original weighted average cost example, but with different proportions of costs being divided between the finished goods and ending work-in-process accounts.

The Hybrid Accounting System

A hybrid costing system is a cost accounting system that includes features of both a job costing and process costing system. It is also known as an *operation costing system*.

A hybrid costing system is useful when a production facility handles groups of products in batches and charges the cost of materials to those batches (see the Job Costing chapter), while also accumulating labor and overhead costs at the departmental or work center level, and allocating these costs at the individual unit level (as is the case in a process costing environment).

Hybrid costing is most commonly used in situations where there is identical processing of a baseline product, as well as individual modifications that are made beyond the baseline level of processing. For example, this situation arises when identical products are manufactured until they reach a painting operation, after which each product receives a different coating, with each coat having a different cost.

As another example, a company produces a variety of refrigerators, all of which require essentially the same processing, but differing amounts of materials. It can use a job costing system to assign varying amounts of materials to each refrigerator, while using the process costing method to allocate the cost of labor and overhead equally across all of the refrigerators produced.

EXAMPLE

Puller Corporation uses process costing to calculate the cost of its ubiquitous plastic door knobs, which are identical in all respects, and cost $0.25 each. Puller stores its plastic door knobs in an unfinished state and waits for customer orders before applying additional finishing operations.

The final finishing operation can involve either a chrome lamination operation, a spray-on mahogany finish, or rolling in a tumbler that simulates distressed furniture. Each of these operations results in a different cost. The cost of additional finishing in chrome is $0.15, the mahogany finish is $0.05, and the tumbler operation is $0.12. Thus, the additional costs are significantly different from each other, and will be completed in small batches, depending upon the size of customer orders.

Based on the variety of possible outcomes and the smaller size of production runs for finishing operations, Puller elects to keep its process costing system for the initial creation of plastic door knobs, but to switch to a job costing system to calculate finishing costs.

The key issue in choosing to use a hybrid system is whether certain parts of the production process are more easily accounted for under a different system than the one used by the bulk of the manufacturing operation. Many companies do not realize that they are using a hybrid costing system - they have simply adapted their cost accounting systems to the operational requirements of their business models.

Process Costing Journal Entries

Process costing is really just a simplified version of job costing, because it treats an entire production process as a single job. That being the case, it is possible to use the same journal entries shown in the Job Costing chapter to record process costs.

To use the weighted average process costing example used earlier in this chapter, the allocation of direct materials to production units results in $24,286 being allocated to completed units, and $9,714 to ending work-in-process units. The journal entry for this calculation would be:

	Debit	Credit
Finished goods inventory	24,286	
Work-in-process inventory	9,714	
Raw materials inventory		34,000

To continue with the same example, $15,179 of conversion costs were allocated to completed units, and $1,821 to ending work-in-process units. The journal entry for this calculation would be:

	Debit	Credit
Finished goods inventory	15,179	
Work-in-process inventory	1,821	
Conversion cost pool		17,000

If one were to use a standard costing variation on the process costing system, the only additional entry is to charge any variances to the cost of goods sold. To use the variances calculated earlier in the standard costing example, there is a $50 unfavorable variance for direct materials, and a $200 unfavorable variance for conversion costs. The journal entry to record these variances would be:

	Debit	Credit
Cost of goods sold	250	
Raw materials inventory		50
Conversion cost pool		200

The journal entries used for the FIFO method are quite similar in structure to those used for the weighted average method, though the proportions of costs recorded between the work-in-process and finished goods accounts differ somewhat. Also, the entries do not include the amount of costs in beginning work-in-process, which were recorded in the preceding period. The journal entries to record the results of the example in the earlier FIFO section are:

	Debit	Credit
Finished goods inventory	18,000	
Work-in-process inventory	12,000	
Raw materials inventory		30,000

To allocate direct materials to finished goods and work-in-process

	Debit	Credit
Finished goods inventory	13,044	
Work-in-process inventory	1,956	
Conversion cost pool		15,000

To allocate conversion costs to finished goods and work-in-process

In the last journal entry, the $13,044 addition to finished goods inventory is comprised of both the $9,783 that was directly allocated to completed units in the earlier example, and the $3,261 allocated to the units in beginning work-in-process (which assumes that beginning work-in-process was converted to finished goods during the reporting period).

Problems with Process Costing

The single largest problem with the process costing concept is the use of an estimated percentage of completion of work-in-process at the end of a reporting period. This percentage is a key part of the calculation to assign costs to work-in-process inventory, and so can be used to shift costs into or out of the current period to modify reported levels of profitability.

EXAMPLE

The production manager of Colossal Furniture, Mr. Mammoth, will receive a bonus if the company records a profit of $10,000 in November. The company uses a hybrid accounting system for its production of high chairs for oversized infants. Mr. Mammoth has control over the percentage of completion for units in process in the process costing portion of the cost accounting system.

The actual percentage of completion for units in process is 42%, but Mr. Mammoth calculates that if he authorizes a change to 45% completion, this will cause a higher allocation of costs to work-in-process, and thereby increases profits just enough to earn him the bonus.

The cost accounting manager is not aware of the bonus situation, and does not complain about what appears to be a minor increase in the percentage of completion. Mr. Mammoth receives his bonus.

A simple method that avoids manipulation of the percentage of completion is to use a standard percentage that is never changed in any reporting period. This technique does eliminate the risk of management override of the percentage; however, it introduces a new risk, which is that management can initiate a large amount of new work-in-process at the end of a reporting period, to which the standard percentage of completion now applies. Thus, management could potentially shift into a new form of reporting fraud if new controls are placed elsewhere in the system.

EXAMPLE

The internal audit staff of Colossal Furniture recommends to senior management that the percentage of completion used in its process costing calculation be fixed at 50%, thereby eliminating the type of manipulation described in the preceding example.

In December, the production manager (still Mr. Mammoth, despite his earlier manipulations) can earn yet another bonus if the company records a profit of $20,000. Near the end of the month, it appears that the company will be $5,000 short of its profit goal. To meet his target, Mr. Mammoth releases a large amount of work into the production area on December 31. No work is actually performed on any of these new projects, but because they are now categorized as work-in-process, the cost accountant must apply the standard percentage of completion to them.

The cost accountant allocates $5,000 of conversion costs to the new work-in-process items, which shifts these costs into the balance sheet as assets, thereby reducing the cost of goods sold by $5,000. Mr. Mammoth again earns his bonus.

Summary

Process costing is a common method for calculating the cost of standardized products that are produced in large quantities. It results in reasonably accurate results, so long as all of the products for which costs are being derived are actually the same in all respects. If not, it is better to incorporate some aspects of a job costing system into the process costing system, resulting in a hybrid system that yields a higher level of costing accuracy.

Chapter 7
Standard Costing

Introduction

Standard costing is the practice of substituting an expected cost for an actual cost in the accounting records, and then periodically recording variances that are the difference between the expected and actual costs. Standard costing appeared in the early twentieth century, when transaction volumes were overwhelming the record keeping systems in use at that time. Since then, the prevalent use of computer systems and automated data entry systems have reduced the need for standard costing, though not entirely eliminated it.

In this chapter, we will discuss how a standard costing system functions, where it should be used, how to calculate the many variances associated with it, and how to report these variances.

Overview of Standard Costing

Standard costing involves the creation of estimated (i.e., standard) costs for some or all activities within a company. The core reason for using standard costs is that there are a number of applications where it is too time-consuming to collect actual costs, so standard costs are used as a close approximation to actual costs.

Standard costs only work within a certain range of constraints, beyond which they are no longer a close match for actual costs. For example, the cost of a purchased component may only be accurate if it is purchased in quantities of 1,000; the price would double if a business were to order it in quantities of 100.

Since standard costs are usually slightly different from actual costs, the cost accountant periodically calculates variances that break out differences caused by such factors as labor rate changes and the cost of materials. The cost accountant may also periodically change the standard costs to bring them into closer alignment with actual costs.

Advantages of Standard Costing

Though most companies do not use standard costing in its original application of calculating the cost of ending inventory, it is still useful for a number of other applications. In most cases, users are probably not even aware that they are using standard costing, only that they are using an approximation of actual costs. Here are some potential uses:

- *Budgeting*. A budget is always composed of standard costs, since it would be impossible to include in it the exact actual cost of an item on the day the budget is finalized. Also, since a key application of the budget is to compare it to actual results in subsequent periods, the standards used within it continue to appear in financial reports through the budget period.

- *Inventory costing.* It is extremely easy to print a report showing the period-end inventory balances (if a business is using a perpetual inventory system), multiply it by the standard cost of each item, and instantly generate an ending inventory valuation. The result does not exactly match the actual cost of inventory, but it is close. However, it may be necessary to update standard costs frequently, if actual costs are continually changing. It is easiest to update costs for the highest-dollar components of inventory on a frequent basis, and leave lower-value items for occasional cost reviews.
- *Overhead application.* If it takes too long to aggregate actual costs into cost pools for allocation to inventory, use a standard overhead application rate instead, and adjust this rate every few months to keep it close to actual costs.
- *Price formulation.* If a company deals with custom products, it uses standard costs to compile the projected cost of a customer's requirements, after which it adds on a margin. This may be quite a complex system, where the sales department uses a database of component costs that change depending upon the unit quantity that the customer wants to order. This system may also account for changes in the company's production costs at different volume levels, since this may call for the use of longer production runs that are less expensive.

Nearly all companies have budgets and many use standard cost calculations to derive product prices, so it is apparent that standard costing will find some uses for the foreseeable future. In particular, standard costing provides a benchmark against which management can compare actual performance.

Disadvantages of Standard Costing

Despite the advantages just noted for some applications of standard costing, there are substantially more situations where it is *not* a viable costing system. Here are some problem areas:

- *Cost-plus contracts.* If there is a contract with a customer under which the customer pays for costs incurred plus a profit (known as a cost-plus contract), one must use actual costs, as per the terms of the contract. Standard costing is not allowed. Cost-plus contracts are particularly common when dealing with the government.
- *Drives inappropriate activities.* A number of the variances reported under a standard costing system will drive management to take incorrect actions to create favorable variances. For example, they may buy raw materials in larger quantities in order to improve the purchase price variance, even though this increases the investment in inventory. Similarly, management may schedule longer production runs in order to improve the labor efficiency variance, even though it is better to produce in smaller quantities and accept less labor efficiency in exchange.

- *Fast-paced environment.* A standard costing system assumes that costs do not change much in the near term, so it is possible to rely on standards for a number of months or even a year, before updating the costs. However, in an environment where product lives are short or continuous improvement is driving down costs, a standard cost may become out-of-date within a month or two.
- *Ignores scrap.* The standard costing system relies upon the bill of materials (the record of materials used to construct a product) to accumulate the standard costs of the component parts that comprise a finished product. It is customary to include in the bill of materials an estimated amount of scrap that will result from the production process. However, this means that the system is presupposing the existence of scrap, which tends to focus the attention of a company away from eliminating scrap.
- *Slow feedback.* A complex system of variance calculations is an integral part of a standard costing system, which the accounting staff completes at the end of each reporting period. If the production department is focused on immediate feedback of problems for instant correction, the reporting of these variances is much too late to be useful.
- *Unit-level information.* The variance calculations that typically accompany a standard costing report are accumulated in aggregate for a company's entire production department, and so are unable to provide information about discrepancies at a lower level, such as the individual work cell, batch, or unit.

The preceding list shows that there are a multitude of situations where standard costing is not useful, and may even result in incorrect management actions. Nonetheless, as long as the accountant is aware of these issues, it is usually possible to profitably adapt standard costing into some aspects of a company's operations.

How to Create a Standard Cost

At the most basic level, one can create a standard cost simply by calculating the average of the most recent actual cost for the past few months. In many smaller companies, this is the extent of the analysis used. However, there are some additional factors to consider, which can significantly alter the standard cost that will be used. They are:

- *Equipment age.* If a machine is nearing the end of its productive life, it may produce a higher proportion of scrap than was previously the case.
- *Equipment setup speeds.* If it takes a long time to setup equipment for a production run, the cost of the setup, as spread over the units in the production run, is expensive. If a setup reduction plan is contemplated, this can yield significantly lower overhead costs.
- *Labor efficiency changes.* If there are production process changes, such as the installation of new, automated equipment, this impacts the amount of labor required to manufacture a product.
- *Labor rate changes.* If employees are about to receive pay raises, either through a scheduled raise or as mandated by a labor union contract, incorpo-

rate these changes into the new standard. This may mean setting an effective date for the new standard that matches the date when the cost increase is supposed to go into effect.

- *Learning curve*. As the production staff creates an increasing volume of a product, it becomes more efficient at doing so. Thus, the standard labor cost should decrease (though at a declining rate) as production volumes increase.
- *Purchasing terms*. The purchasing department may be able to significantly alter the price of a purchased component by switching suppliers, altering contract terms, or by buying in different quantities.
- *Push or pull*. The type of materials flow system used in a production facility can have a vast impact on the cost of goods produced. A pull system, such as a just-in-time system, only produces when customers place orders, while a push system, such as a material requirements planning system, produces from a forecast, irrespective of customer orders. Pull systems generally result in less expensive total costs for a product.

Any one of the additional factors noted here can have a major impact on a standard cost, which is why it may be necessary in a larger production environment to spend a significant amount of time formulating a standard cost.

The cost accountant is unlikely to be familiar with all of the factors just noted, which is why standard costs are more commonly derived by either the engineering or purchasing departments (or both). The primary role of the cost accountant is to manage the process of deriving standard costs, with inputs coming from the engineers and purchasing staff.

Historical, Attainable, and Theoretical Standards

An additional factor to consider when deriving a standard cost is whether to set it at a historical actual cost level that has been proven to be attainable, or at a rate that should be attainable, or one that can only be reached if all operations work perfectly. Here are some considerations:

- *Historical basis*. This is an average of the costs that a company has already experienced in the recent past, possibly weighted towards just the past few months. Though clearly an attainable cost, a standard based on historical results contains all of the operational inefficiencies of the existing production operation.
- *Attainable basis*. This is a cost that is more difficult to reach than a historical cost. This basis assumes some improvement in operating and purchasing efficiencies, which employees have a good chance of achieving in the short term.
- *Theoretical basis*. This is the ultimate, lowest cost that the facility can attain if it functions perfectly, with no scrap, highly efficient employees, and machines that never break down. This can be a frustrating basis to use for a standard cost, because the production facility can never attain it, and so always produces unfavorable variances.

Of the three types of standards noted here, use the attainable basis, because it gives employees a reasonable cost target to pursue. If standards are continually updated on this basis, a production facility will have an incentive to continually drive down its costs over the long term.

How to Account for Standard Costs

Standard costs are stored separately from all other accounting records, usually in a bill of materials for finished goods, and in the item master file for raw materials. The item master is a record that lists the name, description, unit of measure, weight, dimensions, ordering quantity, and other key information for a component part.

At the end of a reporting period, the following steps show how to integrate standard costs into the accounting system:

1. *Cost verification.* Review the standard cost database for errors and make corrections as necessary. Also, if it is time to do so, update the standard costs to more accurately reflect actual costs.
2. *Inventory valuation.* Multiply the number of units in ending inventory by their standard costs to derive the ending inventory valuation.
3. *Calculate the cost of goods sold.* Add purchases during the month to the beginning inventory and subtract the ending inventory to determine the cost of goods sold.
4. *Enter updated balances.* Create a journal entry that reduces the purchases account to zero and which also adjusts the inventory asset account balance to the ending total standard cost, with the offset to the cost of goods sold account.

EXAMPLE

Hodgson Industrial Design is using a standard costing system to calculate its inventory balances and cost of goods sold. The company conducts a month-end physical inventory count that results in a reasonably accurate set of unit quantities for all inventory items. The cost accountant multiplies each of these unit quantities by their standard costs to derive the ending inventory valuation. This ending balance is $2,500,000.

The beginning inventory account balance is $2,750,000 and purchases during the month were $1,000,000, so the calculation of the cost of goods sold is:

Beginning inventory	$2,750,000
+ Purchases	1,000,000
- Ending inventory	(2,500,000)
= Cost of goods sold	$1,250,000

To record the correct ending inventory balance and cost of goods sold, Hodgson records the following entry, which clears out the purchases asset account and adjusts the ending inventory balance to $2,500,000:

	Debit	Credit
Cost of goods sold	1,250,000	
Purchases		1,000,000
Inventory		250,000

Overview of Variances

A variance is the difference between the actual cost incurred and the standard cost against which it is measured. A variance can also be used to measure the difference between actual and expected sales. Thus, variance analysis can be used to review the performance of both revenue and expenses.

Related Podcast Episode: Episode 186 of the Accounting Best Practices Podcast discusses inventory variances. It is available at: **accountingtools.com/podcasts** or **iTunes**

There are two basic types of variances from a standard that can arise, which are the rate variance and the volume variance. Here is more information about both types of variances:

- *Rate variance.* A rate variance (which is also known as a *price* variance) is the difference between the actual price paid for something and the expected price, multiplied by the actual quantity purchased. The "rate" variance designation is most commonly applied to the labor rate variance, which involves the actual cost of direct labor in comparison to the standard cost of direct labor. The rate variance uses a different designation when applied to the purchase of materials, and may be called the *purchase price variance* or the *material price variance*.
- *Volume variance.* A volume variance is the difference between the actual quantity sold or consumed and the budgeted amount, multiplied by the standard price or cost per unit. If the variance relates to the sale of goods, it is called the *sales volume variance*. If it relates to the use of direct materials, it is called the *material yield variance*. If the variance relates to the use of direct labor, it is called the *labor efficiency variance*. Finally, if the variance relates to the application of overhead, it is called the *overhead efficiency variance*.

Thus, variances are based on either changes in cost from the expected amount, or changes in the quantity from the expected amount. The most common variances that a cost accountant elects to report on are subdivided within the rate and volume variance categories for direct materials, direct labor, and overhead. It is also possible to report these variances for revenue. Thus, the primary variances are:

	Rate Variance	Volume Variance
Materials	Purchase price variance	Material yield variance
Direct labor	Labor rate variance	Labor efficiency variance
Fixed overhead	Fixed overhead spending variance	Not applicable
Variable overhead	Variable overhead spending variance	Variable overhead efficiency variance
Revenue	Selling price variance	Sales volume variance

All of the variances noted in the preceding table are explained in the following sections, including examples to demonstrate how the variances are applied.

The Purchase Price Variance

The purchase price variance is the difference between the actual price paid to buy an item and its standard price, multiplied by the actual number of units purchased. The formula is:

(Actual price - Standard price) × Actual quantity = Purchase price variance

A positive variance means that actual costs have increased, and a negative variance means that actual costs have declined.

The standard price is the price that the procurement staff believes a company should pay for an item, given a certain quality level, purchasing quantity, and speed of delivery. Thus, the variance is really based on a standard price that was the collective opinion of several employees based on a number of assumptions that may no longer match a company's current purchasing situation.

EXAMPLE

During the development of its annual budget, the engineers and purchasing staff of Hodgson Industrial Design decide that the standard cost of a green widget should be set at $5.00, which is based on a purchasing volume of 10,000 units for the upcoming year. During the subsequent year, Hodgson only buys 8,000 units, and so cannot take advantage of purchasing discounts, and ends up paying $5.50 per widget. This creates a purchase price variance of $0.50 per widget, and a variance of $4,000 for all of the 8,000 widgets that Hodgson purchased.

There are a number of possible causes of a purchase price variance. For example:
- *Layering issue.* The actual cost may have been taken from an inventory layering system, such as a first-in first-out system, where the actual cost varies from the current market price by a substantial margin.
- *Materials shortage.* There is an industry shortage of a commodity item, which is driving up the cost.

- *New supplier.* The company has changed suppliers for any number of reasons, resulting in a new cost structure that is not yet reflected in the standard.
- *Rush basis.* The company incurred excessive shipping charges to obtain materials on short notice from suppliers.
- *Volume assumption.* The standard cost of an item was derived based on a different purchasing volume than the amount at which the company now buys.

Material Yield Variance

The material yield variance is the difference between the actual amount of material used and the standard amount expected to be used, multiplied by the standard cost of the materials. The formula is:

$$(\text{Actual unit usage - Standard unit usage}) \times \text{Standard cost per unit}$$
$$= \text{Material yield variance}$$

An unfavorable variance means that the unit usage was greater than anticipated.

The standard unit usage is developed by the engineering staff, and is based on expected scrap rates in a production process, the quality of raw materials, losses during equipment setup, and related factors.

EXAMPLE

The engineering staff of Hodgson Industrial Design estimates that 8 ounces of rubber will be required to produce a green widget. During the most recent month, the production process used 315,000 ounces of rubber to create 35,000 green widgets, which is 9 ounces per product. Each ounce of rubber has a standard cost of $0.50. Its material yield variance for the month is:

(315,000 Actual unit usage - 280,000 Standard unit usage) × $0.50 Standard cost/unit

= $17,500 Material yield variance

There are a number of possible causes of a material yield variance. For example:
- *Scrap.* Unusual amounts of scrap may be generated by changes in machine setups, or because changes in acceptable tolerance levels are altering the amount of scrap produced. A change in the pattern of quality inspections can also alter the amount of scrap.
- *Material quality.* If the material quality level changes, this can alter the amount of quality rejections. If an entirely different material is substituted, this can also alter the amount of rejections.
- *Spoilage.* The amount of spoilage may change in concert with alterations in inventory handling and storage.

Labor Rate Variance

The labor rate variance is the difference between the actual labor rate paid and the standard rate, multiplied by the number of actual hours worked. The formula is:

(Actual rate - Standard rate) × Actual hours worked = Labor rate variance

An unfavorable variance means that the cost of labor was more expensive than anticipated.

The standard labor rate is developed by the human resources and industrial engineering employees, and is based on such factors as the expected mix of pay levels among the production staff, the amount of overtime likely to be incurred, the amount of new hiring at different pay rates, the number of promotions into higher pay levels, and the outcome of contract negotiations with any unions representing the production staff.

EXAMPLE

The human resources manager of Hodgson Industrial Design estimates that the average labor rate for the coming year for Hodgson's production staff will be $25/hour. This estimate is based on a standard mix of personnel at different pay rates, as well as a reasonable proportion of overtime hours worked.

During the first month of the new year, Hodgson has difficulty hiring a sufficient number of new employees, and so must have its higher-paid existing staff work overtime to complete a number of jobs. The result is an actual labor rate of $30/hour. Hodgson's production staff worked 10,000 hours during the month. Its labor rate variance for the month is:

($30/hr Actual rate - $25/hour Standard rate) × 10,000 hours = $50,000 Labor rate variance

There are a number of possible causes of a labor rate variance. For example:
- *Incorrect standards*. The labor standard may not reflect recent changes in the rates paid to employees (which tend to occur in bulk for all staff).
- *Pay premiums*. The actual amounts paid may include extra payments for shift differentials or overtime.
- *Staffing variances*. A labor standard may assume that a certain job classification will perform a designated task, when in fact a different position with a different pay rate may be performing the work.

Labor Efficiency Variance

The labor efficiency variance is the difference between the actual labor hours used to produce an item and the standard amount that should have been used, multiplied by the standard labor rate. The formula is:

(Actual hours - Standard hours) × Standard rate = Labor efficiency variance

An unfavorable variance means that labor efficiency has worsened, and a favorable variance means that labor efficiency has increased.

The standard number of hours represents the best estimate of the industrial engineers regarding the optimal speed at which the production staff can manufacture goods. This figure can vary considerably, based on assumptions regarding the setup time of a production run, the availability of materials and machine capacity, employee skill levels, the duration of a production run, and other factors. Thus, the multitude of variables involved makes it especially difficult to create a standard that can be meaningfully compared to actual results.

EXAMPLE

During the development of its annual budget, the industrial engineers of Hodgson Industrial Design decide that the standard amount of time required to produce a green widget should be 30 minutes, which is based on certain assumptions about the efficiency of Hodgson's production staff, the availability of materials, capacity availability, and so forth. During the month, widget materials were in short supply, so Hodgson had to pay production staff even when there was no material to work on, resulting in an average production time per unit of 45 minutes. The company produced 1,000 widgets during the month. The standard cost per labor hour is $20, so the calculation of its labor efficiency variance is:

(750 Actual hours - 500 Standard hours) × $20 Standard rate
= $5,000 Labor efficiency variance

There are a number of possible causes of a labor efficiency variance. For example:
- *Instructions*. The employees may not have received written work instructions.
- *Mix*. The standard assumes a certain mix of employees involving different skill levels, which does not match the actual staffing.
- *Training*. The standard may be based on an assumption of a minimum amount of training that employees have not received.
- *Work station configuration*. A work center may have been reconfigured since the standard was created, so the standard is now incorrect.

Variable Overhead Spending Variance

The variable overhead spending variance is the difference between the actual and budgeted rates of spending on variable overhead. The formula is:

Actual hours worked × (Actual overhead rate - standard overhead rate)
= Variable overhead spending variance

A favorable variance means that the actual variable overhead expenses incurred per labor hour were less than expected.

The variable overhead spending variance is a compilation of production expense information submitted by the production department, and the projected labor hours to be worked, as estimated by the industrial engineering and production scheduling staffs, based on historical and projected efficiency and equipment capacity levels.

EXAMPLE

The cost accounting staff of Hodgson Industrial Design calculates, based on historical and projected cost patterns, that the company should experience a variable overhead rate of $20 per labor hour worked, and builds this figure into the budget. In April, the actual variable overhead rate turns out to be $22 per labor hour. During that month, production employees work 18,000 hours. The variable overhead spending variance is:

$$18,000 \text{ Actual hours worked} \times (\$22 \text{ Actual variable overhead rate} \\ - \$20 \text{ Standard overhead rate}) \\ = \$36,000 \text{ Variable overhead spending variance}$$

There are a number of possible causes of a variable overhead spending variance. For example:

- *Account misclassification.* The variable overhead category includes a number of accounts, some of which may have been incorrectly classified and so do not appear as part of variable overhead (or vice versa).
- *Outsourcing.* Some activities that had been sourced in-house have now been shifted to a supplier, or vice versa.
- *Supplier pricing.* Suppliers have changed their prices, which have not yet been reflected in updated standards.

Variable Overhead Efficiency Variance

The variable overhead efficiency variance is the difference between the actual and budgeted hours worked, which are then applied to the standard variable overhead rate per hour. The formula is:

$$\text{Standard overhead rate} \times (\text{Actual hours - Standard hours}) \\ = \text{Variable overhead efficiency variance}$$

A favorable variance means that the actual hours worked were less than the budgeted hours, resulting in the application of the standard overhead rate across fewer hours, resulting in less expense incurred.

The variable overhead efficiency variance is a compilation of production expense information submitted by the production department, and the projected labor hours to be worked, as estimated by the industrial engineering and production scheduling staffs, based on historical and projected efficiency and equipment capacity levels.

EXAMPLE

The cost accounting staff of Hodgson Industrial Design calculates, based on historical and projected labor patterns, that the company's production staff should work 20,000 hours per month and incur $400,000 of variable overhead costs per month, so it establishes a variable overhead rate of $20 per hour. In May, Hodgson installs a new materials handling system that significantly improves production efficiency and drops the hours worked during the month to 19,000 hours. The variable overhead efficiency variance is:

$20 Standard overhead rate/hour × (19,000 Hours worked - 20,000 Standard hours)
= $20,000 Variable overhead efficiency variance

Fixed Overhead Spending Variance

The fixed overhead spending variance is the difference between the actual fixed overhead expense incurred and the budgeted fixed overhead expense. An unfavorable variance means that actual overhead expenditures were greater than planned. The formula is:

Actual fixed overhead - Budgeted fixed overhead = Fixed overhead spending variance

The amount of expense related to fixed overhead should (as the name implies) be relatively fixed, and so the fixed overhead spending variance should not theoretically vary much from the budget. However, if the manufacturing process reaches a step cost trigger point, where a whole new expense must be incurred, then this can cause a significant unfavorable variance. Also, there may be some seasonality in fixed overhead expenditures, which may cause both favorable and unfavorable variances in individual months of a year, but which cancel each other out over the full year.

EXAMPLE

The production manager of Hodgson Industrial Design estimates that the fixed overhead should be $700,000 during the upcoming year. However, since a production manager left the company and was not replaced for several months, actual expenses were lower than expected, at $672,000. This created the following favorable fixed overhead spending variance:

($672,000 Actual fixed overhead - $700,000 Budgeted fixed overhead) =
$(28,000) Fixed overhead spending variance

There are a number of possible causes of a fixed overhead spending variance. For example:

- *Account misclassification.* The fixed overhead category includes a number of accounts, some of which may have been incorrectly classified and so do not appear as part of fixed overhead (or vice versa).
- *Outsourcing.* Some activities that had been sourced in-house have now been shifted to a supplier, or vice versa.
- *Supplier pricing.* Suppliers have changed their prices, which have not yet been reflected in updated standards.

Selling Price Variance

The selling price variance is the difference between the actual and expected revenue that is caused by a change in the price of a product or service. The formula is:

(Actual price - Budgeted price) × Actual unit sales = Selling price variance

An unfavorable variance means that the actual price was lower than the budgeted price.

The budgeted price for each unit of product or sales is developed by the sales and marketing managers, and is based on their estimation of future demand for these products and services, which in turn is affected by general economic conditions and the actions of competitors. If the actual price is lower than the budgeted price, the result may actually be favorable to the company, as long as the price decline spurs demand to such an extent that the company generates an incremental profit as a result of the price decline.

EXAMPLE

The marketing manager of Hodgson Industrial Design estimates that the company can sell a green widget for $80 per unit during the upcoming year. This estimate is based on the historical demand for green widgets.

During the first half of the new year, the price of the green widget comes under extreme pressure as a new supplier in Ireland floods the market with a lower-priced green widget. Hodgson must drop its price to $70 in order to compete, and sells 20,000 units during that period. Its selling price variance during the first half of the year is:

($70 Actual price - $80 Budgeted price) × 20,000 units = $(200,000) Selling price variance

There are a number of possible causes of a selling price variance. For example:

- *Discounts.* The company has granted various discounts to customers to induce them to buy products.

- *Marketing allowances.* The company is allowing customers to deduct marketing allowances from their payments to reimburse them for marketing activities involving the company's products.
- *Price points.* The price points at which the company is selling are different from the price points stated in its standards.
- *Product options.* Customers are buying different product options than expected, resulting in an average price that differs from the price points stated in the company's standards.

Sales Volume Variance

The sales volume variance is the difference between the actual and expected number of units sold, multiplied by the budgeted price per unit. The formula is:

(Actual units sold - Budgeted units sold) × Budgeted price per unit
= Sales volume variance

An unfavorable variance means that the actual number of units sold was lower than the budgeted number sold.

The budgeted number of units sold is derived by the sales and marketing managers, and is based on their estimation of how the company's product market share, features, price points, expected marketing activities, distribution channels, and sales in new regions will impact future sales. If the product's selling price is lower than the budgeted amount, this may spur sales to such an extent that the sales volume variance is favorable, even though the selling price variance is unfavorable.

EXAMPLE

The marketing manager of Hodgson Industrial Design estimates that the company can sell 25,000 blue widgets for $65 per unit during the upcoming year. This estimate is based on the historical demand for blue widgets, as supported by new advertising campaigns in the first and third quarters of the year.

During the new year, Hodgson does not have a first quarter advertising campaign, since it is changing advertising agencies at that time. This results in sales of just 21,000 blue widgets during the year. Its sales volume variance is:

(21,000 Units sold - 25,000 Budgeted units) × $65 Budgeted price per unit
= $260,000 Unfavorable sales volume variance

There are a number of possible causes of a sales volume variance. For example:

- *Cannibalization.* The company may have released another product that competes with the product in question. Thus, sales of one product cannibalize sales of the other product.

84

- *Competition*. Competitors may have released new products that are more attractive to customers.
- *Price*. The company may have altered the product price, which in turn drives a change in unit sales volume.
- *Trade restrictions*. A foreign country may have altered its barriers to competition.

Problems with Variance Analysis

There are several problems with the variances just described in this chapter, which are:

- *The use of standards*. A central issue is the use of standards as the basis for calculating variances. What is the motivation for creating a standard? Standard creation can be a political process where the amount agreed upon is designed to make a department look good, rather than setting a target that will improve the company. If standards are politically created, variance analysis becomes useless from the perspective of controlling a business.
- *Feedback loop*. The accounting department does not calculate variances until after it has closed the books and created financial statements, so there is a gap of potentially an entire month from when a variance arises and when it is reported to management. A faster feedback loop would be to eliminate variance reporting and instead create a reporting process that provides for feedback within moments of the occurrence of a triggering event.
- *Information drill down*. Many of the issues that cause variances are not stored within the accounting database. For example, the reason for excessive material usage may be a machine setup error, while excessive labor usage may be caused by the use of too much employee overtime. In neither case will the accounting staff discover these issues by examining their transactional data. Thus, a variance report only highlights the general areas within which problems occurred, but does not necessarily tell anyone the nature of the underlying problems.

The preceding issues do not always keep accounting managers from calculating complete sets of variances for management consumption, but they do bring the question of whether the work required to calculate variances is a good use of the accounting staff's time.

The Controllable Variance

A controllable variance refers to the "rate" portion of a variance. A variance is comprised of two primary elements, which are the volume variance and the rate variance. The volume element is that portion of the variance attributable to changes in sales volume or unit usage from a standard or budgeted amount, while the rate element is the difference between the actual price paid and a standard or budgeted price.

The controllable variance concept is usually applied to factory overhead, where the calculation of the controllable variance is:

Actual overhead expense - (Budgeted overhead per unit × Standard number of units)

Thus, the controllable variance within the total factory overhead variance is that portion not related to changes in volume.

From a practical perspective, a controllable variance may be completely uncontrollable if it is calculated from a baseline standard cost that is impossible to attain.

The Favorable or Unfavorable Variance

A favorable variance is the excess amount of a standard or budgeted amount over the actual amount incurred. Obtaining a favorable variance (or, for that matter, an unfavorable variance) does not necessarily mean much, since it is based upon a budgeted or standard amount that may not be an indicator of good performance.

Budgets and standards are frequently based on politically-derived wrangling to see who can beat their baseline standards or budgets by the largest amount. Consequently, a large favorable variance may have been manufactured by setting an excessively low budget or standard. The one time to take note of a favorable (or unfavorable) variance is when it sharply diverges from the historical trend line, and the divergence was not caused by a change in the budget or standard.

Where to Record a Variance

There are always going to be variances in a standard costing system, where the variance is the difference between actual and standard costs. How should they be recorded? There are two schools of thought, which are:

- *Variances are exceptions*. This viewpoint holds that a standard is the cost level that a company should be attaining, so any variance from that amount is an exception, and should be charged to the cost of goods sold in the current period. Thus, if a variance is an exception, only carry forward the standard cost of an item in inventory, and eliminate any other expense in the current period. This is the simplest method, since the variance calculation and subsequent charge to expense are easy.
- *Inventory is valued at actual cost*. According to generally accepted accounting principles, ·the accountant is supposed to value the inventory asset at its actual cost, which in a standard costing system is the standard cost, plus or minus all variances. Thus, this viewpoint holds that one should allocate variances between the period-end inventory asset and the cost of goods sold. This requires additional allocation calculations, which can be time-consuming.

Clearly, it is easier to charge variances to the cost of goods sold. To reduce the validity of the argument that inventory should be valued at its actual cost, update standard costs with sufficient frequency to ensure that all variances from standard costs will be so small that there is no material difference between the value of the inventory at standard cost or actual cost.

Which Variances to Report

A lot of variances have been described in this chapter. Is it really necessary to report them all to management? Not necessarily. If management agrees with a reduced reporting structure, report on just those variances over which management has some ability to reduce costs, and which contain sufficiently large variances to be worth reporting on. The following table provides commentary on the characteristics of the variances:

Name of Variance	Commentary
Materials	
Purchase price variance	Material costs are controllable to some extent, and comprise a large part of the cost of goods sold; possibly the most important variance
Material yield variance	Can contain large potential cost reductions driven by quality issues, production layouts, and process flow; a good opportunity for cost reductions
Labor	
Labor rate variance	Labor rates are difficult to change; do not track unless work can be shifted into lower pay grades
Labor efficiency variance	Can drive contrary behavior in favor of long production runs, when less labor efficiency in a just-in-time environment results in greater overall cost reductions; not recommended
Overhead	
Variable overhead spending variance	Caused by changes in the actual costs in the overhead cost pool, and so should be reviewed
Variable overhead efficiency variance	Caused by a change in the basis of allocation, which has no real impact on underlying costs; not recommended
Fixed overhead spending variance	Since fixed overhead costs should not vary much, a variance here is worth careful review; however, most components of fixed overhead are long-term costs that cannot be easily changed in the short term

Name of Variance	Commentary
Revenue	
Selling price variance	Caused by a change in the product price, which is under management control, and therefore should be brought to their attention
Sales volume variance	Caused by a change in the unit volume sold, which is not under direct management control, though this can be impacted by altering the product price

The preceding table shows that the variances most worthy of management's attention are the purchase price variance, variable overhead spending variance, fixed overhead spending variance, and selling price variance. Reducing the number of reported variances is well worth the cost accountant's time, since reporting the entire suite of variances calls for a great deal of investigative time to track down variance causes and then configure the information into a report suitable for management consumption.

How to Report Variances

A variance is a simple number, such as an unfavorable purchase price variance of $15,000. It tells management very little, since there is not enough information on which to base any corrective action. Consequently, the cost accountant needs to dig down into the underlying data to determine the actual causes of each variance, and then report the causes. Doing so is one of the most important value-added activities of the cost accountant, since it leads directly to specific cost reductions. The following table is an example of the level of variance detail that the cost accountant should report to management:

Variance Item	Amount*	Variance Cause
Purchase Price		
Order quantity	$500	Bought wrappers at half usual volume, and lost purchase discount
Substitute material	1,500	Used more expensive PVC piping; out of stock on regular item
Variable Overhead		
Rush order	300	Overnight charge to bring in grease for bearings
Utility surcharge	2,400	Charged extra for power usage during peak hours
Fixed Overhead		

Variance Item	Amount*	Variance Cause
Property taxes	3,000	Tax levy increased by 8%
Rent override	8,000	Landlord charge for proportional share of full-year expenses
Selling Price		
Marketing discounts	4,000	Customers took discounts for advertising pass-through
Sales returns	11,000	450 units returned with broken spring assembly

* Note: All amounts are unfavorable variances

The preceding table can be expanded to include the names of the managers responsible for correcting each item noted.

Summary

Standard costing is now used less frequently, since it has been largely replaced by actual costs for the bulk of all cost accounting activities. This had led to the elimination of variance analysis in some organizations. In those cases where variance analysis is still used, the cost accountant can save a great deal of time by only reporting on those variances containing information that management can readily act upon.

Nonetheless, there are cases, such as in price setting and budgeting, where standard costing is still used, and will likely still be used in the future. Standard costing remains a simple way to derive costs, especially for applications that do not have ready access to the accounting database, where approximate costs are good enough, or where a company wishes to measure its performance against a standard.

Chapter 8
Joint and By-Product Costing

Introduction

In some industries, a number of products may be derived from a single production process, such as when a meat packing facility cuts up an animal carcass into a number of different finished goods. In these industries, it is not possible to accurately ascribe certain production costs to specific products, if these costs were incurred prior to the point in the production process when individual finished goods are identifiable. These are known as joint costs. A *joint cost* is a cost which benefits more than one product, and for which it may not be possible to separate its contribution to each product.

Several cost allocation methods have been created to deal with joint costs and a similar issue known as by-products. In this chapter, we will describe these issues, and how well (or not) the various allocation methods perform.

Split-Off Points and By-Products

A company needs to use joint costing or by-product costing if it has a production process where it cannot determine the final product until later in the process. The point at which it can finally determine the final product is called the *split-off point*. There may even be several split-off points; at each one, another product can be clearly identified, and is (literally) split off from the production process, possibly to be further refined into a finished product. If the company has incurred any manufacturing costs prior to the split-off point, it must use some method for allocating these costs to the final products. If it incurs any costs after the split-off point, then the costs are likely associated with a specific product, and can more readily be assigned to them.

EXAMPLE

California Chardonnay Corporation operates several wineries that press their own grapes. During this process, there is a split-off point that produces an abundant amount of grape seed oil. The company may then sell the grape seed oil to various cooking oil manufacturers, or it may engage in several straining operations to further refine the grape seed oil into a more pure form that it can then sell to cosmetics manufacturers as the primary ingredient in skin moisturizers; alternatively, the company can then add a stabilizer to the purified oil and sell it to a shaving cream manufacturer as a face shaving lubricant.

California Chardonnay has two split-off points – one where the grape seed oil is separated, and another where the purified oil is split off for sale as a skin moisturizer ingredient.

Besides the split-off point, there may also be one or more by-products. A *by-product* is a product that arises from a manufacturing process, but whose sales are minor in comparison to the sales of the primary products generated by the manufacturing process.

EXAMPLE

Latham Lumber operates a sawmill, which routinely produces large quantities of planks. As part of the milling process, Latham produces a significant amount of sawdust as a by-product, which has little value. The company sells the sawdust to a third party that converts it into "scatter," which is used to simulate the effect of ground cover in dioramas.

Why We Allocate Joint Costs

If a company incurs costs prior to a split-off point, it must allocate them to products, under the dictates of both generally accepted accounting principles and international financial reporting standards. If these costs are not allocated to products, they would instead be treated as period costs (under the assumption that the item purchased is consumed at once), and charged to expense in the current period. This may be an incorrect treatment of the cost if the associated products were not sold until sometime in the future, since one would be charging a portion of the product cost to expense before realizing the offsetting sale transaction.

Allocating joint costs does not help management, since the resulting information is based on essentially arbitrary allocations. Consequently, the best allocation method does not have to be especially accurate, but it should be easy to calculate, and be readily defensible if it is reviewed by an auditor.

How to Allocate Joint Costs

There are two common methods for allocating joint costs. One allocates costs based on the sales value of the resulting products, while the other is based on the estimated final gross margins of the resulting products. The calculation methods follow:

1. *Allocate based on sales value.* Add up all production costs through the split-off point, then determine the sales value of all joint products as of the same split-off point, and then assign the costs based on the sales values. If there are any by-products, do not allocate costs to them; instead, charge the proceeds from their sale against the cost of goods sold. This is the simpler of the two methods.

2. *Allocate based on gross margin.* Add up the cost of all processing costs that each joint product incurs after the split-off point, and subtract this amount from the total revenue that each product will eventually earn. This approach requires additional cost accumulation work, but may be the only viable alternative if it is not possible to determine the sale price of each product as of the split-off point (as was the case with the preceding calculation method).

EXAMPLE

Allocation based on sales value: Hassle Corporation generates three products from a joint manufacturing process that incurs $90 of costs through the split-off point. It allocates costs to these products based on their sales value at the split-off point. The calculation follows:

Product Name	Type	Revenue at Split-Off	Percent of Total Revenue	Cost Allocation
Product Alpha	Joint	$100	67%	$60
Product Beta	Joint	50	33%	30
Product Charlie	By-product	0	0%	0
		$150	100%	$90

Under this method, Hassle Corporation designates Product Charlie as a by-product, so it does not share in the allocation of costs. If the company eventually sells any of Product Charlie, it will net the resulting revenues against the costs assigned to Products Alpha and Beta.

Allocation based on gross margin: Hassle Corporation's controller decides to assign joint costs based on the gross margins of the products after the split-off point. His calculation follows:

Product Name	Final Revenue	Costs Following Split-Off	Margin Following Split-Off	Proportion of Total Margins	Cost Allocation
Product Alpha	$200	$125	$75	53%	$48
Product Beta	100	60	40	29%	26
Product Charlie	25	0	25	18%	16
	$325	$185	$140	100%	$90

The cost allocations are entirely different between the two allocation methods, since the first calculation is based on revenue at the split-off point, and the second is largely based on costs incurred after the split-off point.

How to Determine Prices for Joint Products and By-Products

The costs allocated to joint products and by-products should have no bearing on the pricing of these products, since the costs have no relationship to the value of the items sold. Prior to the split-off point, all costs incurred are sunk costs, and as such have no bearing on any future decisions – such as the price of a product. A sunk cost is an expenditure made in a prior period, which will not be affected by any current or future decisions.

The situation is quite different for any costs incurred from the split-off point onward. Since these costs can be attributed to specific products, never set a product price to be at or below the total costs incurred after the split-off point. Otherwise, the company will lose money on every product sold.

If the floor for a product's price is only the total costs incurred *after* the split-off point, this brings up the odd scenario of potentially charging prices that are lower than the total cost incurred (including the costs incurred *before* the split-off point). Clearly, charging such low prices is not a viable alternative over the long term, since a company will continually operate at a loss. This brings up two pricing alternatives:

- *Short-term pricing.* Over the short term, it may be necessary to allow extremely low product pricing, even near the total of costs incurred after the split-off point, if market prices do not allow pricing to be increased to a long-term sustainable level.
- *Long-term pricing.* Over the long term, a company must set prices to achieve revenue levels above its total cost of production, or risk bankruptcy.

In short, if a company is unable to set individual product prices sufficiently high to more than offset its production costs, and customers are unwilling to accept higher prices, then it should cancel production – irrespective of how costs are allocated to various joint products and by-products.

Special Concerns with By-Product Costing

By-products are, by definition, minor items, but they can cause variations in a company's financial results. The following problems can arise:

- *Definition of a by-product.* If a company defines a product of a production process as a by-product, it can validly assign no cost to that by-product (if it is allocating costs based on sales value). If the company then holds a significant amount of the by-product in inventory and then sells it in a batch, it will record a large amount of revenue with no offsetting cost of goods sold, resulting in an inordinate profit. The solution is to have a corporate policy that limits the by-product designation to those products having a small historical percentage of company sales.
- *Batch sales of by-products.* A company may let its by-products build up for several months and then sell them all in a large batch (which may be mandated by the buyer). If this happens, the company then subtracts all sale proceeds from the cost of goods sold in the month when the sale occurs, which can cause sudden increases in the gross margin.
- *Sale price variation.* By-products are frequently commodities, and so are unusually subject to the supply and demand forces in the marketplace. The result may be significant fluctuations in by-product revenues. Since these revenues are then netted against the cost of joint products (if the allocation is based on sales value), the result may be continual fluctuation in the reported costs of the joint products. To completely avoid this issue, do not designate *any* items as by-products.

Summary

The key point to remember about the cost allocations associated with joint products and by-products is that the allocation is simply a formula – it has no bearing on the value of the product to which it assigns a cost. The only reason we use these allocations is to achieve valid cost of goods sold amounts and inventory valuations under the requirements of the various accounting standards.

Chapter 9
Waste Accounting

Introduction

The typical manufacturing facility generates a significant amount of waste – in some cases, an extraordinary amount that represents a major reduction of corporate profits. Given the significance of the amount of waste, the cost accountant should make a major effort to properly record and report it, so that management can take action to control the issues causing waste.

In this chapter, we review the three primary types of waste, which are spoilage, rework, and scrap, as well as how to account for them.

Definition of Spoilage

Spoilage is produced goods that are defective. A defective product is one that does not meet a predetermined acceptance criterion.

EXAMPLE

The Atlas Machining Company produces a widget that is judged acceptable if its actual thickness is within 5% of the predetermined specification. Therefore all widgets it produces that are more than 5% of this specification are considered spoilage, and are thrown out.

Across the street, the Billabong Machining Company products a similar widget that it considers to be acceptable if its actual thickness is within 2% of the predetermined specification. All widgets outside of this range are thrown out.

Thus, based on the criteria that Atlas and Billabong have settled upon in advance, different quantities of the same product are designated as spoilage.

Spoilage frequently arises at the initiation of a production run, when the production staff is still setting up equipment and manufactures a few products that are outside of the range of acceptable tolerances. Such spoilage may be significant without good setup controls.

Spoilage usually cannot be reworked without spending an inordinate amount on labor, so it is usually scrapped and sold off for a very low price. It is not normally sold off as finished goods, since it is by definition out of specification, and therefore may not work properly, or even be dangerous to the user.

Accounting for Normal Spoilage

If the amount of spoilage occurring is within the normal range of expectations for spoilage in a manufacturing process, then include it in the cost of the related product.

EXAMPLE

Henderson Industrial manufactures plastic cartons for local dairies. The historical amount of spoilage that it experiences is 1% of all production. Each spoiled carton consumes plastic resin having a cost of $0.25. Henderson's cost accountant includes the cost of this resin in the carton bill of materials. The line items in the bill of materials are:

Line Item	Cost
Resin	$0.2500
Plastic cap	0.0200
Label	0.0150
Spoilage	0.0025
Total cost	$0.2875

The spoilage line item in the bill of materials is calculated as:

1% Probability of occurrence × $0.25 Cost per unit

Henderson then multiplies the total cost in the bill of materials by the number of units produced in the period to calculate its cost of goods sold, thereby incorporating the cost of spoilage into its cost of goods.

An alternative method of accounting for normal spoilage is to accumulate its cost during the reporting period, add this cost to the manufacturing overhead cost pool at the end of the month, and then allocate it to the goods produced during the month.

EXAMPLE

To continue with the preceding example, Henderson Industrial decides to stop recording normal spoilage in its bills of material, and instead records the actual cost of spoilage in a manufacturing overhead cost pool. It calculates this cost by adding up the number of spoiled cartons and multiplying by the component cost of each one. In May, the calculation is:

1,500 spoiled cartons × $0.25/unit resin cost = $375

Henderson's cost accountant includes this cost in the manufacturing overhead cost pool, which is comprised of the following costs in May:

Manufacturing Overhead Line Item	Amount
Manufacturing supervisor salaries	$140,000
Building rent	50,000
Utilities	15,000
Spoilage	375
Total	$205,375

During May, Henderson manufactured 10,000,000 cartons. The amount of the overhead cost pool allocated to each carton is:

$205,375 ÷ 10,000,000 cartons = $0.021 per carton

Accounting for Abnormal Spoilage

What happens when there is an abnormal amount of spoilage? The accountant cannot use the preceding method of including it in the bill of materials, since that method only works if there is a consistent and reliable amount of spoilage that does not vary significantly from period to period. Instead, charge the amount of the abnormal spoilage to the cost of goods sold expense in the period when it occurs. If the amount is of sufficient size to warrant it, consider recording the spoilage in a separate account.

EXAMPLE

Quest Clothiers, maker of rugged outdoor wear, experiences abnormal spoilage when it uses substandard thread on some of its outerwear, resulting in burst seams. The cost of the spoilage is $20,000, which it records as follows:

	Debit	Credit
Abnormal spoilage expense	20,000	
Inventory		20,000

Accounting for the Sale of Spoilage

If a company is able to sell its spoiled stock, there are two ways to record it. The first approach is to record it as revenue (usually within a unique revenue account). This alternative is most useful when the revenue is large enough to warrant separate treatment for sales that are expected to continue in the future. However, the amount of revenue from the sale of spoiled stock is usually too minor to make this approach worthwhile.

The more common alternative is to net any proceeds against the recorded cost of the spoilage. This gives management a good idea of the true cost of spoilage, though it does not reveal the amount of any lost profits.

EXAMPLE

To continue with the preceding example, Quest Clothiers sells a group of garments that were subject to abnormal spoilage, in the amount of $2,000. Quest rarely experiences abnormal spoilage, and so prefers to account for the sale as a one-time event, electing to net it against the cost of spoilage with the following entry:

	Debit	Credit
Cash	2,000	
Abnormal spoilage expense		2,000

Cost Allocation to Spoilage

Normally, overhead costs are allocated to manufactured goods. Should this be done for goods that are spoiled? Common practice is to do so, though only through the point in the production process that a product reaches before it is recognized as spoiled and withdrawn. However, this can be time-consuming for the cost accountant to track, especially when spoilage is rare and can occur in a number of areas within the production facility. Consequently, it may be necessary to apply overhead to spoiled goods as though they completed the entire production process, as long as the effect of this change in comparison to a more precise level of cost allocation is minimal.

EXAMPLE

Quest Clothiers discovers spoilage at all stages of its production process, usually in small amounts. Quest does not calculate cost allocations for discrete segments of its production process; instead, it only allocates costs for the entire process from a single cost pool. Quest calculates the amount of overhead that would be applied to the average amount of monthly spoilage, versus applying no overhead to it at all, and finds that the differential is only $10,000, in comparison to its monthly cost of goods sold of $2,000,000. Given the immateriality of the overhead application decision, Quest elects to apply overhead to spoilage as though it had completed the entire production process, and documents its findings in case the auditors wish to review it.

Definition of Rework

Rework is any product that is initially found to be faulty, and which is then repaired and sold; the sale price may be at a reduction from the standard price for a similar product that does not require rework.

The production managers of many companies do not like to deal with rework, since it frequently requires the efforts of the more skilled production staff to repair; also, the lower prices of rework items yield a lower gross margin than would a product that does not require rework. Consequently, given the low level of profitability associated with rework, there is a tendency to let it build up in inventory, which also presents a risk of obsolescence.

Reporting Rework

As just noted, there is an inordinately high risk that goods requiring rework will become obsolete, so the cost accountant should monitor the amount on hand and the amount of estimated effort needed to prepare it for sale, and share this information with management. A sample report that could be used is shown in the following exhibit, which shows the amount of estimated effort required by each of a company's work centers to rework inventory, as well as the current recorded cost of this inventory. The report is useful not only for showing the production planners how much time to schedule at each work center, but also to get a general idea of a company's working capital investment in rework inventory. Working capital is the amount of an entity's current assets minus its current liabilities, and is considered to be a prime measure of its liquidity. The key components of working capital are cash, accounts receivable, inventory, and accounts payable.

Exhibit: Rework Status Report

| Product | Rework Hours Required | | | | ($) |
	Bending	Curing	Painting	Assembly	Valuation
Product Alpha	12	82	6	24	$3,500
Product Beta	14	86	7	28	4,200
Product Charlie	23	100	12	46	8,000
Totals	49	268	25	98	$15,700

An alternative reporting format is shown in the following exhibit, which assigns a job number to each product or group of products that require rework. This report is more specific, itemizing the exact repair steps required to complete a rework item. Production managers prefer this higher level of detail, which gives them sufficient information to properly schedule rework. It is also useful for determining which products can be reworked for the minimum amount of effort, which is useful for clearing rework items from inventory quickly.

Exhibit: Detailed Rework Report

Product	Batch Number	Rework Description	Rework Cost	Estimated Completion
Product Alpha	4003	Re-bend drain corners	$129	May 14
Product Beta	4011	Extend curing time by five hours	340	May 17
Product Charlie	4017	Strip paint and apply new layer	72	May 21
Product Delta	4025	Repackage in undamaged boxes	415	May 27

Accounting for Rework

It takes a great deal of effort to account for the work required to bring rework items back into sellable condition. This accounting requires special tracking codes, and may involve work centers located throughout a production facility. The staff of each work center must record its labor hours and any new materials used to rework an item, after which someone must input the information into a rework database. The cost accountant then periodically extracts this information from the database and reports on rework costs to management.

If the amount of rework that a company normally deals with is minor, there is no need to account for it separately in the general ledger at all. It is more cost-effective to allow the production accounting systems to record rework as a normal part of doing business. The only downside is that the company has no idea of the exact amount of costs it is expending on rework.

The reverse situation may also arise, where a company is operating under the burden of a great deal of rework. Since this may have a major negative impact on profits, the cost accountant must have a system for recording the cost of rework, if only so that management has a good feedback system for how well it subsequently reduces the amount of rework.

Definition of Scrap

Scrap is the amount of unused material that remains after a product has been manufactured. The classic example of rework is in a metal stamping operation, where there is always some scrap remaining after a number of parts have been punched from a metal sheet.

Accounting for Scrap

The accounting for scrap is essentially the same as for spoilage, as described earlier in this chapter. It can be accounted for in one of three ways:

- *Include scrap in the bill of materials.* This approach only works if a standard costing system is in place that uses the bill of materials to calculate the cost of goods sold.
- *Include in a cost pool.* This approach is a reasonable alternative to including the information in the bill of materials, and is somewhat easier to calculate.

- *Charge to the cost of goods sold*. This approach matches the treatment for abnormal scrap, and has the singular advantage of requiring no accounting transactions at all. Though it provides no method for determining the cost of scrap, the amount of scrap may be so small that management is comfortable with the arrangement.

The preceding steps were all noted earlier for spoilage accounting. Another alternative is to precisely track the cost of scrap and then charge it to specific jobs (see the Job Costing chapter). This approach requires considerable effort to accumulate costs, but is useful in a cost reimbursement situation where the customer will reimburse the company for all costs that it can document.

Scrap, by definition, has little residual value, so it rarely makes sense to record its sale in a separate revenue account. Instead, it is most commonly recorded net of the cost of goods sold, thereby reducing a company's cost of goods sold.

EXAMPLE

Micron Metallic runs a large metal stamping machine that creates parts for washing machines. In the June reporting period, it recorded $80,000 of scrap from its stamping operations. Since this amount usually represents about 5% of Micron's cost of goods sold, which is a material amount, the controller always records scrap in a separate account. At the end of each month, a scrap hauler takes away the scrap metal and pays Micron based on the weight of the metal removed. The June payment from the scrap hauler is $800, which the controller records with the following entry:

	Debit	Credit
Cash	800	
Scrap expense		800

If a company elects to allow its scrap to accumulate for some time before selling it to a third party, the value of the scrap may be sufficiently material to call for a journal entry at the end of each reporting period to account for the gain in assets. For example, if there were a $10,000 gain in scrap during a month, the entry could be recorded as:

	Debit	Credit
Inventory - scrap	10,000	
Cost of goods sold		10,000

This entry reduces expenses during the month and creates an asset that is an estimate of the market value of the scrap. Then, when the scrap is eventually sold, eliminate the inventory asset and adjust for any differences between the actual and estimated amounts of the market value. To continue with the example, the scrap is sold early in the following month, for $9,750. There is a residual loss of $250, which is so small that it is not worth recording in a separate account. Instead, it is charged to the cost of goods sold with the following entry:

	Debit	Credit
Cash	9,750	
Cost of goods sold	250	
Inventory - scrap		10,000

Impact of Waste on Manufacturing Systems

Waste is a particular problem for several types of lean manufacturing systems, since they incorporate assumptions about waste that may not be correct. When abnormal waste occurs, the systems are not designed to handle the issue. The two problem areas are:

- *Backflushing systems.* A material requirements planning (MRP) system may use a backflushing option, whereby the system eliminates raw materials from inventory automatically and charges these items to the cost of goods sold, based on the assumption that the standard amount of components were used to create a product. Though backflushing is a very efficient method for recording production activity, it has no way of recording abnormal waste. A separate tracking system must be created for recording abnormal waste, and these transactions are manually recorded in the MRP system. Otherwise, backflushing will result in excessively high inventory balances and an incorrectly low cost of goods sold.
- *Just-in-time systems.* A just-in-time (JIT) system emphasizes the use of very small production lots, so that waste is spotted (and corrected) immediately. A JIT system also uses the least possible amount of data entry. Given these two points, it is difficult to impose a waste recording system on a manufacturing facility where data entry consumes valuable time, and where waste levels are presumably quite low. One alternative approach is to use auditors to sample waste levels and extrapolate its cost from this information. Another option is to accumulate all waste in a central location, and periodically count it. Either approach is minimally intrusive, and gives a reasonable approximation of actual waste levels.

Of the two problems noted here, the more significant one is backflushing. If a manufacturing operation has an ongoing problem with large amounts of abnormal waste, it may render the backflushing system useless, if there is not a compensating data collection system in place to record the waste.

Summary

The typical manufacturing operation creates a significant amount of waste throughout its operations. Not only does this waste have a large negative impact on profits, but it also results in incorrectly high inventory balances. The cost accountant must have recording systems in place that track the amount of waste, its cost, the cost to rework it, and any amounts received from the sale of waste. Depending upon the materiality of waste, it may be necessary to create separate accounts in which to track waste. If there is little waste, it may be acceptable to record it within the cost of goods sold, without attempting to break out the information.

Chapter 10
Product Pricing: What Does This Cost?

Introduction

This chapter is designed to address the key information needed to answer the question, "what does this cost?" for product pricing purposes. Doing so requires one to ask additional questions, resulting in a potential range of answers to the question, "what does this cost?"

What Does This Cost?

The marketing manager walks into the accountant's office, holds up the green widget that the company just started producing, and asks, "what does this cost?" The question is a simple one, but the answer is not – in fact, it brings up a number of issues to be aware of before answering the marketing manager. Cost is the expenditure required to create and sell products and services, or to acquire assets. When sold or consumed, a cost is charged to expense. Thus, if the business pays $10,000 for parts that will eventually be assembled into a product, the $10,000 is part of the cost of the product, but it is not charged to expense until the product is sold. Consider the following issues before answering the "what does this cost" question:

- *Pricing duration.* The marketing manager usually wants to know about the cost of a product for one reason only, which is to add a profit margin to it, thereby creating a price. This price tends to be much higher if the intent is to cover the entire cost of the business over the long term. However, if the marketing manager is contemplating a one-time deal with a customer, he may want to use the product cost to establish a minimum price that only generates a small profit over the product cost.
- *Proportion of overhead costs.* Well over half of all manufacturing costs are part of manufacturing overhead in almost any company, and it is very difficult to reliably associate most costs with any products.
- *Application of overhead costs.* If overhead costs are allocated to products, there are a number of methods for doing so. None of them will yield perfectly justifiable results, so the emphasis should be on selecting a small number of allocation methods that are reasonably justifiable, and which can be efficiently and correctly calculated over time.
- *Corporate overhead costs.* Costs generated at the corporate level have nothing to do with products manufactured at the division level, so do not allocate corporate overhead costs to products.
- *Production bottleneck.* If there is a work center in the production department that cannot process all of the existing customer orders, the marketing man-

ager should not set prices on any new orders that result in profits lower than the profits of the orders already queued up in front of the bottleneck operation.

All of these issues are discussed at greater length in the following sections.

The Issue of Pricing Duration

If someone wants cost information for a product in order to set a price, this brings up several issues. The key point is that the proper price for a product is some variation on the market price at which other, similar products are selling. The market price may be many times more than the cost of a product, or it may be less than the cost of the product. Supply and demand issues drive product price, not necessarily the cost of the product.

There is one interrelationship between a product's cost and its price, and that is to use the cost in order to set a *minimum* price. This is not necessarily the optimal price at which the company earns the largest profit, it is simply a threshold below which the price should not be set. If a product's price is set lower than its cost, the company will lose money on every unit it sells. However, even the concept of a minimum pricing threshold is not an entirely concrete concept when dealing with product cost, because the accountant can subdivide the issue into deriving a cost for short-term pricing and for long-term pricing. The issues are:

- *Short-term pricing.* When the marketing manager is dealing with a potential one-time order from a customer that is unlikely to be repeated, he needs a product cost that only includes the totally variable cost of the product – which means the cost of the materials used to build the product, as well as any shipping and handling costs directly associated with acquiring those materials. With this information, he can bid a low price in order to obtain the business, but not so low that the company is losing money on the specific deal.

- *Long-term pricing.* Short-term pricing does not work very well over the long-term, because there is a temptation with short-term pricing to offer prices that are unsustainably low. At these lower price points, a company does not generate sufficient revenue to pay for all of its expenses, and it will eventually go out of business. Consequently, if the marketing manager explains that he wants to establish a long-term price, provide him with not only the totally variable cost of the product, but also an indication of how much overhead should be assigned to the product in order to cover all of the company's costs.

EXAMPLE

Snyder Corporation manufactures small, compact global positioning satellites. All of the personnel involved in their production are so highly qualified that the company will retain them even if production levels decline. The product requires a great deal of research and development expenditures, as well as prolonged quality testing. The cost breakdown for a satellite is:

	Variable Costs	Overhead Costs
Components	$125,000	
Assembly staff		$400,000
Quality control staff		150,000
Research staff		200,000
Building overhead		75,000
Manufacturing supervision		50,000
Totals	$125,000	$875,000

The totally variable cost of a single satellite is only $125,000, so Snyder could theoretically make money by pricing its satellites in short-term pricing situations for any amount over $125,000. However, it would soon go out of business if it were to do so for an extended period of time, since the company must also pay for a significant amount of overhead costs. If Snyder hopes to be in business for any length of time, it will need to use the long-term cost per satellite of $1,000,000 as the minimum threshold for setting prices (not including a profit margin).

Tip: To obtain information about the totally variable cost of a product, a good source is the bill of materials. This is a listing of all the component parts of a product, as well as the standard cost of each part (which should approximate its actual cost). A bill of materials may also include an allowance for material scrap that arises during the production process, which is an acceptable part of the product cost.

The Issue of Overhead Costs

When a product is manufactured, the only cost that can be clearly traced to the product is the cost of the materials used to create it, which is called *direct materials*. That is all. It is impossible to trace any other cost directly to a product.

Historically, the cost of production labor was also assumed to be traceable to a product, and was called *direct labor*. However, consider how production people work – they start work at the beginning of their shift, and stop work at the end of the shift. They do not stop work even if they run out of products to assemble; instead, managers generally have them complete "make work" tasks until there are more products to work on. Managers do this because sending employees home as soon as they run out of work is an excellent way to drive employees into the arms of competitors who are willing to offer them a more stable work environment. Consequently, there is no clear relationship between direct labor and a product, which means that direct labor is really part of the cost category called manufacturing overhead. Manufacturing overhead encompasses *all* of the costs of a factory, other than those costs that can be proven to be actually used in a product. Manufacturing overhead includes a lot of costs, such as:

- Building rent
- Building supplies
- Equipment depreciation
- Fringe benefits
- Insurance

- Janitorial costs
- Production planning salaries
- Materials handling salaries
- Supervisor salaries
- Utilities

Since most of the costs of a factory are part of manufacturing overhead, there is a major issue – should these costs be assigned to products, or not? The following example illustrates the issue.

EXAMPLE

Horton Corporation incurs the following manufacturing costs during the month of May:

	Overhead	Direct Costs
Building rent	$60,000	
Direct labor	150,000	
Fringe benefits	50,000	
Insurance	8,000	
Janitorial costs	9,000	
Materials		$280,000
Production-related salaries	80,000	
Utilities	34,000	
Other	29,000	
Totals	$420,000	$280,000
Percent of total	60%	40%

In the example, 60 percent of the manufacturing costs of Horton Corporation involve overhead (in which direct labor is included), while it can only trace 40 percent of its costs directly to its products. This proportion is, if anything, conservative in the modern corporation. It is not at all uncommon to see materials costs of only 20 percent of the total cost of a factory. Consequently, the majority of all manufacturing costs are not tied directly to specific products.

The Issue of Overhead Application

There is clearly a great deal of overhead that can be allocated to products. If overhead costs are assigned to a product, this is easy only if there is a single product. For example, if the total manufacturing overhead of a production facility is $1,000,000 and that facility produces 100,000 widgets per year, then one can safely assign $10 of overhead cost to each widget. However, the situation is rarely so simple as that. Instead, what if the factory produces a number of different products? How are overhead costs assigned to each of the products within each product line? And does it matter if overhead costs are assigned at all?

The basic problem with overhead allocation is that there is no direct linkage between a product and an overhead cost. For example, if one less unit of a product is manufactured, does the overhead cost associated with a production supervisor decline by some small amount at the same time? Of course not. If there were a linkage, the cost would be treated as a direct cost, rather than an overhead cost. Consequently, it does not seem to matter if we allocate overhead costs to products, since there is no linkage between the overhead and the products, other than the fact that the entire block of overhead costs must be incurred in order to manufacture the products.

Then why do we allocate overhead costs to products at all? A slightly defensible reason is that we must ensure that product prices remain high enough for the company to generate a sufficient amount of revenue to cover its costs, and including overhead costs in the product costs will keep the marketing department from setting prices too low.

If we agree with this reasoning, then we need to find a method for allocating manufacturing overhead to products. This is a two-stage process:

1. *Allocate any costs traceable to a subset of the factory.* It is possible that some components of manufacturing overhead are only related to a specific part of the factory. For example, a quality control person may be employed to review only a single product line. If this is the case, allocate these costs only to the products to which they are linked.

2. *Allocate all remaining manufacturing costs.* Assign all remaining costs to cost pools, and find a reasonable and consistent method for allocating each of the cost pools to products.

EXAMPLE

Ambivalence Corporation has $500,000 of annual manufacturing overhead that it must assign to its three product lines. Of the $500,000, $100,000 is directly associated with the Red Potion product line, while the remaining $400,000 is only associated with the entire factory, and so must be allocated across all three products. Ambivalence produced 50,000 capsules of the Red Potion during the year, so it assigns $2 of manufacturing overhead to each capsule, thereby fully allocating the $100,000 that was traceable to that product line.

Product Pricing: What Does This Cost?

The cost accountant decides to allocate $250,000 of the remaining $400,000 of overhead based on the usage by the various products of the brewing vat, since all of them use it through a substantial proportion of the production process, and because he can trace all $250,000 to the monitoring, management, or operation of the brewing vat. The allocation is as follows:

Product Line	Minutes of Vat Usage	Percentage of Vat Usage	Overhead Allocation
Red Potion	165,000	55%	$137,500
Blue Toadstools	90,000	30%	75,000
Green Potion	45,000	15%	37,500
Totals	300,000	100%	$250,000

Finally, the cost accountant must allocate the remaining $150,000 of factory overhead, which is related to the cost of the building – its rent, maintenance, and insurance. He decides to use the square footage taken up by each product within the facility as the best way to allocate the expense. This is a somewhat questionable basis of allocation, since it relates primarily to the storage portion of the facility and not the production area – nonetheless, it is a reasonable basis of allocation for a portion of the building overhead, and he decides to extend it to all parts of the building. The allocation is as follows:

Product Line	Square Feet Used	Percentage of Building Usage	Overhead Allocation
Red Potion	35,000	35%	$52,500
Blue Toadstools	40,000	40%	60,000
Green Potion	25,000	25%	37,500
Totals	100,000	100%	$150,000

The total allocation of $500,000 to the various product lines is as follows:

Product Line	Red Potion Line Allocation	Vat Usage Allocation	Square Footage Allocation	Total Allocation
Red Potion	$100,000	$137,500	$52,500	$290,000
Blue Toadstools	--	75,000	60,000	135,000
Green Potion	--	37,500	37,500	75,000
Totals	$100,000	$250,000	$150,000	$500,000

> **Tip:** Do not allocate overhead based on something that products use only a small amount of. For example, do not allocate based on the direct labor cost if this cost is 10% or less of the total product cost. Otherwise, a large amount of cost may be allocated that is several multiples higher than the basis of allocation. An example of a bad allocation is when $10 of overhead is assigned based on $1 of direct labor.

In the example, the cost accountant knew that his reason for using square footage as the basis for allocating $150,000 of building overhead was somewhat flawed, since it was only possible to clearly measure square footage usage by products in the warehouse area, and not in the rest of the facility. This is a common problem with overhead allocation, since any method used will not result in an overly high level of precision. Consequently, the emphasis is more on using a reasonable basis for allocation, rather than on the most absolutely correct basis of allocation.

> **Tip:** Only alter the cost allocation methodology infrequently, such as once a year, to avoid large swings in overhead cost allocations to individual products.

> **Tip:** Do not use too many cost pools or allocation methods to allocate overhead costs to products. Remember, we call this an *allocation* because it is not exact –an overly high level of precision cannot be achieved, so instead focus on creating a reasonable and supportable methodology that can be efficiently calculated with few mistakes.

A quite reasonable alternative to allocating overhead costs to products is to simply tell the marketing manager the size of the total pool of manufacturing overhead costs. This gives the marketing manager a target amount of costs that he must offset with a sufficient amount of profit from all of the products that he sells. By using this approach, the marketing manager can price some products quite close to their totally variable costs, while setting extremely high prices for other products, if the market will tolerate such high prices. This approach gives the marketing manager more room to maneuver (since his minimum price points are lower), while focusing his attention on the high-level goal of achieving a profit for the entire company.

Corporate Overhead Costs

Manufacturing overhead costs have just been applied to a product. What if corporate management also wants an additional amount of corporate overhead costs to be applied to the product? After all, the corporation as a whole must generate sufficient revenue to cover its costs, and applying corporate costs to products will force the marketing manager to set an even higher price for those products. What should be done?

If there seemed to be few valid bases for assigning manufacturing overhead costs to products, the situation with corporate costs is even worse. There is absolutely no justifiable method for allocating these costs, other than a completely arbitrary formula. Thus, cost information is not being handed off to the marketing manager that is incrementally more useful than the costs that had been previously compiled. In fact, since these additional costs bear no relevance to the underlying product, a strong case can be made that the information now being provided is *less* meaningful than costs that do not include corporate overhead.

Based on the argument of reduced relevance, do not allocate corporate overhead to the cost of a product. Instead, the marketing manager should be responsible for building it into the profit margin that he applies to the product. This may sound like splitting hairs, since responsibility for applying the cost is simply being shifted to the marketing manager. However, this also means that the marketing manager is fully aware of the need to cover the cost of corporate overhead, and he can alter profit margins across the full range of company products in order to do so. If the accountant had added it to the baseline cost of the product, the cost of *all* products would have risen, so that the marketing manager would have less flexibility to alter pricing.

EXAMPLE

Horton Corporation's corporate staff costs $400,000. The corporate controller decides that this cost should be formally incorporated into the company's product pricing. Of the $400,000, the controller decides that its Widget Division should cover $250,000, with the remaining $150,000 assigned to other divisions.

The cost accountant for the Widget Division decides that it will be easiest to assign the $250,000 across all four of the division's products using an identical allocation percentage that is assigned based on the budgeted cost of goods sold for the four products for the full year. The allocation calculation is:

Product	Budgeted Cost of Goods	Allocation at 12.5% of Cost of Goods	Revised Budgeted Cost of Goods	Budgeted Unit Sales	Revised Cost per Unit
Three-tone widget	650,000	$81,250	$731,250	15,000	$48.75
Two-tone widget	350,000	43,750	393,750	15,000	26.25
Black widget	200,000	25,000	225,000	10,000	22.50
Blue widget	800,000	100,000	900,000	60,000	15.00
Totals	$2,000,000	$250,000	$2,250,000	100,000	$22.50

The preceding calculation means that the cost of all four products has now risen by 12.5%, as shown in the following table:

	Budgeted Cost	Revised Cost
Three-tone widget	$43.33	$48.75
Two-tone widget	23.33	26.25
Black widget	20.00	22.50
Blue widget	13.33	15.00

The marketing manager usually applies a 30% markup to the cost of each product in order to calculate its price, which is reflected in the following table of before-and-after pricing:

	Budgeted Price	Revised Price
Three-tone widget	$56.33	$63.38
Two-tone widget	30.33	34.13
Black widget	26.00	29.25
Blue widget	17.33	19.50

The trouble is that the market prices for the two-tone widget and the blue widget are lower than the revised price, and customers are highly sensitive to price. Because of the company's rigid system for calculating the price of a product, it is about to lose all sales of these two products, which leaves fewer products over which the cost of corporate overhead can be spread.

What Does This Cost, Part Two

We now return to the marketing manager, who is still standing in the accountant's office, holding up the green widget. A number of concepts have now been reviewed regarding his question, and it is apparent that the accountant needs to answer his question with another question, which is "how are you going to use the information?" Since the person asking the question is the marketing manager, one can safely assume that he wants to set a price for the widget. Here is how the accountant can respond, depending on his answer:

"I want to set a long-term price." In this case, tell the marketing manager not only about the direct material cost of the widget, but also include a fair allocation of the manufacturing overhead. The marketing manager then adds a profit percentage to the cost he has been given, and the company ends up selling widgets at a price that allows the company as a whole to earn a reasonable profit over time.

An even better answer is to give him just the totally variable cost of the product, plus the total amount of manufacturing overhead cost that must also be covered. This information does not obscure the incremental cost (the extra cost to manufacture one additional unit) of the product, and the marketing manager now knows exactly how much profit he must generate in total to offset the cost of manufacturing overhead.

"I have a one-time deal with a customer." In this case, the marketing manager wants to know what the cost of the product is without any additional overhead cost, so that he can craft a one-time price that will secure a deal with the customer for a single order. As long as the price is higher than the materials cost of the product, the company will earn some incremental profit that will allow it to defray the cost of its manufacturing overhead.

The Issue of the Bottleneck

There is a significant issue that bears on the two responses given by the marketing manager to the accountant in the last section – the bottleneck. In many manufacturing operations, there is one work center that is running flat out all the time, and which has a significant pile of work-in-process inventory positioned in front of it, waiting to be processed. This work center can be anything at all – a simple quality control inspection station, a stamping machine, perhaps a paint shop. For whatever reason, a significant part of the work in the shop flows through this work center, and there is not enough capacity to handle all of the work. Capacity is the maximum sustainable rate of output that an operation can achieve.

What if the marketing manager responded that he had a one-time deal with a customer, so he was given the cost of the materials used to construct the green widget? Let's say that the cost of materials was $10, and the marketing manager decided to add a 30 percent markup and quote the widget to his special customer at a price of $13. This means that the company will earn a profit of $3 on every widget sold. However, what if the manufacturing bottleneck is its paint shop, and the widgets all have to be painted green in the paint shop? We already know that the paint shop is currently overwhelmed with work, so the green widgets, sporting their $3 profit margins, will have to replace some other products that had already been scheduled into the paint shop. What if the company is currently selling blue widgets for a $5 profit, and the special order of green widgets can only be sold by stopping production of the blue widgets and running the green widgets through the paint shop instead (and assume that both widgets require the same amount of processing time by the paint shop). The result is that the new, specially-priced green widgets will earn $2 less per unit than the blue widgets they are replacing. This concept is called *throughput analysis*, and we will address it further in the Constraint Analysis chapter.

The key issue to be aware of for now is that if there is a bottleneck, it is necessary to know the amount of throughput (revenue minus totally variable expenses) being generated per minute on other products, in order to point out to the marketing manager the minimum price point he needs to set for the green widget in order to generate an incremental increase in the company's *total* amount of profit.

What Does This Cost, Part Three

Given the preceding discussion of throughput, the accountant can now give a more comprehensive answer to the marketing manager if he needs the cost of the green widget in order to set a price for a special order. As noted before, the accountant should certainly state that the cost of the widget is its direct material cost, which is $10. However, if there is a manufacturing bottleneck, it is also necessary to point out the minimum amount of throughput per minute that is currently or which is scheduled to run through that operation, and what the price of the green widget will have to be in order to at least equal the current rate of throughput.

EXAMPLE

Horton Corporation currently has four products that it is processing through its paint shop, which is its bottleneck operation. The paint shop is available for use 24 hours a day, which is 1,440 minutes per day. However, it requires substantial downtime for cleaning, so the paint shop is really only available for 1,200 minutes per day. The following production schedule shows the jobs that are scheduled to run through the paint shop during the next month, in descending order by throughput per minute.

Product Description	Throughput per Minute of Bottleneck	Required Bottleneck Usage	Scheduled Production in Units	Bottleneck Usage (minutes)	Throughput per Product
Three-tone widget	$36	3	150	450	$16,200
Two-tone widget	25	2	125	250	6,250
Black widget	18	1	200	200	3,600
Blue widget	5	1	300	300	1,500
		Totals	775	1,200	$27,550

The table shows that the paint shop bottleneck is fully utilized, and that the minimum amount of throughput per minute scheduled through it is three hundred minutes of time to paint blue widgets, at $5 of throughput per minute.

Based on the information in the exhibit, the accountant would point out that any additional sales during the month will bump out one of the other jobs that is scheduled for production, and the minimum margin on any of those projects is $5 of throughput per minute. Consequently, and on the assumption that a green widget requires one minute of processing time at the bottleneck, one should also point out that the marketing manager should establish a price of at least $5 more than the cost of the widget; otherwise, the company will not earn any additional profit from the deal.

Of course, volunteering throughput pricing information goes well beyond the original "what does this cost?" question, but the accountant would be remiss in not volunteering the information, since the marketing manager's intent in asking the question is clear, and he can be prevented from making a bad pricing decision by giving him this extra information.

Summary

It should be clear by now that the question "what does this cost?" is by no means an easy one to answer. The accountant is always safe in giving a minimum cost that is the totally variable cost of the product. It is questionable whether one should also include a per-unit allocation of manufacturing overhead costs, and it is even less supportable to also include corporate overhead costs at the per-unit level. However, the recipient of the cost information may need to know about the total amount of manufacturing overhead and corporate overhead cost that the company must pay for, and should also know about the throughput of other products that are currently scheduled to be worked on by the bottleneck operation in the manufacturing area. Thus, a reasonable sample answer to the question "what does this cost?" is:

"The totally variable cost of the [product name] is $50. In addition, there are $482,000 of manufacturing overhead costs and $178,000 of corporate overhead costs per year that we have to pay for. Finally, the minimum throughput per minute at the bottleneck is $10, so we should not price any products to have a throughput below that amount. Please consider all of these factors when you set product prices."

Chapter 11
Target Costing

Introduction

A fundamental flaw in the role of the traditional cost accountant is that he reports on the costs that *are* – the costs that are already in existence. Costs tend to continue in the same proportions into the future, so the cost accountant cannot do a great deal to improve a company's profitability based on its existing cost structure.

The primary management concept that can change this situation is *target costing*, under which a company plans in advance for the product price points, product costs, and margins that it wants to achieve. If it cannot manufacture a product at these planned levels, then it cancels the product entirely. With target costing, a management team has a powerful tool for continually monitoring products from the moment they enter the design phase and onward throughout their product life cycles.

This chapter describes how target costing works, and the cost accountant's key role in the process.

> **Related Podcast Episode:** Episode 57 of the Accounting Best Practices Podcast discusses target costing. It is available at: **accountingtools.com/podcasts** or **iTunes**

The Basic Steps of Target Costing

Target costing has been in existence for a number of years and is used by many companies, so the primary steps in the process are well defined. They are:

1. *Conduct research.* The first step is to review the marketplace in which the company wants to sell products. The team needs to determine the set of product features that customers are most likely to buy, and the amount they will pay for those features. The team must learn about the perceived value of individual features, in case they later need to determine what impact there will be on the product price if they drop one or more of them. It may be necessary to later drop a product feature if the team decides that it cannot provide the feature while still meeting its target cost. At the end of this process, the team has a good idea of the target price at which it can sell the proposed product with a certain set of features, and how it must alter the price if it drops some features from the product.

2. *Calculate maximum cost.* The company provides the design team with a mandated gross margin that the proposed product must earn. By subtracting the mandated gross margin from the projected product price, the team can easily determine the maximum target cost that the product must achieve before it can be allowed into production.

3. *Engineer the product.* The engineers and procurement personnel on the team now take the leading role in creating the product. The procurement staff are particularly important if the product has a high proportion of purchased parts; they must determine component pricing based on the necessary quality, delivery, and quantity levels expected for the product. They may also be involved in outsourcing parts, if this results in lower costs. The engineers must design the product to meet the cost target, which will likely include a number of design iterations to see which combination of revised features and design considerations results in the lowest cost.

4. *Ongoing activities.* Once a product design is finalized and approved, the team is reconstituted to include fewer designers and more industrial engineers. The team now enters into a new phase of reducing production costs, which continues for the life of the product. For example, cost reductions may come from waste reductions in production (known as kaizen costing, which is the process of continual cost reduction after a product is being manufactured), or from planned supplier cost reductions. These ongoing cost reductions yield enough additional gross margin for the company to further reduce the price of the product over time, in response to increases in the level of competition. Kaizen costing does not generate the size of cost reductions that can be achieved through initial design changes, but it can have a cumulatively significant impact over time.

EXAMPLE

SkiPS is a maker of global positioning systems (GPS) for skiers, which they use to log how many vertical feet they ski each day. SkiPS conducts a marketing survey to decide upon the features it needs to include in its next generation of GPS device, and finds that skiers want a device they can strap to their arm or leg, and which does not require recharging during a multi-day vacation.

The survey indicates that skiers are willing to pay no more than $150 for the device, while the first review of costs indicates that it will cost $160 to manufacture. At a mandated gross margin percentage of 40%, this means that the device must attain a target cost of $90 ($150 price × (1 − 40% gross margin). Thus, the design team must reduce costs from $160 to $90.

The team decides that the GPS unit requires no display screen at all, since users can plug the device into a computer to download information. This eliminates the LCD display and one computer chip. It also prolongs the battery life, since the unit no longer has to provide power to the display. The team also finds that a new microprocessor requires less power; given these reduced power requirements, the team can now use a smaller battery.

Finally, the team finds that the high-impact plastic case is over-engineered, and can withstand a hard impact with a much thinner shell. After the team incorporates all of these changes, it has reached the $90 cost target. SkiPS can now market a new device at a price point that allows it to earn a generous gross profit.

Value Engineering Considerations

The product engineering process noted above in step three involves many considerations. Here are examples of ways to reduce the cost of a product in order to meet a target cost:

- *Revise the manufacturing process.* The industrial engineering staff may be called upon to create an entirely new manufacturing process that uses less labor or less expensive machinery. It is entirely possible that multiple processes will be entirely eliminated from the production process. In particular, there may be an opportunity to eliminate various quality reviews from the process if product quality can be ensured by other means.

- *Reduce durability.* It is possible that the preliminary product design incorporates a product durability level that is actually *too* robust, thereby creating an opportunity to carefully decrease the level of product durability in order to cut costs. The typical result of this change is to completely eliminate some types of structural reinforcement from the product, or to at least downgrade to a less durable material in some parts of the product.

- *Reduce product features.* It may turn out to be quite expensive to offer certain features in a product. If so, the team needs to decide if it can delete one or more of these features while accepting a lower projected product price for which the net effect is an improved product margin. This type of value engineering must be carefully weighed against the problem of eliminating so many key features that the product will no longer be attractive to customers.

- *Reduce the number of parts.* It may be possible to simplify the design by using fewer parts, especially if doing so reduces the cost of assembling the final product. However, this concept can be taken too far, especially when many standard parts are replaced by a smaller number of customized (and therefore more expensive) parts.

- *Replace components.* It is possible that slightly different components are available at a substantially reduced cost; if so, the design engineers can modify the product to accommodate the different components. This is an especially common avenue when a product is initially designed to include components that have a high per-unit cost, and which can be replaced with components on which the company already earns significant volume discounts by using them across multiple product lines.

- *Design for easier manufacture.* To avoid time-consuming mistakes in the manufacturing process, consider designing the product so that it can only be assembled in a single way – all other attempts to assemble the product in an incorrect manner will fail. By doing so, there will be fewer product failures or recalls, which reduces the total cost of the product. It may be necessary to *increase* the cost of a product in order to create the optimum design for manufacturing, thereby reducing the total cost of the product over its full life span.

- *Ask suppliers*. Suppliers may have significant insights into how to reduce the costs of the various components they are contributing to the final product design, particularly in regard to altering material content or changing the manufacturing process. Suppliers may be willing to serve on design teams and contribute their expertise in exchange for being the sole source of selected components.

If the project team finds that it can comfortably meet the target cost without engaging in all of the preceding steps, then it should work through the activity list anyways. By doing so, it can generate sufficient room between the actual and target gross margins that management now has the option to reduce the product price below the target level, which may attract additional sales.

The Cost Reduction Program

The methods used by the design team are more sophisticated than simply saying, "folks, we need to cut $150 in costs – anyone have any ideas?" Instead, the team uses one of two approaches to more tightly focus its cost reduction efforts:

- *Tied to components*. The design team allocates the cost reduction goal among the various product components. This approach tends to result in incremental cost reductions to the same components that were used in the last iteration of the product. This approach is commonly used when a company is simply trying to refresh an existing product with a new version, and wants to retain the same underlying product structure. The cost reductions achieved through this approach tend to be relatively low, but also result in a high rate of product success, as well as a fairly short design period.
- *Tied to features*. The product team allocates the cost reduction goal among various product features, which focuses attention away from any product designs that may have been inherited from the preceding model. This approach tends to achieve more radical cost reductions (and design changes), but also requires more time to design, and also runs a greater risk of product failure or at least greater warranty costs.

Of the two methods noted here, companies are more likely to use the first approach if they are looking for a routine upgrade to an existing product, and the second approach if they want to achieve a significant cost reduction or break away from the existing design.

The Milestone Review Process

What if the project team simply cannot meet the target cost? Rather than completing the design process and creating a product with a substandard profit margin, the correct response is to stop the development process and move on to other projects instead. This does not mean that management allows its project teams to struggle on for months or years before finally giving up. Instead, they must come within a set percentage of the cost target on various milestone dates, with each successive milestone requirement coming closer to the final target cost. Milestones may occur on specific dates, or when key completion steps are reached in the design process, such as at the end of each design iteration.

EXAMPLE

Milagro Corporation is developing a new espresso machine that only works with its specially-developed strain of coffee bean. Milagro conducts market research and concludes that the product cannot sell for more than $200. At the company's required gross margin of 40%, this means that the target cost of the product is $120. Management sets a maximum design duration of six months, with milestone reviews at one-month intervals. The results of the month-end milestone reviews are:

Review Date	Cost Goal	Actual Cost Estimate	Actual Cost Variance from Goal	Allowance Variance From Cost Goal
Jan. 31	$120	$150	25%	30%
Feb. 28	120	143	19%	20%
Mar. 31	120	138	15%	15%
Apr. 30	120	134	12%	10%
May 31	120	Cancelled	--	5%
June 30	120	Cancelled	--	0%

As the table reveals, the Milagro project team was able to stay ahead of the cost target at the end of the first two months, but then was barely able to meet the allowable variance in the third month, and finally fell behind in the fourth month. Management then cancelled the project, saving itself the cost of continuing the project team for several more months when it was becoming obvious that the team would not be able to achieve the target cost.

Though management may cancel a design project that cannot meet its cost goals, this does not mean that the project will be permanently shelved. Far from it. Instead, management should review old projects at least once a year to see if the circumstances have changed sufficiently for them to possibly become viable again. A more precise review approach is to have each project team formulate a set of variables that should initiate a product review if a trigger point is reached (such as a decline in the price of a commodity that is used in the product design). If any of these trigger points are reached, the projects are immediately brought to the attention of management to see if they should be revived.

Problems with Target Costing

Target costing is difficult to initiate, because of the uncertainty surrounding the eventual release of a product. A company that allows its engineering department sole responsibility for creating products will achieve product releases on a fairly consistent schedule, even though some of the products may not be overly profitable. Under target costing, it is quite possible that a company may cancel a series of projects before they reach fruition, resulting in a frantic marketing department that sees no new products entering the pipeline. The solution is a combination of firm support by senior management and ongoing questioning of whether the target gross margin is too high to be achievable. It is entirely possible that an overly enthusiastic management team sets an excessively high gross margin standard for its new target costing process, and then sees no products survive the process. Consequently, it may take some time before management understands what gross margin levels will result in a target costing process that can churn out an acceptable number of products.

Another problem with target costing is the unwillingness of management to cancel a project. They do not want to see their investment in a project thrown away, and so they keep funding it for "just one more month," hoping that the team will find a way to achieve the target cost. The end result is a very long design process that absorbs more design costs than expected, and which still does not achieve the target cost. The only way to resolve this issue is an iron resolve to terminate projects in a timely manner.

Finally, a design team needs a strong leader to keep control of the opinions of the various departments that are represented on the team. For example, the marketing department may hold out for certain product features, while the design engineers claim that those same features introduce too many costs into the product. The best team leader is not one who unilaterally decides on the product direction, but rather one who can craft a group decision, and if necessary weed out those who are unwilling to work with the rest of the group.

The Members of a Design Team

The members of the design team are drawn from multiple disciplines, and their contributions are all essential to the success of a product launch. These positions are:

- *Design engineering.* The design engineers play the most prominent role on the team, since they must create a series of product iterations that incorporate the cost reductions needed to achieve the target cost.
- *Industrial engineering.* A significant part of a product's cost arises during the production process, so industrial engineers must become involved in order to give feedback to the design engineers regarding which design elements should be used that require the lowest production costs.
- *Cost accounting.* A cost accountant should be with the team at all times, constantly compiling the expected cost of a design as it goes through a series of iterations. The cost accountant also compares the expected cost to the target cost, and communicates the status of the product cost situation to both the team members and management on a periodic basis.
- *Procurement.* The purchasing department is a valuable contributor to the team, since many components will likely be sourced to third parties, and an

experienced procurement person can have a significant positive impact on the cost of purchased components.

- *Marketing.* The marketing department is particularly useful during the initial stages of target costing, where it investigates the prices of competing products and conducts polls to determine the value of specific product features.

The Role of the Cost Accountant in Target Costing

The cost accountant's role on a design team is to continually compile the projected cost of the product as it moves forward through the design process. He compares this cost to the total target cost, and communicates the variance between the two figures to management, along with qualitative information about where projected costs are expected to decline further, what design changes are most likely to achieve further cost declines, and how these design changes will affect the value proposition of the final product. Management uses this information to periodically monitor the progress of the design project, and to cancel the project if it appears likely that the product cannot be designed within the cost and value parameters of the project.

It may be necessary to purchase new manufacturing equipment to create a new product. If so, the cost accountant is the best person to create purchase requests for this equipment, since his normal responsibilities include the review of capital expenditure proposals. Also, since he obviously has a working relationship with the accounting department, he is the best intermediary for relaying any accounting questions about capital proposals.

A key part of the cost accountant's role is to obtain cost information from suppliers, which in turn is predicated on the assumption of a certain amount of purchasing volume, which may not ultimately prove to be correct. If there are significant cost differences at varying purchase volume levels, it may be necessary for the cost accountant to present several possible product costs, one for each volume level.

EXAMPLE

Active Exercise Machines is designing a new treadmill for the home exercise market, and is having trouble pricing the laminated rubber conveyor belt. Since Active is creating a treadmill in a non-standard length, the conveyor belt supplier will incur a setup cost, and must spread this cost over the projected number of treadmills to be produced. Since the setup cost is significant, the cost per unit will decline dramatically if Active orders more conveyor belts. The cost is $95 per unit if Active only orders 5,000 belts, and drops to $50 if Active orders 10,000 belts. Since the total cost of the treadmill is projected to be $500, this difference represents 9% of the total cost, which is significant enough to bring to the attention of management. Consequently, the cost accountant presents management with two projected costs for the treadmill – one at a unit volume of 5,000, and another at a unit volume of 10,000.

The cost accountant's cost information is likely to be vague when the project is initiated, since he is working with general design concepts and rough estimates of production volumes. Consequently, his initial cost reports are likely to be within a range of possible costs, which gradually tighten up as the team generates more precise designs and better sales estimates.

A final task is for the cost accountant to continue monitoring the cost of the product after its release, and throughout its product life. This is a key role, because management needs to know immediately if the initial cost structure that the design team worked so hard to create is no longer valid, and why the cost has increased.

The tasks ascribed to a cost accountant in his role as a member of a design team are not minor. For a larger design project, it is entirely possible that he will be released for special duty to the project, so that no other routine tasks will interfere with his work on the team. In a larger company where product design is the lifeblood of the entity, the cost accountant may find himself permanently assigned to a series of project teams.

Data Sources for Target Costing

The cost accountant may have a difficult time obtaining data from which to develop the cost of a new product design. Here are some of the data sources needed for a target costing project:

- *New components*. The design team may be creating entirely new components from scratch, so there is no cost information available. In this case, the cost accountant needs to locate roughly comparable components and extrapolate from them what the new components might cost, including tooling costs.

- *Materials sourcing*. Some materials that the design team wants to include in a product may be difficult to obtain, or be subject to significant price swings. The cost accountant needs to highlight these issues, particularly by using outside sources of historical commodity prices to note the range of price swings that have occurred in the recent past. It is dangerous to only report to management the current market price of these materials, since management may decide to continue product development when it might otherwise drop the project in the face of large potential cost increases.

- *Competitor costs*. It is extremely useful to disassemble competing products to determine what they cost to produce. The cost accountant can assemble this information into a database, which is useful for not only calculating the likely gross margins that competing products are earning, but also for comparing the design team's choice of components to those used by competitors. In many instances, the design team can copy some aspects of a competing design in order to quickly achieve a lower cost.

- *Production costs*. If a company has engaged in product design for a number of years, it may have developed a table that contains the cost to produce specific components or the cost of the production functions used to create those components. This type of information is difficult to obtain, and requires a great deal of analysis to compile, so having the information available from previous design projects is a significant advantage in the design of new products.

- *Downstream costs.* When the design team modifies a product design, there is a good chance that it will cause modifications in other parts of the design, in a ripple effect. The only source of information for what these changes may be is the design team itself, which the cost accountant must regularly interview for clues about the cost effects of these changes.
- *Supplier performance data.* Suppliers are likely going to provide a significant proportion of the components of a new product, so the cost accountant needs access to the company's database of supplier performance to see if key suppliers are capable of supplying goods within the performance constraints required by the new design. This is less of a cost issue than a qualitative review of the ability of a supplier to perform within the company's specifications.

Clearly, the cost accountant must have access to a broad array of data sources in order to be a fully functioning member of a design team. These data sources frequently do not contain the high degree of data accuracy that the cost accountant needs, so the result is likely to be a significant degree of uncertainty in costing information, especially during the initial stages of product design.

The Product Life Cycle and Target Costing

Target costing generates a significant and immediate cost reduction at the beginning of a product's life cycle. Kaizen costing then generates an ongoing series of smaller cost reductions that gradually decline as the number of cost reduction opportunities are eliminated. A company that wants to stay competitive with its product offerings should carefully track the gradual decline in product costs, and replace the original product with a new one when there are minimal cost reductions still to be garnered from the old product. The new product is subjected to the same target costing approach in order to create a new value proposition for the consumer, to be followed by another round of kaizen costing.

In order to remain competitive over the long term, it is clear that a company must be aware of where its products stand within their product cycles, and be willing to replace them when there are minimal costs to be eliminated from the old designs.

Summary

Target costing is most applicable to companies that compete by continually issuing a stream of new or upgraded products into the marketplace (such as consumer goods). For them, target costing is a key survival tool. Conversely, target costing is less necessary for those companies that have a small number of legacy products that require minimal updates, and for which long-term profitability is more closely associated with market penetration and geographical coverage (such as soft drinks).

Target costing is an excellent tool for planning a suite of products that have high levels of profitability. This is opposed to the much more common approach of creating a product that is based on the engineering department's view of what the product should be like, and then struggling with costs that are too high in comparison to the market price. Given the extremely cooperative nature of target costing across multiple departments, it can be quite a difficult change for the engineering manager to accept.

The cost accountant plays a key role in target costing, as the key compiler of information for the project team, keeping both them and management continually informed of their progress toward the cost goals that a product must reach.

Chapter 12
Transfer Pricing

Introduction

Some companies have chosen to become vertically integrated, which means that one subsidiary creates a component that is used by another subsidiary in its products. Companies do this either to have an assured source of components, or because suppliers are earning an inordinate profit on the components.

Vertical integration is important to the cost accountant, because a company must sell these components from one subsidiary to another, and it does so with a transfer price, which the cost accountant assists in creating. This chapter addresses the importance of the transfer price and a number of methods for creating it.

Overview of Transfer Pricing

Transfer pricing can be of considerable importance, because it strongly impacts the behavior of the subsidiaries that use it as the basis for transferring components to each other. Here are the key issues:

- *Revenue basis.* The manager of a subsidiary treats it in the same manner that he would the price of a product sold outside of the company. It forms part of the revenue of his subsidiary, and is therefore crucial to the financial performance on which he is judged.
- *Preferred customers.* If the manager of a subsidiary is given the choice of selling either to a downstream subsidiary or to outside customers, an excessively low transfer price will lead the manager to sell exclusively to outside customers, and to refuse orders originating from the downstream subsidiary.
- *Preferred suppliers.* If the manager of a downstream subsidiary is given the choice of buying either from an upstream subsidiary or an outside supplier, an excessively high transfer price will cause the manager to buy exclusively from outside suppliers. As a result, the upstream subsidiary may have too much unused capacity, and will have to cut back on its expenses in order to remain profitable.

Conversely, these issues are not important if corporate headquarters uses a central production planning system, and *requires* upstream subsidiaries to ship components to downstream subsidiaries, irrespective of the transfer price.

An additional topic that impacts the overall level of corporate profitability is the total amount of income taxes paid. If a company has subsidiaries located in different tax jurisdictions, it can use transfer prices to adjust the reported profit level of each subsidiary. Ideally, the corporate parent wants to recognize the most taxable income in those tax jurisdictions where corporate income taxes are lowest. It can achieve this by lowering the transfer prices of components going into the subsidiaries located in those tax jurisdictions having the lowest tax rates.

A company should adopt those transfer prices that result in the highest total profit for the consolidated results of the entire entity. Almost always, this means that the company should set the transfer price to be the market price of the component, subject to the issue just noted regarding the recognition of income taxes. By doing so, subsidiaries can earn more money for the company as a whole by having the option to sell to outside entities, as well as in-house. This gives subsidiaries an incentive to expand their production capacity to take on additional business.

EXAMPLE

Entwhistle Electric makes compact batteries for a variety of mobile applications. It was recently purchased by Razor Holdings, which also owns Green Lawn Care, maker of low-emission lawn mowers. The reason for Razor's purchase of Entwhistle was to give Green an assured supply of batteries for Green's new line of all-electric lawn mowers. Razor's corporate planning staff mandates that Entwhistle set a transfer price for batteries shipped to Green that equals its cost, and also requires that Entwhistle fulfill all of Green's needs before it can sell to any other customers. Green's orders are highly seasonal, so Entwhistle finds that it cannot fulfill orders from its other customers at all during the high point of Green's production season. Also, because the transfer price is set at cost, Entwhistle's management finds that it no longer has a reason to drive down costs, and so its production efficiencies stagnate.

After a year, Razor's corporate staff realizes that Entwhistle has lost 80% of its previous customer base, and is now essentially relying upon its sales to Green to stay operational. Entwhistle's profit margin has vanished, since it can only sell at cost, and its original management team, faced with a contracting business, have all left to work for competitors.

Transfer prices do not have to match the market price to achieve optimal results. There are cases where there is no market price at all, so a company needs to create a price in order to spur management behavior that is favorable to the company as a whole.

EXAMPLE

Entwhistle Electric creates five tons per year of black plastic shavings as part of its production of battery casings. Since there is no market for black plastic scrap, the company has traditionally thrown it into the trash. The annual trash haulage and environmental disposal fees associated with this scrap are about $1,000.

Entwhistle's fellow corporate subsidiary, Green Lawn Care, learns of the black plastic scrap situation, and offers to buy it from Entwhistle for a token $10 a ton, as well as haul it away for free. Green can melt down this scrap and use it in the black plastic trim on its electric lawn mowers.

Entwhistle agrees to the deal, not only because of the minor $50 in annual revenues, but also because of the eliminated disposal fees and the mitigated risk of having any environmental issues related to the scrap.

In short, transfer prices can have a significant impact on how the managers of subsidiaries run their operations, and on how much the company as a whole pays in income taxes. Though we have pointed out that market prices are the best basis for developing transfer prices, there are a number of pricing methods available. We will explore both market pricing and these other methods next.

Market Price Basis for Transfer Pricing

The simplest and most elegant transfer price is to use the market price. By doing so, the upstream subsidiary can sell either internally or externally and earn the same profit with either option. It can also earn the highest possible profit, rather than being subject to the odd profit vagaries that can occur under mandated pricing schemes. Downstream subsidiaries will also be indifferent to where they receive components from, since the price is the same from all suppliers. If the price is simple to obtain, such as through industry trade journals or price sheets, there is also little reason for buying and selling subsidiaries to argue over the price.

However, market-based prices are not always available. Here are several areas of concern:

- *Product differentiation.* The most common problem is that the products being sold in the market are differentiated from each other by a variety of unique features, so there is no standard market price.
- *Quality differentiation.* Product features may be the same, but quality differences between products cause significant pricing differences.
- *Specialty products.* The components in question may be of such a highly specialize nature that there is no market for them at all.
- *Internal costs.* The cost of selling internally to another subsidiary is somewhat lower than the cost of selling to an external customer, since there are fewer selling costs and bad debts associated with an internal sale; this means that comparing potential sales based just on the market price is not correct.
- *Corporate planning.* If there is a centralized planning staff, they may not want the subsidiaries to make decisions based on the market price, because they want all components routed to internal subsidiaries to relieve supply shortages. This is not necessarily a problem, as long as the internal sales are conducted at the market price.

In short, market-based pricing is highly recommended, but it does not apply in many situations. If market pricing cannot be used, then consider using one of the alternative methods outlined in the following sections.

Adjusted Market Price Basis for Transfer Pricing

If it is not possible to use the market pricing technique just noted, consider using the general concept, but incorporating some adjustments to the price. For example, the market price can be reduced to account for the presumed absence of bad debts, since corporate management will likely intervene and force a payment if there is a risk of non-payment. The market price could also be reduced to account for the absence of any sales staff in transactions, since these internal sales should not require any sales effort to complete – a sale is reduced to some paperwork between the purchasing and planning staffs of the two subsidiaries.

If these bad debt and selling costs are actually eliminated from the selling subsidiary and the buying subsidiary can make purchases at lower prices, then both entities benefit from the price reductions. The result may be a tendency to prefer selling within the company rather than to outside parties, which is what corporate managers want to see.

The main problem with adjusted market prices will be arguments between the subsidiaries over the size of the downward adjustments. There should be a procedure in place for how the adjustments are determined. If not, the subsidiary manager with the better negotiating ability will win, which may result in the other subsidiary taking its business elsewhere. The corporate staff should monitor these negotiations and intervene as necessary.

Negotiated Basis for Transfer Pricing

It may be necessary to negotiate a transfer price between subsidiaries, without using any market price as a baseline. This situation arises when there is no discernible market price because the market is very small or the goods are highly customized.

Negotiated prices can vary wildly, depending on the negotiating skills of the participants. The variable cost of production for the selling subsidiary should be used as the minimum possible price, so that it does not lose money. The resulting price usually gives both participants some ability to earn a profit. However, there are some issues with it:

- *Unfairness.* If the negotiated price excessively favors one subsidiary, the other subsidiary will likely search outside of the company for better deals.
- *Negotiation time.* If a component represents a large amount of revenue for the selling subsidiary, or a large cost for the buying subsidiary, they may spend an inordinate amount of time negotiating the price.

For the reasons noted here, negotiated prices are considered to be a suboptimal solution, and so should only be used in a minority of transfer pricing situations, for items representing a small proportion of total business activity.

Contribution Margin Basis for Transfer Pricing

If there is no market price at all from which to derive a transfer price, an alternative is to create a price based on a component's contribution margin. Contribution margin is a product's price minus its variable costs, resulting in the incremental profit earned for each unit sold. To create a transfer price based on contribution margin, a company follows these steps:

1. Determine the price at which a finished product will sell to an outside entity after all subsidiaries of the company have finished their processing of the product.
2. Determine the contribution margin of the finished product.
3. Allocate the contribution margin back to the various subsidiaries that contributed to its construction, based on each subsidiary's share of the total cost incurred.

This approach creates a fair allocation of the contribution margin to the subsidiaries. However, it also suffers from the following problems:

- *Allocation methodology.* Since the allocation of contribution margin is based on each subsidiary's share of the total cost, a subsidiary can increase its share if it *increases* its costs. Also, if a subsidiary reduces its costs, the cost savings is essentially apportioned among all of the subsidiaries, which gives a subsidiary little reason to reduce its costs. Thus, the allocation method drives subsidiaries to engage in behavior that does not benefit the company as a whole.
- *Complicated allocation.* If a company has many subsidiaries, there may be so many transfers of parts associated with a specific product that it is difficult to determine which subsidiaries should be credited with the contribution margin, or the amount of the allocation. This also requires a large amount of accounting staff time, and requires an allocation procedure that is rigidly adhered to; otherwise, the subsidiaries will bicker over how much contribution margin they receive.

Despite the problems noted here, the contribution margin approach can be a workable alternative to using market prices to develop transfer prices.

Cost Plus Basis for Transfer Pricing

If there is no market price at all on which to base a transfer price, consider using a system that creates a transfer price based on the cost of the components being transferred. The best way to do this is to add a margin onto the cost, where the accountant compiles the standard cost of a component, adds a standard profit margin, and uses the result as the transfer price. While this method is useful, be aware of two flaws that can cause problems:

- *Cost basis.* When the pricing system is based on adding a margin to the underlying cost, there is no incentive to reduce the underlying cost. If anything, subsidiary managers will be tempted to alter their cost accounting systems to shift more costs *into* those components being sold to another subsidiary, thereby dumping costs onto a different entity.

- *Standard margin.* The margin added to the cost may not relate to the margin that a subsidiary earns on its sales to outside customers. If it is too low, subsidiary managers have no incentive to manufacture the component. If the margin is too high, and this margin is incorporated into the final product price, the subsidiary selling the completed product may find that its cost is too high to earn a profit.

Despite the issues noted here, the cost plus method can still work, as long as corporate management mandates ongoing cost reductions throughout the company, and also verifies whether the margins added to costs are reasonable. Also, it may work if there are so few transfers that the economic benefits to be gained from rigging the system are minimal.

Cost Anomalies in a Cost-Based Transfer Price

Of the transfer pricing methods described here, the contribution margin basis and the cost plus basis both involve cost inputs. When collecting the cost information used to derive transfer prices, be aware of a number of issues that can impact costs, and which may result in a great deal of variability in the transfer price. These issues are:

- *Cost allocations.* When a selling subsidiary can shift its costs to a buying subsidiary, there is a tendency to shift more overhead costs into the components being sold to the buying subsidiary.
- *Cost reduction incentive.* When the manager of a selling subsidiary knows he can sell products to a buying subsidiary and cover his costs, there is no incentive to reduce those costs. It would be egregious to let costs increase, but there is no longer any incentive to decrease costs. This problem is less critical if the selling subsidiary still sells most of its products to outside entities, since it must still maintain control over its costs in order to be competitive.
- *Volume changes.* If the unit volume ordered by a buying subsidiary changes substantially over time, the selling subsidiary will have to manufacture parts in varying batch sizes, which may result in very different costs, depending on the volume produced. If the transfer price is fixed for a relatively long-term period, the selling subsidiary may find itself either benefiting from these volume changes or experiencing very low profits that are caused by small batch sizes.

A partial solution to several of these problems is to agree on a standard cost at the beginning of the year, and review it periodically. Corporate management should be involved in this process, both to impose cost reduction goals and to verify whether any shifting of overhead costs to downstream subsidiaries is being attempted. Using a standard cost allows buying subsidiaries to plan for costs with considerable certainty, while selling subsidiaries can improve their profits if they reduce costs to below the agreed-upon standard costs.

Pricing Problems Caused by Transfer Pricing

Transfer pricing between subsidiaries causes a problem for the marketing department of whichever subsidiary is selling the final product to outside customers, because it does not know which part of the transferred-in price is variable costs, and which is fixed costs. If the marketing department is developing long-term sustainable costs, then it knows the price needs to be higher than both types of costs combined, in order to assure long-term sustainable profitability. However, this is not the case for short-term pricing situations where a customer may be asking for a pricing discount in exchange for a large order. In this latter situation, the costing system needs to clearly differentiate which product costs are variable, and which are not.

Another issue with price setting arises when several subsidiaries in a row add as many costs as they can to the transfer price, as well as a profit margin. By the time the final product arrives at the subsidiary that sells it to an outside customer, the cost may be so high that the last subsidiary cannot possibly earn a profit on the sale. The following example illustrates the problem:

EXAMPLE

Razor Holdings adopts a transfer pricing policy under which each of its subsidiaries can add a 30% margin to the additional costs transferred to buying subsidiaries. In the following scenario, its Lead Supply subsidiary sends lead components to Entwhistle Electric, which incorporates the lead into its batteries. Entwhistle sends the batteries to Green Lawn Care, which includes the batteries in its electric lawn shears.

	Lead Supply	Entwhistle Electric	Green Lawn Care
Transferred cost	$0	$5.85	13.98
Additional cost	4.50	6.25	15.00
30% markup	1.35	1.88	4.50
Transfer price	$5.85	$13.98	$33.48

Unfortunately, the market price for electric lawn shears is $30, so the Green Lawn Care subsidiary will only earn a profit of $1.02, or 3%, on each sale. However, the company as a whole will earn a profit of $4.25 ($1.35 for Lead Supply + $1.88 for Entwhistle + $1.02 for Green), or 14%.

Thus, Green Lawn Care likely questions why it is bothering to sell electric lawn shears, while corporate management is somewhat more pleased with the overall result.

Possible solutions are to allow the furthest downstream subsidiary to buy its components elsewhere, or to have corporate management reduce the margins allowed to upstream subsidiaries.

Product pricing is addressed in greater detail in the chapter Product Pricing: What Does This Cost?

The Tax Impact of Transfer Prices

We have discussed various methods for developing transfer prices in most of the preceding sections, but they may all be overridden by corporate management if it wants to achieve the lowest possible amount of income taxes paid. This is a major area of corporate planning, because it causes a permanent reduction in income taxes paid, not just a deferral of tax payments to a later period.

The essential tax management concept is to set a high transfer price for buying subsidiaries located in tax jurisdictions that have a high income tax rate, so that they report a high cost of goods sold, and therefore pay the minimum amount of high-percentage income tax. Conversely, the transfer price should be as low as possible for those buying subsidiaries located in tax jurisdictions that have a low income tax rate, so that they report a low cost of goods sold, and therefore pay the maximum amount of low-percentage income tax. The overall impact for the corporate parent should be a reduction in income taxes paid.

EXAMPLE

Razor Holdings owns Entwhistle Electric, which is located in the United States, and Green Lawn Care, which is located in Ireland. The corporate tax rate in the United States is 35%, and the rate in Ireland is 12.5%. Because of the disparity in tax rates, Razor wants Entwhistle to sell all of its components to Green at a low price. By doing so, Entwhistle earns a minimal profit on these inter-company sales and therefore has minimal income on which to pay taxes, while Green has a very low cost of goods sold and a correspondingly high net profit, on which it pays the reduced Irish income tax. Razor implements this strategy for the current fiscal year, with the following results:

	Entwhistle Subsidiary (United States)	Green Lawn Care (Ireland)
Revenue	$10,000,000	$35,000,000
Cost of goods sold and administrative expenses	8,000,000	21,000,000
Profit	$2,000,000	$14,000,000
Profit %	20%	40%
Income tax rate	35%	12.5%
Income tax	$700,000	$1,750,000

If Entwhistle had sold its products to other customers, rather than internally, it would have realized a profit of an additional $1,000,000, which would have called for an additional $350,000 income tax payment to the United States government. However, the transfer pricing strategy essentially shifted the additional $1,000,000 of profit to the Ireland tax jurisdiction, which was then taxed at only 12.5%. Thus, Razor created a permanent tax savings of $225,000 through its transfer pricing strategy, which is calculated as:

(35% United States tax rate – 12.5% Ireland tax rate) × $1,000,000 Taxable profit

There are other forms of transfer pricing that can also be used to the same effect. For example, the corporate parent can charge royalty or licensing fees to subsidiaries in such a manner that they have the largest impact on those tax jurisdictions having the highest tax rates.

EXAMPLE

The tax attorneys for Razor Holdings suggest that the Green Lawn Care subsidiary in Ireland purchase the patents from all other subsidiaries and license them back for a fee. In the case of the Entwhistle subsidiary in the United States, this means that it accepts a $100,000 payment (which is the market rate) to sell its rights to several battery-related patents to Green, which in turn charges Entwhistle a $20,000 annual licensing fee for the rights to the patented technology. By doing so, Entwhistle's taxable income drops by $20,000 and Green's taxable income increases by $20,000. Since Entwhistle has a tax rate of 35% and Green has a tax rate of 12.5%, this results in a net savings to the company as a whole of $4,500, which is calculated as:

(35% United States tax rate – 12.5% Ireland tax rate) × $20,000 Taxable profit

The practices just noted could lead a company to adopt outrageous transfer pricing practices that shift virtually all profits to whichever tax jurisdictions have the lowest tax rates. To keep such egregious behavior from occurring, the Internal Revenue Service has issued guidelines in Section 482 of the Internal Revenue Code that specify how transfer prices can be formulated. Section 482 contains multiple alternative formulations, with the preferred practice being to use market rates as the transfer price, followed by variations on the cost plus profit methodology. These formulations allow for the inclusion of a variety of adjustments, which can alter a transfer price significantly. A company usually takes advantage of the Section 482 guidelines to the greatest extent possible in order to achieve the lowest possible consolidated tax payment. The IRS prefers to have companies use transfer prices that are largely based on market prices, leaving the minimum amount of additional adjustments for a company's cost accountants to manipulate.

There is always a chance that auditors from a taxing jurisdiction will take issue with the transfer pricing methods used by a company, which may lead to substantial fines and penalties. This is a particular problem when a company is being audited by multiple tax jurisdictions, with each one trying to maximize its tax receipts at the expense of the other jurisdictions.

To avoid these audit costs, larger companies frequently enter into an advance pricing agreement (APA) with multiple tax jurisdictions, which is known as a *bilateral APA*. The APA outlines in advance the procedure that the company will take to establish its transfer prices. An APA application involves a presentation by the company of why it plans to use a certain transfer pricing method, why alternate methods were not chosen, and a description of the transactions to which the transfer pricing method will be applied. Having an APA in place means that the company will be much less likely to incur penalties and fines, though it may still be subject to audits, to ensure that it is complying with the terms of the APA.

In short, transfer pricing can have a major impact on the amount of income tax payments that a company must make, by shifting reported net income amongst subsidiaries located in various tax jurisdictions. The transfer prices used to effect these tax reductions are subject to regulation by the various tax jurisdictions, which can lead to an ongoing series of audits. To avoid the aggravation of audits and any resulting additional payments, consider entering into bilateral advance pricing agreements.

Summary

The key point to remember about all of the transfer pricing systems noted in this chapter is that no one system is likely to work perfectly in all situations. Instead, it may be necessary to use several systems at once to most closely align with the circumstances surrounding various transfers. In general, it is best to adopt market-based prices as the default transfer pricing system, and to incorporate modifications to market prices as needed.

Also, incorporate a well-documented procedure into the transfer pricing system, in order to minimize bickering between the various subsidiaries regarding which transfer prices to use. Otherwise, subsidiary managers will spend an inordinate amount of time negotiating prices, instead of improving the sales and operations of their companies.

Chapter 13
Direct Costing

Introduction

Direct costing is a specialized form of cost analysis that only uses variable costs to make decisions. It is extremely useful for short-term decisions, but can lead to harmful results if used for long-term decision making. In this chapter, we will describe the concept, as well as those situations in which it is most useful, and the scenarios where it can lead to incorrect conclusions.

Overview of Direct Costing

In brief, direct costing is the analysis of incremental costs. Direct costs are most easily illustrated through examples, such as:
- The costs actually consumed when a product is manufactured.
- The incremental increase in costs when production is ramped up.
- The costs that disappear when a production line is shut down.
- The costs that disappear when an entire subsidiary is shut down.

The examples show that direct costs can vary based upon the level of analysis. For example, when reviewing the direct cost of a single product, the only direct cost may be the materials used in its construction. However, if management is contemplating shutting down an entire company, the direct costs are *all* costs incurred by that company – including all of its production and administrative costs. The main point to remember is that a direct cost is any cost that changes as the result of either a decision or a change in volume.

Direct costs do not necessarily align with the way in which costs are accumulated in an accounting system, which calls for some selective cost extraction from various sources to arrive at the proper set of direct costs.

EXAMPLE

The management of Dude Skis wants to know how much it will cost to increase production of its Drag Knuckle Skis from 5,000 units to 8,000 units, so that it can sell the additional 3,000 skis for a wholesale price (in aggregate) of $900,000. The most obvious direct cost is the cost of the wood core and graphite laminate used in the skis, at a cost of $150 per pair of skis. In addition, the company will require three additional staff whose labor cost will be $25 per pair of skis. Finally, the company must lease a lamination machine for $30,000, which it can then return to the lessor after the production run is complete.

For the purposes of this specific production-increase decision, then, the associated direct costs are:

Incremental revenue	$900,000
Cost of materials ($150 × 3,000 units)	450,000
Cost of labor ($25 × 3,000 units)	75,000
Cost of lamination machine	30,000
Total of all direct costs	555,000
Contribution margin	$355,000

Note in the preceding example that the cost accountant could probably obtain the cost of materials from the existing bill of materials for the Drag Knuckle ski, but would have to obtain the labor cost from the production manager, and the lamination machine's lease cost from the industrial engineering manager. Thus, it is clear that much of the information needed for a direct costing analysis does not come from the accounting database; in addition, it may involve nothing more than estimated costs, since the analysis involves an action that has not yet taken place, and for which there is no exact cost information.

A key issue with direct costing is the large variety of costs that are ignored. In the preceding example, note the absence of any costs related to the management of the production facility, or an administrative charge, or machine setup labor by the engineering staff. The reason these costs are not included is that the costs are the same, whether or not the company elects to increase its ski production. Only costs exhibiting incremental changes as a result of the decision are included in a direct costing analysis.

Contribution Margin versus Gross Margin

The typical direct costing question may simply be "how much money do I *save* if..." but it may also be, "how much money do I *make* if..." In the latter case, the answer requires giving management not only a listing of direct costs, but also the projected amount of earnings. Doing so usually involves the *contribution margin*, which is calculated as revenues minus all direct costs. This measurement varies from the more common gross margin, which also includes a deduction for allocated overhead costs. Since overhead costs are almost never categorized as direct costs, the contribution margin should be used.

EXAMPLE

Dude Skis wants to create an entirely new line of skis that can be used separately to ski uphill, and then lock together into a single monoski for downhill use. It is called the Chump Ski. The company projects incremental revenues from the new line of skis of $1,000,000, as well as incremental labor costs of $200,000, incremental material costs of $400,000, overhead that is directly traceable to the new product of $120,000, and a general manufacturing overhead allocation of $80,000. The existing production equipment can accommodate the new product with no changes. The calculation of the margin on the Chump Ski line is:

	Contribution Margin Calculation	Gross Margin Calculation
Revenue	$800,000	$800,000
Expenses		
Materials	400,000	400,000
Labor	200,000	200,000
Traceable overhead	120,000	120,000
General overhead	--	80,000
Total expenses	720,000	800,000
Margin	$80,000	$0
Margin percentage	10%	0%

The contribution margin reveals a positive outcome of $80,000, while the gross margin calculation (which includes the general overhead allocation) shows no profit at all. If management only saw the gross margin calculation, it might elect to avoid rolling out the Chump Ski line, whereas the contribution margin might be sufficiently positive to encourage an alternative course of action.

Direct Costing as an Analysis Tool

Direct costing is of great use as an analysis tool. The following decisions all involve the use of direct costs as inputs to decision models. What is immediately noticeable in the examples accompanying these decision models is the simplicity and clarity of the direct costing format, because it deals with only a small subset of total costs – those that are impacted by the decision. All other costs are irrelevant for the purposes of the decision being addressed, and so can be excluded from the model. In particular, they contain no allocations of overhead, which are not only irrelevant for many short-term decisions, but which can be difficult to explain to someone not trained in accounting.

Automation investments. A common scenario is for a company to invest in automated production equipment in order to reduce the amount it pays to its direct labor staff. Under direct costing, the key information to collect is the incremental labor cost of any employees who will be terminated, as well as the new period costs to be incurred as part of the equipment purchase, such as the depreciation on the equipment and maintenance costs.

EXAMPLE

Dude Skis plans to acquire an automated graphics lamination machine, which it will use to laminate graphics onto its high-end skis. It plans to eliminate three direct labor positions and add one maintenance technician as a result of this change. The lamination machine costs

138

$100,000 and will be depreciated over five years. The fully burdened cost of all three direct labor positions is $90,000, while the fully burdened cost of the new maintenance technician is $55,000. Dude's cost accountant constructs the following table to summarize the situation:

Direct cost additions	
Annual machine depreciation	+$20,000
Maintenance technician	+55,000
Direct cost deductions	
Direct labor positions	-90,000
Net change in direct costs	-$15,000

The table reveals that Dude should install the machine, since there will be a net decline in direct costs. Additional factors to consider might be any history of machine breakdowns that could lead to the rehire of the laid off workers, as well as the risk that the machine's manufacturer will go out of business and can therefore no longer support the machine. These are qualitative risk factors.

Cost reporting. Direct costing is very useful for controlling variable costs (which are costs that vary in relation to changes in production volume), because a variance analysis report can be created that compares the actual variable cost to what the variable cost per unit should have been. Fixed costs are not included in this analysis, since they are associated with the period in which they are incurred, and so are not direct costs. A simple reporting format follows, which focuses the attention of management solely on direct costs.

EXAMPLE

Dude Skis closely tracks the direct cost of its skis, and does so by comparing actual variable costs per unit to budgeted costs. The following report shows its direct cost analysis for January production of its low-cost line of children's introductory skis.

Actual unit production = 2,703 ski pairs			
Variable Cost Item	Actual Cost per Unit	Budgeted Cost per Unit	Variance per Unit
Wood core	$42.50	$41.75	-$0.75
Fiberglas wrap	38.84	37.52	-1.32
Edging	4.11	4.03	-0.08
Tip and tail caps	0.39	0.42	+0.03
Lamination	4.72	4.73	+0.01
Totals	$90.56	$88.45	-$2.11

The report does not include direct labor, since Dude's management does not feel that labor costs vary sufficiently with production volumes to warrant being included in the report.

The example only shows direct costs. Management will likely want to also track its ability to control fixed costs, so it can use a separate report for those items that notes total period costs by expense type, as compared to budgeted amounts. For example:

Fixed Cost Item	Actual Cost	Budgeted Cost	Variance
Accounting and legal	$12,500	$12,000	-$500
Insurance	7,400	7,200	-200
Salaries, administration	29,000	27,400	-1,600
Rent	18,000	18,000	0
Utilities	4,700	4,000	-700
Totals	$71,600	$68,600	-$3,000

Note that the direct cost variance analysis report was designed for costs at the individual unit level, while the fixed cost variance analysis report was designed for total costs in a period. It is easier for management to take remedial action by using these differing formats for different types of costs.

Customer profitability. Some customers require a great deal of support, but also place such large orders that a company still earns a notable profit from the relationship. If there are such resource-intensive situations, it makes sense to occasionally calculate how much money the company really earns from each customer. This analysis may reveal that the company would be better off eliminating some of its customers, even if this results in a noticeable revenue decline.

EXAMPLE

Dude Skis sells to Stuffy Skis, which is a high-end retailer of the most expensive all-mountain skis, as well as Warehouse Sports, which retails the lowest-cost skis through many outlets to beginner skiers. The skis that Dude sells to Stuffy have the highest margins, and Stuffy requires little administrative support. Warehouse buys in massive volume, but only buys low-margin items, and returns 20% of its purchases under various pretexts in order to clear out its inventory at the end of the season. Dude's management wants to know how much it earns from each customer, and whether it should drop either one. Dude's cost accountant constructs the following table:

	Stuffy Customer	Warehouse Customer
Revenue	$520,000	$2,780,000
Direct costs		
Materials	210,000	1,390,000
Direct labor	100,000	550,000
Customer service cost	0	130,000
Sales returns cost	0	600,000
Total direct costs	310,000	2,670,000
Contribution margin ($)	$210,000	$110,000
Contribution margin (%)	40%	4%

In the table, there is no customer service cost at all for Stuffy Skis, since no customer service positions would be eliminated if Dude were to drop Stuffy as a customer. On the other hand, there are four customer service employees assigned to the Warehouse Sports account who would be laid off if Dude were to drop that account.

The analysis reveals that Stuffy Skis produces far more contribution margin than Warehouse Sports, despite much lower revenues. However, this does not mean that Dude should eliminate Warehouse as a customer, since it still produces $110,000 of contribution margin. If Dude has a large amount of overhead to cover, it may be quite necessary to continue dealing with Warehouse Sports in order to retain the associated amount of contribution margin.

The preceding format can be expanded to include not just a single customer, but also sales for an entire region or product line.

Internal inventory reporting. Generally accepted accounting principles and international financial reporting standards require that a company allocate indirect costs to its inventory asset for external reporting purposes. Overhead allocation can require a prolonged amount of time to complete, so it is relatively common for company controllers to avoid updating the overhead allocation during reporting periods when there will be no external reporting. Instead, they rely mostly on direct cost updates, and either avoid all changes to the overhead allocation, or make an approximate guess at the correct overhead allocation based on a proportion of direct costs, and make a more accurate adjustment when a reporting period arrives for which the company must report financial statements to outside parties.

Profit-volume relationship. Direct costing is useful for plotting changes in profit levels as sales volumes vary. It is relatively simple to create a direct costing table, such as the one in the following example, which points out the volume levels at which additional direct costs will be incurred, so that management can estimate the amount of profit at different levels of corporate activity.

EXAMPLE

Dude Skis is conducting its annual budgeting process, and the cost accountant is called upon to create a profit-volume table that shows the amount of profit before taxes that Dude is likely to earn at different unit volume sales levels. The company currently produces 50,000 pairs of skis per year, and this figure is unlikely to decline. He learns that the company can produce an additional 10,000 pairs of skis without incurring any additional overhead costs. However, if the company expands production by an additional 20,000 pairs, it will incur an additional $750,000 in annual overhead expenses, and will likely also have to reduce its prices by 10% in order to achieve that volume level. Based on this information, he constructs the following table:

	Number of Skis Sold		
Number of ski pairs	50,000	60,000	70,000
Direct cost per pair of skis	$210	$210	$210
Net sales price per pair sold	380	380	342
Total revenue	19,000,000	22,800,000	23,940,000
Total direct cost	10,500,000	12,600,000	14,700,000
Total period cost	8,000,000	8,000,000	8,750,000
Profit	$500,000	$2,200,000	$490,000
Profit %	3%	10%	2%

The analysis reveals that Dude should certainly make every effort to increase its sales by an additional 10,000 units, since this will result in a significant improvement in its profitability. However, expanding by yet another 10,000 units may be a bad idea, since the company must accept lower per-unit prices as well as more overhead. In fact, the additional growth by 20,000 units, when coupled with an increased need for working capital and reduced profitability, may put the company in serious operating difficulties.

As just noted in the preceding example, a working capital analysis should be included with any profit-volume analysis, so that management can see the cost of expansion in terms of the increased investment in accounts receivable, payables, and inventory.

EXAMPLE

To continue with the preceding example, the management of Dude Skis is concerned about the working capital impact of expanding the business by 20,000 pairs of skis, and so it asks the cost accountant for a revised analysis that includes projected working capital costs for the baseline scenario of 50,000 units, and for the highest-volume scenario of 70,000 units. The following table presents this information:

	Number of Skis Sold	
Number of ski pairs	50,000	70,000
Total revenue	$19,000,000	$23,940,000
Profit	500,000	490,000
Working capital components		
+ Accounts receivable	+$1,600,000	+$2,400,000
+ Inventory	+3,200,000	+4,480,000
- Accounts payable	-1,100,000	-1,300,000
Total working capital	$3,700,000	$5,580,000

The working capital assumptions in the table are that the same proportions of inventory and accounts payable will carry forward from the 50,000 unit activity level to the 70,000 unit activity level. However, the accounts receivable investment is assumed to increase, since the company will be making many of the incremental sales to a new group of retailers who are assumed to pay slower than the current group of retailers.

The working capital analysis reveals that Dude Skis would have to invest an extra $1,880,000 in its business in order to grow to a 70,000 unit level, while earning a somewhat lower profit. Clearly, the company should avoid this expansion, though the 60,000 unit sales level noted in the preceding example has a much better payoff, and should be considered.

Outsourcing. Direct costing is useful for deciding whether to manufacture an item in-house or maintain a capability in-house, or whether to outsource it. If the decision involves manufacturing in-house or elsewhere, it is crucial to determine how many staff and which machines will actually be eliminated; in many cases, these resources are simply shifted elsewhere within the company, so there is no net profit improvement by shifting production to a supplier.

EXAMPLE

Dude Skis currently has a small plastic injection molding operation in-house, from which it molds the tip and tail guards for its skis. A local plastic injection molding firm visits Dude Skis and offers to produce these items for $0.41 per set. Management asks the cost accountant to determine whether this will result in improved profits for the company, using the assumption that the company would sell its injection molding machine if the supplier's offer is accepted.

According to Dude's cost records, the cost of a set of tip and tail guards is $0.56, which is comprised of the following items:

Cost Items	Direct Costs	Overhead
Resin	$0.25	
Color	0.02	
Scrap	0.01	
Injection molder depreciation	0.03	
Injection molder maintenance	0.02	
Injection molding labor	0.05	
Injection molding labor benefits	0.01	
Manufacturing overhead		$0.12
Administrative overhead		0.5
Total	$0.39	$0.17

In the preceding table, the injection molder depreciation cost of $0.03 per unit would not have been included if the company had chosen to keep the machine. However, since it plans to sell the machine if it accepts the supplier's offer, the depreciation is directly related to the decision, and so is a direct cost.

The costs comprising the overhead allocations will not decline if the company outsources this component, so the overhead is not a direct cost.

The table reveals that the direct costs associated with the analysis are lower than the supplier's offered price, so the company should reject the outsourcing option and continue to produce the tip and tail guards in-house. This decision is also reasonable from a risk management perspective, since Dude Skis would otherwise be permanently eliminating its capability to produce the part in-house, which could potentially leave it at the mercy of any price increases later imposed by the supplier.

Direct Costing Pitfalls

Direct costing is an analysis tool, but it is only usable for certain types of analysis. In some situations, it can provide incorrect results. This section describes the key issues with direct costing to be aware of. They are:

- *External reporting.* Direct costing is prohibited for the reporting of inventory costs under both generally accepted accounting principles and international financial reporting standards. This means that the accountant cannot report the cost of inventory as though it only includes direct costs; one must also include a proper allocation of indirect costs. If direct costing is being used for external reporting, fewer costs would be included in the inventory asset on the balance sheet, resulting in more costs being charged to expense in the current period.

It is unfortunate that direct costing is not allowed for external reporting, because it presents a more accurate picture of how costs are incurred over time; if a company incurs an indirect cost, it is charged to expense at once, where it is clearly visible. Under the current system of absorption costing that is required for external reporting, these costs are allocated to inventory, where they may remain for some months, until the inventory is sold. Thus, overhead expenditures recorded under an absorption costing system are less visible to users of a company's financial statements.

If direct costing were allowable for reporting the cost of inventory, and the quantity of inventory increased during a reporting period, direct costing would charge more cost to expense in the current period, while absorption costing would tend to increase the value of inventory, thereby shifting this cost into a future period. Absorption costing is a methodology under which all fixed and variable manufacturing costs are assigned to products, while all non-manufacturing costs are charged to expense in the period incurred. Conversely, if the quantity of inventory decreased during a reporting period, then absorption costing would charge more cost to expense in the current period, since costs previously recorded in the inventory asset in prior periods would now be charged to the cost of goods sold.

- *Increasing costs.* Direct costing is sometimes targeted at whether to increase production by a specific amount in order to accept an additional customer order. For the purposes of this specific decision, the analyst usually assumes that the direct cost of the decision will be the same as the historical cost. However, the cost may actually increase. For example, if a machine is already running at 80% of capacity and a proposed decision will increase its use to 90%, this incremental difference may very well result in a disproportionate increase in the maintenance cost of the machine. Thus, be aware that a specific direct costing scenario may contain costs that are only relevant within a narrow range; outside of that range, costs may be substantially different.

EXAMPLE

Dude Skis has received an inquiry from a Japanese ski manufacturer that wants to outsource a production run of 5,000 skis. The total revenue from the proposed deal is $1,000,000 and Dude's direct cost is projected to be $800,000, which is based on the $700,000 of materials and $100,000 of labor required to manufacture the skis. Initially, it therefore appears that Dude can earn $200,000 on the deal.

However, Dude's production equipment is fully utilized during its single shift of operation, so this order will require employing a second shift that is paid a 10% shift differential, as well as an on-site supervisor and maintenance technician. There will also be an assumed 10%

scrap rate caused by having a less well-trained work force on that shift. These additional costs are:

Cost Item	Amount
Overtime	$10,000
Scrap	70,000
Supervisor	65,000
Maintenance technician	45,000
Total	$190,000

Given that these additional costs leave a paltry $10,000 profit, Dude should either reject the inquiry or negotiate a higher price. The increased costs caused by the production being outside of Dude's normal operating range caused the deal (as proposed) to fail.

- *Indirect costs.* Direct costing does not account for indirect costs, because it is designed for short-term decisions where indirect costs are not expected to change. However, all costs change over the long term, which means that a decision that can impact a company over a long period of time should address long-term changes in indirect costs. Consequently, if a company uses an ongoing series of direct cost analyses to drive its pricing decisions, it may end up with an overall pricing structure that is too low to pay for its overhead costs. This is an especially pernicious problem for companies with a very high proportion of overhead costs, such as information technology companies that invest heavily in new products.

EXAMPLE

Dude Skis has a new software development group that has created a downloadable software product that allows skiers to track which runs they have skied each day, when tied into the global positioning chips on their smart phones. Under a direct costing analysis, the only cost to the company when a sale is made is a 2% credit card fee. However, Dude's programming team costs $200,000 per year, and charging a vanishingly small fee for the product will never pay for the overhead cost.

Instead, Dude's marketing manager conducts a survey of the market, learns that there is a potential market of 50,000 users at a price point of $10 per download, and accordingly prices the product at $10. This approach comfortably generates enough cash to pay for the related amount of overhead, also creates an additional profit, and is not based in any way on the direct cost of the product.

- *Relevant range.* A direct costing analysis is usually only valid within the constraints of the current capacity level. It requires a more sophisticated form of direct costing analysis to account for changes in costs as sales volumes or production volumes increase. This shortcoming can be overcome by consulting with the industrial engineering staff to determine additional capacity costs.

EXAMPLE

Dude Skis is considering an expansion of a prototype skiing platform for disabled skiers. It constructed 100 units as a pilot project, and sold them easily at a price of $2,000 and a direct cost of $750 each. Initial forecasts indicate that Dude could sell 5,000 units per year. Thus, the initial analysis indicates that Dude could earn a contribution margin of $6,250,000 on this new opportunity.

The trouble is that the direct costing analysis is based on the costs incurred during a pilot project. Launching a fully-equipped and properly managed product line will introduce an additional $1,000,000 per year of depreciation costs, as well as $4,000,000 of overhead costs that are directly related to the product. Consequently, the new product will be more likely to earn $1,250,000 per year than the $6,250,000 that was initially indicated.

Summary

Direct costing is an excellent analysis tool. It is almost always used to create a model to answer a question about what actions management should take. It is not a costing methodology for constructing financial statements – in fact, accounting standards specifically exclude direct costing from financial statement reporting. Thus, it does not fill the role of a standard costing, process costing, or job costing system, which contribute to actual changes in the accounting records. Instead, it is used to extract pertinent information from a variety of sources and aggregate the information to assist management with any number of tactical decisions. It is most useful for short-term decisions, and least useful when a longer-term time frame is involved - especially in situations where a company must generate sufficient margins to pay for a large amount of overhead. Though useful, direct costing information is problematic in situations where incremental costs may change significantly, or where indirect costs may be pertinent to the decision.

Chapter 14
Activity-Based Costing

Introduction

A large part of a company's expenses is comprised of overhead, which is difficult to trace back to any specific product, product line, geographic region, customer, or any other item that managers want to learn about. Instead, managers have had to put up with overhead allocations that do not relate to how the overhead costs were actually incurred. Instead, they are allocated based on how many direct labor hours something uses, because that was the basis of allocation many years ago, when direct labor was a much higher proportion of total expenses than it is today. The result is startling allocations that may be several multiples higher than the direct labor upon which they are based.

The sheer size of overhead and the problems with allocating it led to the invention of activity-based costing (ABC), which is a methodology for more precisely allocating overhead to those items that actually use it. In this chapter, we will explore why overhead allocation is such a problem, how ABC works, how to install it, and both the advantages and disadvantages of using it.

The Problem with Overhead Allocation

Under generally accepted accounting principles and international financial reporting standards, the accountant is required to allocate overhead to products, so that these items are recorded in inventory at their full costs. Full cost is the aggregation of all costs associated with a product or other item, so that one can see the total cost of all materials, labor, and overhead that relate to that item. Most companies deal with this requirement by accumulating all of their manufacturing overhead costs into a spreadsheet and allocating it to products by any means – they really do not care what allocation method is used, since they are just fulfilling an accounting requirement.

Over time, the amount of overhead as a proportion of a company's costs has swelled, until it comprises the bulk of all expenditures. When management is interested in interpreting where these costs come from, their cost accountants dredge up the same allocation model used for allocating costs to inventory, and apply it to every question that managers ask. For example, if a manager wants to know the cost of a specific product, the answer is to apply the entire pool of overhead costs to that product, so that the allocation includes a number of expenses that bear no relationship to the product at all.

Managers usually react to these generic allocations in one of two ways. They may feel that the accountants do not know what they are doing and throw out the allocations as pure rubbish. Or, they may believe that the accountants are experts, and therefore trust their pronouncements with the same gravity accorded those of a religious leader. The first reaction is unfortunate but justified, while the second can result in a dangerous dependence on information that is not appropriately matched to the circumstances.

We have thus far addressed the general problem posed by overhead – it is an amorphous mass that is difficult to apply to specific situations. Here are a more targeted set of issues:

- *Automation cost allocation.* If a company uses automated production equipment to eliminate direct labor personnel and it is using direct labor as its allocation base, overhead costs will be under-applied to those jobs using the automation, and over-applied to those jobs not using automation. The reason is that the automated jobs use less direct labor, so the allocation system will not assign them as much overhead. Meanwhile, jobs not using the automation are still using a sizeable amount of direct labor, so a proportionally greater amount of overhead (which is also increased by the depreciation expense associated with the automated machinery) is allocated to those jobs. This makes labor-intensive jobs look less profitable than they really are, while the reverse situation occurs for jobs using more automation.

EXAMPLE

Lowry Locomotion produces toy cars. Its engineering manager is considering installing an automated packaging machine on one production line located in its Chicago facility that makes toy fire trucks. Doing so will require an investment in new machinery that will add $50,000 of depreciation to overhead, and will eliminate $1.50 per unit of direct labor. The company currently allocates overhead based on the amount of direct labor consumed.

After the installation is complete, the total amount of overhead has increased from $450,000 to $500,000, while the total amount of direct labor consumed by a toy fire truck has declined from $6.00 to $4.50. The total direct labor used throughout the Chicago facility has declined from $400,000 to $350,000. The calculation of its overhead allocation before and after the installation of automated equipment is:

Overhead Per Dollar of Direct Labor Calculation	
Before automation	$450,000 overhead ÷ $400,000 labor = $1.13 per $ of direct labor
After automation	$500,000 overhead ÷ $350,000 labor = $1.43 per $ of direct labor

Before automation, the toy fire truck consumed $6.00 of direct labor, so the amount of overhead assigned to each truck was $6.78 ($6.00 direct labor × $1.13 overhead allocation). After automation, the toy fire truck consumes $4.50 of direct labor, so the amount of overhead assigned to each truck declines to $6.44 ($4.50 direct labor × $1.43 overhead allocation). Consequently, the method of overhead allocation drives down the full cost of the fire truck.

After automation, the entire Chicago facility still uses $350,000 of direct labor, of which $250,000 is used on another production line that manufactures toy racing cars. Prior to the automation, the racing car line had a total overhead allocation of $282,500 ($250,000 direct labor × $1.13 overhead allocation). Following automation, the racing car line still uses the same amount of labor, but its overhead allocation has increased to $357,500 ($250,000 direct labor × $1.43 overhead allocation).

Thus, the overhead allocation to the fire truck has declined, because its allocation base has declined, while the additional overhead has now shifted to the racing car product, simply because its allocation base did not decline. The shift in allocation between the two product lines is so extreme that the racing car line is now absorbing an additional $75,000 of overhead, even though the total amount of overhead only increased by $50,000; this is because the racing car line has proportionally more of the allocation base than it did before the automation project was completed.

- *Batch-level allocations.* A large amount of overhead cost is associated with the initiation and termination of product batches, which involve machine configurations and testing, as well as the pre-positioning of materials and tools at the production line. Consequently, small-batch jobs have high batch costs on a per-unit basis, while large-batch jobs have low batch costs on a per-unit basis. When an overhead application system only has one basis of allocation, overhead costs are under-applied to small jobs and over-applied to large jobs, so that the smaller jobs look more profitable. This mis-allocation may lead management to seek out smaller orders from customers, which ultimately lowers overall profitability.

EXAMPLE

Lowry Locomotion's Denver facility has two product lines. One produces toy tractors, and the other manufactures toy dump trucks. The toy tractors are produced in a multitude of different sizes and features, since customers demand it. Customers are less discriminating with dump trucks, so that Lowry can operate very long-term production runs of the same model. The facility produces 20,000 tractors and 280,000 dump trucks per year.

The total cost of batch setups in the Denver facility is $150,000, which is spread across the 300,000 toys produced at a standard overhead charge of $0.50 per unit. The trouble is that the dump trucks have run under a single batch setup for the entire year, while there have been 299 batch setups for the tractor line. Consequently, the allocation is wildly incorrect. Nearly all of the batch setup cost should be charged to the tractors. The calculation is:

$150,000 Total setup cost × (299/300) = $149,500 Setup cost related to tractors

The $149,500 should be allocated to the 20,000 tractors that were produced in the measurement period, which is $7.48 per unit, rather than the $0.50 that is currently used.

- *Large proportion of overhead to allocation base.* A very common problem is that the amount of overhead to be allocated greatly exceeds the size of the allocation base, so that a small change in the allocation base results in a large change in the amount of overhead applied. The most common example is using direct labor as the allocation base – if the amount of direct labor in a company is $1 million and the amount of overhead is $5 million, then $5 of overhead is being allocated to a product that only uses $1 of direct labor. This situation can arise with any excessively small allocation base, and results in unjustifiable swings in applied overhead costs.

- *Single allocation base*. There can be a great variety of costs in overhead, and many of them have no cause-and-effect relationship with the single allocation base that is normally used. For example, the most common allocation base is direct labor, and yet such common overhead costs as rent, depreciation, and utilities are not impacted in any way by direct labor.

We have just mentioned the allocation base. This is the basis upon which an entity allocates its overhead costs. It takes the form of a quantity, such as machine hours used, kilowatt hours consumed, or square footage occupied. The allocation base should be a cause, or driver, of the cost being allocated. A good indicator that an allocation base is appropriate is when changes in the allocation base roughly correspond to changes in the actual cost. Thus, if machine usage declines, so too should the actual cost incurred to operate the machine.

After perusing this list of allocation problems, one may feel that any overhead allocation is only accurate by mistake, because the typical system is not really designed to allocate overhead with any degree of precision. Activity-based costing was designed to side-step these shortcomings and provide overhead allocations that represent meaningful costing information.

Overview of Activity-Based Costing

Activity-based costing is designed to give better information about how to allocate overhead costs. It works best in complex environments, where there are many machines and products, and tangled processes that are not easy to sort out. ABC has nothing to do with the assignment of direct materials or direct labor to products or services; that assignment is already handled adequately by bills of material and labor routings. A labor routing is a document showing the work steps required to complete the manufacture of a product, and includes the time required for each work step.

Activity-based costing is best explained by walking through its various steps. They are:

1. *Identify costs*. The first step in ABC is to identify those costs that we want to allocate. This is the most critical step in the entire process, since we do not want to waste time with an excessively broad project scope. For example, if we want to determine the full cost of a distribution channel, we will identify advertising and warehousing costs related to that channel, but will ignore research costs, since they are related to products, not channels.

2. *Load secondary cost pools*. Create cost pools for those costs incurred to provide services to other parts of the company, rather than directly supporting a company's products or services. The contents of secondary cost pools

typically include computer services and administrative salaries, and similar costs. These costs are later allocated to other cost pools that more directly relate to products and services. There may be several of these secondary cost pools, depending upon the nature of the costs and how they will be allocated. For example, if there is a large cost associated with computer services, then store these costs separately in a cost pool and allocate it based on computer usage. If there is another cost pool that contains building costs, then allocate these costs based on square footage used.

3. *Load primary cost pools.* Create a set of cost pools for those costs more closely aligned with the production of goods or services. It is very common to have separate cost pools for each product line, since costs tend to occur at this level. Such costs can include research and development, advertising, procurement, and distribution. Similarly, cost pools could be created for each distribution channel, or for each facility. If production batches are of greatly varying lengths, then consider creating cost pools at the batch level, in order to adequately assign costs based on batch size. It is not common to create cost pools at the individual product level, since only direct material costs are usually aggregated at this level.

4. *Measure activity drivers.* Use a data collection system to collect information about the activity drivers that are used to allocate the costs in secondary cost pools to primary cost pools, as well as to allocate the costs in primary cost pools to cost objects. An activity driver is the most significant cause of an activity. An example of an activity driver is the number of customer orders, which is used to allocate order entry costs to individual customers. A defensible activity driver is one where there is a strong causal relationship between the cost pool and the activity. Thus, if the activity does not occur, the cost in the related cost pool is not incurred. It can be expensive to accumulate activity driver information, so use activity drivers for which information is already being collected, where possible.

5. *Allocate costs in secondary pools to primary pools.* Use activity drivers to apportion the costs in the secondary cost pools to the primary cost pools.

6. *Charge costs to cost objects.* Use an activity driver to allocate the contents of each primary cost pool to cost objects. A cost object is any item for which costs are being separately measured. Examples of cost objects are products, services, departments, machining operations, processes, suppliers, customers, distribution channels, and geographic regions. There will be a separate activity driver for each cost pool. To allocate the costs, divide the total cost in each cost pool by the total amount of activity in the activity driver, to establish the cost per unit of activity. Then allocate the cost per unit to the cost objects, based on their use of the activity driver.

7. *Formulate reports.* Convert the results of the ABC system into reports for management consumption. For example, if the system was originally designed to accumulate overhead information by geographical sales region, report on revenues earned in each region, all direct costs, and the overhead

derived from the ABC system. This gives management a full cost view of the results generated by each region.

8. *Act on the information.* The most common management reaction to an ABC report is to reduce the quantity of activity drivers used by each cost object. Doing so should reduce the amount of overhead cost being used (though see the Incremental Cost Reduction Fallacy section later in this chapter).

We have now arrived at a complete ABC allocation of overhead costs to those cost objects that deserve to be charged with overhead costs. By doing so, managers can see which activity drivers need to be reduced in order to shrink a corresponding amount of overhead cost. For example, if the cost of a single purchase order is $100, managers can focus on letting the production system automatically place purchase orders, or on using procurement cards as a way to avoid purchase orders. Either solution results in fewer purchase orders and therefore lower purchasing department costs.

EXAMPLE

Lowry Locomotion's president commissions a benchmarking study of various company processes, which concludes that the company's purchasing function is more expensive than the purchasing functions of competing companies. The president supports the creation of an ABC project to determine why Lowry's purchasing is so expensive.

The project is assigned to the cost accountant, David Johnston. Mr. Johnston accesses the general ledger accounts for the purchasing department, and finds that its annual expenditures are:

Expense Item	Amount
Salaries	$500,000
Benefits	75,000
Travel and entertainment	65,000
Payroll taxes	40,000
Rent	20,000
Office supplies	10,000
Total	$710,000

He then conducts a time study in the purchasing department to determine which activities consume the staff's time. He compiles the following information:

Purchasing Activity	Time Spent
Researching purchase orders	50%
Purchase order follow up	30%
Supplier visits	20%
Total	100%

Mr. Johnston creates a separate cost pool for each of the three activities and allocates the $710,000 of expenses consumed by the department to them, using the following calculation:

Cost Pool	Time Spent	Direct Allocation	Proportional Allocation	Total Allocation
Research purchase orders	50%		$322,500	$322,500
Purchase order follow up	30%		193,500	193,500
Supplier visits	20%	$65,000	129,000	194,000
Totals	100%	$65,000	$645,000	$710,000

The travel and entertainment portion of the department's expenses are clearly associated with the supplier visits activity, so he shifts that entire cost to the Supplier Visits cost pool. All remaining costs are allocated among the cost pools based on the staff time spent on each one.

Mr. Johnston then investigates which activity drivers would be most appropriate for each cost pool. His conclusions are:

Cost Pool	Activity Driver	Reasoning
Researching purchase orders	Number of jobs released	Purchase orders are compiled and issued at the start of every production job
Purchase order follow up	Number of purchase orders	The department has a policy of contacting suppliers about every purchase order one week before they are due for delivery
Supplier visits	Number of suppliers	The department visits every supplier once every three years

Next, Mr. Johnston compiles volume information for the activity drivers. Job information is readily available from the logistics department, purchase orders are already compiled within the purchasing department, and the supplier count is available in the accounting database. Thus, all three activity measures cost little to monitor.

He then adds the activity volume to the following table to derive the cost per unit of activity driver:

Activity Driver	Activity Volume	Related Cost Pool	Cost in Related Cost Pool	Activity Driver Cost/Unit
Number of jobs released	3,000	Researching purchase orders	$322,500	$107.50
Number of purchase orders	20,000	Purchase order follow up	193,500	$9.68
Number of suppliers	400	Supplier visits	194,000	$485.00
Total			$710,000	

At this point, there is no need to allocate the purchasing costs even further, at the product level. There are several obvious conclusions from the research project, which Mr. Johnston includes in the following memo to the president:

- *Researching purchase orders.* Purchase orders are tied to job releases, and it is unlikely that the company will substantially alter the number of jobs.
- *Purchase order follow up.* Follow up calls are based on a department policy to follow up on 100 percent of all purchase orders. This can be restricted to monitor only those suppliers who have a history of faulty deliveries.
  Recommendation: Create a receiving procedure to create a supplier ranking system, and eliminate all suppliers who persist in faulty deliveries. The result should be the complete elimination of purchase order follow up.
- *Supplier visits.* There is a substantial $485 cost associated with visiting every supplier on a rotating basis. This is a policy issue, and so can be fixed with a policy change.
  Recommendation: To only visit those suppliers with whom the company spends at least $100,000 per year. This will eliminate 75% of the supplier visits, and thereby reduce costs by $145,500 (300 eliminated visits × $485 per visit).

The ABC study indicates high costs at the activity driver level for all three cost pools. The key issue was how the ABC research uncovered the existence of two purchasing department policies that were significant factors in driving up the cost of the department. By altering the policies, Lowry was able to eliminate a large part of its purchasing expense.

The inner workings of an ABC system can directly affect its cost. Here are several issues to consider:

- *Number of cost pools.* It is quite possible for an overly enthusiastic cost accountant to create a blizzard of cost pools, and end up monitoring dozens of them. This introduces too much complexity to the ABC calculations. Instead, try to limit the system to no more than a dozen cost pools.
- *Refresh rate for activity drivers.* Consider the amount of time it takes to accumulate information about activity drivers, and incorporate this information into the number of times per year that the information about them is refreshed. For example, if the purchasing staff spends 40% of its time creating purchase orders, and this number rarely varies more than a few percent

from month to month, do not impose a timekeeping regimen on the purchasing staff to refresh this information every month. Instead, just conduct an annual study. A common finding is that many activity levels do not change much, and so can be refreshed at long intervals and minimal cost.

EXAMPLE

Lowry Locomotion's cost accountant has not installed an ABC system before, and is overcome with zeal to create a highly detailed system with many cost pools and associated activity drivers. His first iteration of the implementation plan calls for data collection in the following areas:

- *Purchasing*. Track the number of purchase orders issued, reminder contacts made to suppliers, and supplier visits.
- *Manufacturing*. Track the number of machine minutes per batch, the number of machine setups, and the amount of time spent on rework.
- *Engineering*. Track the time spent on production line layouts, engineering change orders, and research and development.
- *Marketing*. Track the time spent on designing new ad campaigns, the number of ad placements, and the time spent on target costing projects.

In short, the cost accountant wants to track everything about everyone. The best estimate of the cost of tracking the time usage of the 300 affected employees is one hour per week, at an average cost per hour of $30. The total data collection cost is therefore $468,000 (300 employees × $30/hour × 52 weeks). After learning of the projected data entry cost, the president prevails upon the cost accountant to begin with a pilot project that only encompasses the purchase order activity in the purchasing department. Since the purchasing department already tracks the number of purchase orders created, there is no additional data entry cost at all.

- *Use existing activity drivers*. Few companies already compile information about activity volumes, so deciding to use a new activity driver for cost pool allocation purposes means that a business will have to create a new data collection system. To avoid this cost, see if there is an existing activity driver already in use that has a reasonable causal relationship with the cost pool in question, and use that instead.
- *Focus on strong causal relationships*. If there is a strong causal relationship between an activity driver and a cost pool, by all means use it! A causal relationship means that a change in the activity driver changes the amount of costs incurred in the related cost pool. Therefore, if management focuses on reducing the number of activity driver occurrences, total costs will decline.

There are many possible activity drivers to choose from. The following table shows a selection of some more commonly used activity drivers.

Sampling of Activity Drivers

Department Cost	Activity Driver with Causal Relationship
Accounts payable	Number of supplier invoices processed
	Number of checks paid
Accounts receivable	Number of customer invoices issued
	Number of collection calls made
	Number of cash receipts recorded
Facilities	Square footage used
Human resources	Number of full-time equivalent employees
	Number of training hours
Logistics	Number of purchase orders
	Number of parts in stock
	Number of receipts
	Number of shipments
	Number of warehouse picks
Order entry	Number of customer orders processed
	Number of customer service contacts
Product engineering	Hours charged to product design
	Number of engineering change orders
	Hours charged to product line process design
Production	Number of jobs scheduled
	Number of machine hours
	Number of maintenance work orders
Quality control	Number of receiving inspections
	Number of supplier certification visits

To summarize activity-based costing, we shift costs from expense accounts into cost pools and then allocate these costs to cost objects using activity drivers. The activity drivers have a direct impact on changes in the cost pools with which they are associated. Cost objects are anything that incurs costs and which management wants to collect information about, such as products and services.

Activity-Based Management

The mechanics of activity-based costing have just been noted, but what has been described thus far is really just a tool, and creates no benefit unless it is actively used. A formal methodology for doing so is activity-based management (ABM), which uses ABC information to improve company operations. ABM focuses on three primary improvement areas, which are:

1. *Eliminate secondary activities.* Determine which activities are directly related to the production of products or services, and which are administrative activities, and then work on reducing the proportion of costs spent on administrative activities. A ratio of 80:20 for production-related activities to administrative activities is very good. ABC information is needed to determine the full cost of both types of activities.

2. *Waste reduction.* Determine which activities (in both the production and administrative areas) causes waste in terms of either excessive costs or time used, and work on process streamlining that reduces or eliminates these costs.

3. *Change reinforcement.* Set up policies and procedures to reinforce all changes made, as well as periodic training sessions. The internal audit staff reviews the improved areas periodically and reports to management about whether the changes are taking hold in the organization. This may result in follow-up actions if slippage is detected.

The ABM activities just noted are all oriented inward, toward the reduction of a company's cost structure. However, it can also be used to force management thinking outward, toward better product pricing. For example, it may show that profitability on a customer order is closely tied to the frequency of delivery, the distance to the customer, and/or the size of the order. Management can then structure its pricing policies to take account of these factors.

EXAMPLE

Lowry Locomotion conducts several ABC studies and learns that a large proportion of its distributors are located outside of the local United Parcel Service (UPS) shipping zone, so that the standard shipping fee charged by Lowry is lower than the actual freight cost that it incurs. Accordingly, Lowry determines the specific UPS shipping zone for all of its customers, loads this information into the customer master file for each customer, and charges them a more accurate freight fee based on the zone in which they are located.

A note of caution regarding ABM: it can focus excessively on cost reduction at the expense of interfering with the optimization of work through a company's bottleneck operation. For example, not allowing overtime pay at a bottleneck operation reduces the amount of production generated, and may reduce company profits far more than the savings generated by eliminating overtime pay. See the Constraint Analysis chapter for more information.

Advantages of Activity-Based Costing

The fundamental advantage of using an ABC system is to more precisely determine how overhead is used. Once an ABC system is installed, better information can be obtained about the following issues:

- *Activity costs.* ABC is designed to track the cost of activities, so it can be used to see if activity costs are in line with industry standards. If not, ABC is an excellent feedback tool for measuring the ongoing cost of specific services as management focuses on cost reduction.
- *Customer profitability.* Though most of the costs incurred for individual customers are simply product costs, there is also an overhead component, such as unusually high customer service levels, product return handling, and cooperative marketing agreements. An ABC system can sort through these additional overhead costs and help to determine which customers are actually earning the company a reasonable profit. This analysis may result in some unprofitable customers being turned away, or more emphasis being placed on those customers who are earning the company its largest profits.

EXAMPLE

Lowry Locomotion's Chicago facility has several thousand customers, most of which are retail stores and distributors. The company experiences a wide range of customer support issues with each customer, with some demanding rapid restocking intervals, cooperative marketing reimbursements, and early payment discounts. After conducting an ABC analysis that is focused on the cost of customers, Lowry arrives at the following results:

Customer Levels	Number of Customers	Profits Earned	Cumulative Profits	Revenue Earned	Cumulative Revenue
Top 10%	197	$800,000	$800,000	$3,200,000	$3,200,000
Next 40%	507	400,000	1,200,000	2,600,000	5,800,000
Next 40%	483	200,000	1,400,000	4,000,000	9,800,000
Low 10%	204	-150,000	1,250,000	1,500,000	11,300,000

The analysis shows that Lowry should drop the 204 customers in its lowest 10th percentile, since it is losing money on them, even though it will give up $1,500,000 of revenues by doing so. This will also allow Lowry to spend more time focusing on the customers in its highest percentile, who are generating one-half of the company's profits. Also, eliminating the bottom percentile of customers will create additional production capacity, which Lowry may be able to use to bring in more profitable business.

- *Distribution cost.* The typical company uses a variety of distribution channels to sell its products, such as retail, Internet, distributors, and mail order catalogs. Most of the structural cost of maintaining a distribution channel is overhead, so if it is possible to make a reasonable determination about which distribution channels are using overhead, one can make decisions to alter how distribution channels are used, or even to drop unprofitable channels.

EXAMPLE

Lowry Locomotive's Memphis facility has three distribution channels, which are Internet sales, distributors, and catalog sales. Sales through the Internet are at full retail price, but comprise only a small proportion of total sales. Distributors buy in large quantities, but also receive a 35% discount from the retail price. The catalog sales are at full retail price and have large sales volume, but the cost of creating and mailing the catalogs has increased recently. The marketing manager commissions an ABC study to examine the full cost of each channel. The results are shown in the following table:

	Revenue	Variable Costs	Contribution Margin	Overhead Allocation	Net Profit
Catalog	$1,500,000	$900,000	$600,000	$575,000	$25,000
Distributors	3,250,000	2,600,000	650,000	365,000	285,000
Internet	250,000	150,000	100,000	60,000	40,000
Totals	$5,000,000	$3,475,000	$1,350,000	$1,000,000	$350,000

The analysis reveals that the overhead allocated to the catalog channel is so large that its net profitability has declined to near zero. In fact, the Internet channel absorbs so much less overhead that it now generates more profit than the catalog channel, despite having six times less revenue.

The marketing manager commissions a historical ABC analysis for just the catalog channel, and finds that its net profit has declined precipitously through the past three years. Accordingly, he decides to notify all catalog recipients of how to access the Internet channel, and then eliminate the catalog channel over the following year.

- *Make or buy.* ABC provides a comprehensive view of every cost associated with the in-house manufacture of a product, so that one can see precisely which costs will be eliminated if an item is outsourced, versus which costs will remain.

EXAMPLE

Lowry Locomotion receives an offer from a local plastic injection molding company to take on the basic fabrication of its toy racing car production line, though Lowry would still have to paint and package the cars. The offer is to provide Lowry with the cars at a price of $5.00 each. Lowry's variable cost of producing the cars (not including paint and packaging) is $3.50, while an ABC analysis at the product line level reveals that the overhead cost is $2.25 per car. Thus, Lowry's full cost per car is $5.75.

It appears that Lowry can save $0.75 per car by outsourcing the plastic molding work. However, the savings only applies if Lowry eliminates the overhead associated with the product line, which involves terminating the production manager and two maintenance technicians, selling off three plastic injection molding machines, and sub-leasing the space in which the product line is currently located. Doing so also eliminates Lowry's ability to ever bring the work back in-house.

Given the strategic implications of completely dismantling the production line and putting the company at the mercy of outside suppliers, Lowry's president elects to forego the $0.75 per unit savings, and rejects the supplier's offer.

- *Margins*. With proper overhead allocation from an ABC system, the margins of various products, product lines, and entire subsidiaries can be determined. This can be quite useful for determining where to position company resources to earn the largest margins.
- *Minimum price*. Product pricing is really based on the price that the market will bear, but the marketing manager should know what the cost of the product is, in order to avoid selling a product that will lose a company money on every sale. ABC is very good for determining which overhead costs should be included in this minimum cost, depending upon the circumstances under which products are being sold. This topic is addressed in detail in the Product Pricing: What Does This Cost? chapter.
- *Production facility cost*. It is usually quite easy to segregate overhead costs at the plant-wide level, so the costs of production between different facilities can be compared.

Clearly, there are many valuable uses for the information provided by an ABC system. However, this information will only be available if the system is designed to provide the specific set of data needed for each decision. If a generic ABC system is installed and *then* used for the above decisions, the accountant may find that it does not provide the needed information. Ultimately, the design of the system is determined by a cost-benefit analysis of which decisions it will assist with, and whether the cost of the system is worth the benefit of the resulting information.

Problems with Activity-Based Costing

Many companies initiate ABC projects with the best of intentions, only to see a very high proportion of the projects either fail, or eventually lapse into disuse. There are several reasons for these issues, which are:
- *Cost pool volume*. The advantage of an ABC system is the high quality of information that it produces, but this comes at the cost of using a large number of cost pools – and the more cost pools there are, the greater the cost of managing the system. To reduce this cost, run an ongoing analysis of the cost to maintain each cost pool, in comparison to the utility of the resulting

information. Doing so should keep the number of cost pools down to manageable proportions.

- *Installation time.* ABC systems are notoriously difficult to install, with multi-year installations being the norm when a company attempts to install it across all product lines and facilities. For such comprehensive installations, it is difficult to maintain a high level of management and budgetary support as the months roll by without installation being completed. Success rates are much higher for smaller, more targeted ABC installations.

- *Multi-department data sources.* An ABC system may require data input from multiple departments, and each of those departments may have greater priorities than the ABC system. Thus, the larger the number of departments involved in the system, the greater the risk that data inputs will fail over time. This problem can be avoided by designing the system to only need information from the most supportive managers.

- *Project basis.* Many ABC projects are authorized on a project basis, so that information is only collected once; the information is useful for a company's current operational situation, and it gradually declines in usefulness as the operational structure gradually changes over time. Management may not authorize funding for additional ABC projects later on, so ABC tends to be "done" once and then discarded. To mitigate this issue, build as much of the ABC data collection structure as possible into the existing accounting system, so that the cost of these projects is reduced; at a lower cost, it is more likely that additional ABC projects will be authorized in the future.

- *Reporting of unused time.* When a company asks its employees to report on the time spent on various activities, they have a strong tendency to make sure that the reported amounts equal 100% of their time. However, there is a large amount of slack time in anyone's work day that may involve breaks, administrative meetings, playing games on the Internet, and so forth. Employees usually mask these activities by apportioning more time to other activities. These inflated numbers represent misallocations of costs in the ABC system, sometimes by quite substantial amounts.

- *Reporting.* The content of ABC reports may vary substantially from what company managers are used to seeing in their old budget-versus-actual financial reports. It may call for periodic retraining to show them how to use these new reports.

- *Separate data set.* An ABC system rarely can be constructed to pull all of the information it needs directly from the general ledger. Instead, it requires a separate database that pulls in information from several sources, only one of which is existing general ledger accounts. It can be quite difficult to maintain this extra database, since it calls for significant extra staff time for which there may not be an adequate budget. The best work-around is to design the system to require the minimum amount of additional information other than that which is already available in the general ledger.

- *Targeted usage.* The benefits of ABC are most apparent when cost accounting information is difficult to discern, due to the presence of multiple product lines, machines being used for the production of many products, numerous machine setups, and so forth – in other words, in complex production environments. If a company does not operate in such an environment, it may spend a great deal of money on an ABC installation, only to find that the resulting information is not overly valuable.

The broad range of issues noted here should make it clear that ABC tends to follow a bumpy path in many organizations, with a tendency for its usefulness to decline over time. Of the problem mitigation suggestions noted here, the key point is to construct a highly targeted ABC system that produces the most critical information at a reasonable cost. If that system takes root in a company, then consider a gradual expansion, during which the system is only expanded further if there is a clear and demonstrable benefit in doing so. The worst thing one can do is to install a large and comprehensive ABC system, since it is expensive, meets with the most resistance, and is the most likely to fail over the long term.

The Incremental Cost Reduction Fallacy

Though many problems with ABC were listed in the preceding section, there is one large issue worth discussion in a separate section, which is the incremental cost reduction fallacy. ABC is designed to focus the attention of management on how overhead is actually used, and its primary method of doing so is the activity driver. In essence, if the use of an activity driver by a cost object can be reduced, the amount of overhead expense related to that activity driver will decline, and the company will save money. The trouble is that overhead costs are usually incurred as step costs, so that it takes a large reduction of activity driver units to yield any overhead cost reduction – though when it occurs, the cost reduction is large. A step cost is a cost that does not change steadily, but rather at discrete points.

Examples of overhead costs that are step costs are the salary of a customer service person, rent paid on a building, or the utilities paid for that building. To use the rent and utilities as a further example, they would be accumulated into a facilities cost pool and allocated based on square footage used. Management might then attempt to reduce this cost by shrinking the amount of square footage used. However, the cost does not decline at all until management can completely empty the building, and even then the company may be obligated to make payments until the building lease expires. Thus, an underlying precept of ABC, that overhead costs can be controlled at a unit level, is not correct in many situations.

EXAMPLE

Lowry Locomotion conducts a targeted ABC analysis of its customer service function, and concludes that it costs $10 every time a customer calls with a complaint. The cost pool is comprised of the cost of 10 customer service representatives, as well as the cost of the facility in which they are located, depreciation on their cubicles, and a fixed monthly charge for their 10 telephone lines. The entire annual cost of this cost pool is $425,000.

Lowry receives 42,500 calls per year. Management elects to reduce the cost of customer service by reducing a variety of issues about which customers are calling. After three months, the company has reduced the number of calls by 3,800, or 9 percent of the total number of calls. However, costs have not declined at all. Upon further investigation, Lowry's management realizes that it has to reduce costs by 10 percent to eliminate one customer service employee, along with the cost of the phone line associated with that position. The cost of cubicle depreciation will not decline, since it is not practical to eliminate a single cubicle. Further, the cost of facility rent will not be eliminated under any circumstances, since the company has committed to a five-year lease.

Lowry eliminates another 450 customer calls, which drops the total number of calls by 10 percent, and is able to lay off one worker and eliminate one phone line. Management now realizes that it only reduces overhead costs when it reduces customer calls in increments of 4,250 calls.

The Bill of Activities

In the production world, a key document is the bill of materials, which contains an itemization of the components needed to build a product. A similar document for the ABC function is the bill of activities, which lists the overhead components of a product. An example of a bill of activities is shown in the following exhibit:

Sample Bill of Activities

Cost Pool	Total Pool Cost	Activity Measure	Relevant Volume	Cost per Unit
Product design	$250,000	Units produced	100,000/life cycle	$2.50
Industrial design	75,000	Units produced	100,000/life cycle	0.75
Batch level costs	5,000	Batch size	5,000/batch	1.00
Marketing	40,000	Annual units	20,000/year	2.00
Totals	$370,000			$6.25

The bill of activities in the example contains a sufficient number of cost pools to show the primary sources of overhead cost, clearly states how these costs are allocated, and derives a cost per unit. This information concisely shows how overhead is applied to a product, rather than the usual undefined allocation methodology found in a basic cost accounting system.

The bill of activities contains valuable information for defining the overhead component of a product's costs. Thus, when combined with a bill of materials and labor routing, the user has a complete set of information about the cost structure of a product.

System Scope Issues

Finding the correct scope of an ABC installation is an important consideration, because a project with an excessively large scope may never reach completion, while a small one addressing an unimportant area will not be seen as creating enough value. Generally, it is better to err on the side of too small an installation than the reverse. A large, comprehensive ABC system calls for a massive investment of time and money, and may irritate so many department heads that they eventually band together to stop the project. Conversely, a small, carefully selected project that yields valuable information may very well result in department heads requesting additional ABC work in other areas. Here are some recommendations that may assist in the construction of a well-positioned ABC system:

- *Focus on complexity.* The results of an ABC system should be seen to extract valuable information from a snarled process. Therefore, if a process is too simple, it does not need an ABC system.
- *Start with a pilot.* Expect those subjected to an ABC system to be suspicious of how it works and their level of involvement in it. To allay their concerns, start with a very small pilot project that involves the minimum amount of effort and maximum results, and then trumpet the results.
- *Initial manual links.* If a pilot project is being created which may or may not later be ramped up into a larger project, avoid installing expensive interfaces to the existing accounting system. Instead, manually rekey any information needed for this initial project. Doing so keeps the startup costs low, which may lead management to authorize a broader installation that uses more expensive systems integration.
- *Departmental inclusions.* The main focus of an ABC system is usually the production department, but there may be significant overhead in other areas, such as the engineering department, that should be allocated to products and services. Be careful about providing ABC coverage to these additional departments, both because their total overhead amounts may be minimal, and because it may be difficult to establish a causal linkage between their overhead costs and the cost objects targeted by the ABC system.

In short, ABC calls for a substantial amount of planning to ensure that the system is properly positioned within a company to have the best possible outcome. Greater success usually equates to a smaller installation that is precisely targeted at resolving a specific issue.

System Integration Issues

Activity-based costing is frequently initiated as a project for which information is accumulated separately from the accounting system. This is fine for a one-time project, where there is some willingness to rekey information into the ABC system, but is not a viable proposition if the ABC project transitions into a permanent installation. For a full integration with the accounting system, consider making the following changes:

- *Chart of accounts*. Alter the chart of accounts to include accounts that are used as cost pools.
- *Cost centers*. Additional cost centers may be needed to more accurately accumulate costs. For example, instead of having a single set of expense accounts for an engineering department, consider splitting these accounts in two, so that one set of accounts accumulate costs for the research and development cost center, and another set of accounts accumulate costs for the industrial engineering cost center.
- *Cost defaults*. The accounts payable system likely contains an account code default, so that when a new supplier invoice is entered, it automatically charges the amount of that invoice to the default account code. The ABC system may require that this default be redirected to a different account code.
- *Billing defaults*. The billing software may contain a default revenue account for each product or service billed, which is automatically loaded when an invoice is created. The ABC system may require that this default be redirected to a different account code.

It may not be necessary to make all of the changes noted here. An easier approach is to make incremental changes to the existing accounting system only for those ABC projects that management decides should be rendered permanent, and integrated more fully into the infrastructure of the company.

Summary

This chapter has shown the significant uses to which ABC can be put. These advantages are all related to cost analyses, so one should consider ABC to be an analysis tool – it is much too expensive a method to use for creating a more accurate inventory valuation. Other, more primitive methods of allocation are entirely adequate for valuing inventory.

The primary problem with ABC is that it requires a data collection system that is different from the one used by any accounting system, so it requires the creation of an entirely new system that runs in conjunction with the main accounting system – and that requires both money and employee time to create and maintain. Because of the significant investment in time and money, it is best to carefully define the mission of an ABC system before implementing it, in order to spend the minimum amount in exchange for receiving a precisely defined set of information.

A final thought about ABC systems is that the results they generate may be quite different from the results issued by the normal accounting system, so be prepared to defend the results of the analysis with reports on exactly how the information was derived.

Chapter 15
Constraint Analysis

Introduction

Most types of analysis require the accountant to pass judgment on a management situation without taking account of the greater corporate structure within which it takes place. For example, the accountant may be called upon to judge whether a product should be cancelled because of an excessively low margin, or to choose between two possible capital investments based on their cash flows. However, management rarely considers the impact of these decisions on a company's entire capability, as an integrated unit, to earn a profit.

Constraint analysis does the reverse – its starting point is determining which company operation is constraining the entire company from earning a greater profit, and then focuses all decision-making upon how they impact this constraint (or "bottleneck"). To use the previous two examples, it may not be judicious to cancel a product that generates *any* amount of profit, since that profit helps to pay for the overhead cost of the entire system. Further, it may not be necessary to invest in a fixed asset unless it improves the capacity of the bottleneck operation.

This chapter gives an overview of constraint analysis, and then delves into a number of management decisions where using it can alter one's perception of how to manage a company.

Related Podcast Episodes: Episodes 43 through 47 of the Accounting Best Practices Podcast discuss constraint analysis. They are available at: **accounting-tools.com/podcasts** or **iTunes**

Constraint Analysis Operational Terminology

Constraint analysis makes use of several unique terms, so we will begin with a set of definitions before proceeding to an overview of constraint analysis. The key operational terms are:

- *Drum.* This is a third variation of the *constraint* term, along with *bottleneck*. It is the operation, person, or (occasionally) the materials within a company that prevent the business from generating additional sales. Since the ultimate profitability of the company depends on this one item, it sets the pace for how the company operates. Picture the drum beating on a rowed galley, which indicates why it is called a *drum*.

- *Buffer.* The drum operation should operate at as close to 100% of capacity as possible, but this is impossible when the flow of materials from upstream operations is unreliable. The buffer is inventory that is positioned in front of the drum operation, and which protects the drum from any stoppage in mate-

rials coming from upstream operations. The buffer may need to be quite large if there is considerable variability in the inflow of materials, or it may be of more modest proportions if the inflow is more stable.
- *Rope*. The rope represents the date and time when jobs must be released into the production process in order to have inventory arrive at the buffer just when it is needed by the drum; thus, it is really the total time duration needed to bring work-in-process to the drum.

These three terms are sometimes strung together in a single phrase, and are called the *drum-buffer-rope* system. As a group, they describe the essential operational components of constraint analysis.

Overview of Constraint Analysis

The key points in understanding constraint analysis are the following two concepts:
1. A company is an integrated set of processes that function together to generate a profit; and
2. There is a chokepoint somewhere in a company that absolutely controls its ability to earn a profit.

The chokepoint is also known as the drum operation (as defined above, or the bottleneck, or the constrained resource). We will refer to it as bottleneck, since the word most clearly describes its impact on an organization.

The first concept, that of a company being an integrated set of processes, applies very strongly at the product line level, but less so at the corporate parent level. At the product line level, there is almost certainly a bottleneck that restricts the ability to generate more profit. At the corporate parent level, there may be multiple subsidiaries, each with a multitude of product lines. Thus, from the perspective of the corporate parent, there are still bottlenecks, but there may be a number of them scattered throughout the operations of the subsidiaries.

The second concept, that of the bottleneck, is most typically characterized by a machine that can only process a certain number of units per day. To improve profits, a company must focus all of its attention on that machine by taking such steps as:
- Adding supplemental staff to cover any employee breaks or downtime during shift changes
- Reviewing the quality of work-in-process going into the operation, so that it does not waste any time processing items that are already defective
- Positioning extra maintenance personnel near it to ensure that service intervals are short
- Reducing the amount of processing time per unit, so that more units can be run through the machine
- Adding more capacity to the machine
- Outsourcing work to suppliers

It is also possible that the bottleneck is not in the production area at all. It may be caused by a materials shortage, or by a lack of sales staff. In those rare cases where there is simply no bottleneck to be found, then the company has excess capacity, and can choose to either reduce its capacity (and the related cost) or try to sell more volume, possibly at a lower price.

EXAMPLE

Hammer Industries produces construction equipment. Its products are large, complex, and mostly sold through a request for proposals process. Its cost accountant has reviewed all production operations in detail and concluded that there is no bottleneck operation to be found. Instead, the real chokepoint appears to be in the sales department.

Hammer has a multi-tiered sales process, where one group makes initial contacts with prospective customers, another group of technical writers responds to requests for proposal (RFP), yet another group conducts sales presentations, and a final group conducts final contract negotiations. A brief analysis shows that the technical writers are completely overwhelmed with writing RFP responses, and have missed several RFP filing deadlines. The sales staff positioned ahead of them in the process flow, those making contacts with prospective customers, are aware of the problem and have scaled back their activities to meet with new customers, since they know the company is not capable of making timely RFP responses. Thus, it is evident that the sales department is the true company bottleneck.

The cost accountant reports this issue to management, and recommends a combination of additional technical writer hiring and the purchase of RFP response software to simplify the writing task.

One can usually tell where the bottleneck is located, because it has a large amount of work piled up in front of it, while the work operation immediately downstream from it is starved for work.

A major part of the management of the bottleneck operation is the inventory buffer located immediately in front of it. Constraint analysis holds that there will always be flaws in the production process that result in variability in the flow of materials to the bottleneck, so it is necessary to build up a buffer to insulate the bottleneck from these issues. The buffer should be quite large if there are lots of upstream production problems, or much smaller if the production flow is relatively placid.

If production problems start to eat into the size of the inventory buffer, then the bottleneck is in danger of having a stock-out condition, which may cause it to run out of work. To avoid this, have a large *sprint capacity* in selected upstream production operations. Sprint capacity is essentially excess production capacity. There should be sufficient sprint capacity available to rapidly rebuild the inventory buffer. If the company has invested in a significant sprint capacity, there is also less need for a large inventory buffer.

Finally, there is the concept of the *rope* that was mentioned earlier as a key definition. It is very important to only release new jobs into the production queue so that they arrive at the inventory buffer just in time to be used. The natural inclination of a production scheduler would be to release jobs too soon, to ensure that there is always a healthy flow of jobs arriving at the inventory buffer. However, doing so represents an excessive inventory investment, and also confuses the production staff, which does not know which of the plethora of jobs to process next. Thus, the rope concept represents a fine balance between overloading the system and starving it of work.

In summary, the bottleneck operation is the most important operation in a company. The management team needs to know where it is located, and spend a great deal of time figuring out how to maximize its operation so that it hardly ever stops.

The Cost of the Bottleneck

How expensive is it when a bottleneck operation is not running? The traditional cost accounting approach would be to calculate the foregone gross margin on any products that would otherwise have been produced if it had been operational. Under constraint analysis, the calculation is the entire operating cost of the facility, divided by the bottleneck's operating hours. We use the entire cost of the facility, because the bottleneck drives the profitability of the entire facility.

For example, a bottleneck operation is running 160 hours a week, which is three shifts, less eight hours for maintenance downtime. The facility has operating expenses of $1,600,000 per week. Therefore, the cost of *not* running the bottleneck operation is $10,000 per hour. When viewed from this perspective, it very expensive indeed to stop a bottleneck operation.

EXAMPLE

Mole Industries incurs $250,000 of operational expenses per week for its Digger equipment line. The bottleneck work center is operational 150 hours per week, with the remaining 18 hours of the week being used for necessary maintenance. Thus, the cost of not running the bottleneck is $1,667 per hour ($250,000 operational expenses ÷ 150 hours per week).

The shift supervisor has received a demand from the union to give a one-hour lunch break to the three people working in the bottleneck operation, in each of the three shifts. The shift supervisor has the choice of shutting down the operation for 21 hours per week to accede to this request (7 days × 3 shifts × 1 hour per shift), or of bringing in additional staff at an astronomical $100 per hour per person to run the operation in their absence. Which is the better alternative?

Option 1, Stop the Bottleneck: The cost of not running the bottleneck is $1,667 per hour, so the total cost over 21 hours would be $35,000 per week.

Option 2, Use Supplemental Staff: The cost of using supplemental staff is $6,300 (21 hours × 3 staff × $100 per person).

Though the use of supplemental staff initially appears excessive, the cost is still far lower than shutting down the bottleneck operation.

The example makes it quite clear that a bottleneck operation should never be shut down. It is always less expensive to add staff to it, or do whatever else is necessary, to ensure that it keeps running.

An ancillary question is, what is the cost of running an operation that is not the bottleneck operation? It is zero. Since company operations do not hinge on any other operation, it is usually acceptable to shut them down for short periods. The only exception is when doing so may impact the bottleneck operation.

Local Optimization

The concept of the constraint is very much at odds with the traditional concept of local optimization, where the target is to improve the efficiency of every operation throughout a company. The cost accountant is involved in many of these decisions, trying to decide whether to invest in any number of efficiency projects. In many cases, these improvements do nothing to increase overall company profits, because the primary driver of profits is still the bottleneck operation. Consequently, if investments are made in local optimization projects, profits do not improve, but the investment in the company increases, so the only logical outcome is that the return on investment declines. Here are several examples of how constraint analysis alters one's view of local optimization:

Situation	Local Optimization Solution	Constraint Analysis Solution
Overtime is 10% of payroll	Restrict all overtime	Do not restrict overtime if it is being spent on the bottleneck operation, or on any operations feeding the bottleneck
A machine is not being utilized	Sell the machine	Keep the machine if it provides sprint capacity for the bottleneck operation
A product can be redesigned	Only do so if the product is at the end of its normal life cycle	Do so if the redesign reduces the product processing time at the bottleneck operation
The production staff is not fully utilized	Cut back on operations and lay off staff	If there is no bottleneck operation, lower prices to attract more sales
A machine is reaching its maximum utilization	Buy an additional machine	Only buy an additional unit if it will provide more sprint capacity. Do not buy if it is located downstream from the bottleneck operation
A supplier is asking us to outsource production	Do so if it passes a cost-benefit analysis	Do so if it reduces the load on the bottleneck operation

In all of the cases noted in the table, it is necessary to step back from the individual decision and see what the impact will be on the entire company before determining the correct course of action.

In particular, be aware of two problems that are caused by local optimization:

1. *Excess inventory.* If a production operation is optimized that is not the bottleneck operation, all that has been accomplished is give it the ability to churn out even more inventory than was previously the case, and which the bottleneck will be unable to process. Thus, management has not only needlessly invested in the operation, but also needlessly invested in additional inventory that must now wait to be processed.

2. *Overly efficient labor.* When a good manufacturing process was considered to be one with very long production runs, there was an emphasis on highly efficient labor. If the focus is instead on maximizing the amount of production passing through the bottleneck – and nowhere else – the bottleneck operation can be grossly overstaffed to make sure that it is always operating; much less attention is paid to labor efficiencies elsewhere. Employees should only work if inventory is actually needed. In short, it is better to have employees be underutilized and produce less inventory than to be more efficient and produce inventory that is not needed.

In summary, a company does not even have to be especially efficient in production areas located away from the bottleneck operation. Instead, the one and only focus is on maximizing the efficiency of the bottleneck. This change in focus alters most of the decisions that would be reached if one were to only focus on local optimization.

Constraint Analysis Financial Terminology

By now it should be apparent that constraint analysis is quite a valuable tool from an operational perspective. But what about from a financial perspective? How does the cost accountant use it to make decisions? There is a model for using constraint analysis in this role, but first we need to define the terms in the model. They are:

- *Throughput.* This is the margin left after totally variable costs have been subtracted from revenue. This tends to be a large proportion of revenues, since all overhead costs are excluded from the calculation.
- *Totally variable costs.* This is usually just the cost of materials, since it is only those costs that vary when one incremental unit of a product is manufactured. This does not normally include the cost of labor, since employees are not usually paid based on one incremental unit of output (unless they are paid under a piece rate plan, where they are paid for the number of units produced). There are a few other possible costs that may be totally variable, such as commissions, subcontractor fees, customs duties, and freight costs.
- *Operating expenses.* This is all company expenses other than totally variable costs. There is no differentiation between overhead costs, administrative

costs or financing costs – quite simply, *all* other company expenses are lumped into this category.

- *Investment*. This is the amount invested in assets. "Investment" includes changes in the level of working capital resulting from a management decision.
- *Net profit*. This is throughput, less operating expenses.

Constraint Analysis from a Financial Perspective

When a company is looked at from the perspective of constraints, it no longer makes sense to evaluate individual products, because overhead costs do not vary at the individual product level. In reality, most companies spend a great deal of money to maintain a production infrastructure, and that infrastructure is what really generates a profit – the trick is making that infrastructure produce the maximum profit with the best mix of products having the highest possible throughput. Under the constraint analysis model, there are three ways to improve the financial position of the entire production infrastructure. They are:

- *Increase throughput*. This is by either increasing revenues or reducing the amount of totally variable costs.
- *Reduce operating expenses*. This is by reducing some element of overhead expenses.
- *Improve the return on investment*. This is by either improving profits in conjunction with the lowest possible investment, or by reducing profits slightly along with a correspondingly larger decline in investment.

Note that only the increase in throughput is related in any way to decisions made at the product level. The other two improvement methods may be concerned with changes anywhere in the production system.

The Constraint Analysis Model

There is an excellent constraint analysis model that was developed by Thomas Corbett, and which is outlined here. The basic thrust of the model is to give priority in the bottleneck operation to those products that generate the highest throughput per minute of bottleneck time. After these products are manufactured, priority is then given to the product having the next highest throughput per minute, and so on. Eventually, the production queue is filled, and the operation can accept no additional work.

The key element in the model is the use of throughput per minute, because the key limiting factor in a bottleneck operation is time – hence, maximizing throughput within the shortest possible time frame is paramount. Note that throughput *per minute* is much more important than total throughput *per unit*. The following example illustrates the point.

EXAMPLE

Mole Industries manufactures trench digging equipment. It has two products with different amounts of throughput and processing times at the bottleneck operation. The key information about these products is:

Product	Total Throughput	Bottleneck Processing Time	Throughput per Minute
Mole Hole Digger	$400	2 minutes	$200
Mole Driver Deluxe	800	8 minutes	100

Of the two products, the Mole Driver Deluxe creates the most overall throughput, but the Mole Hole Digger creates more throughput per minute of bottleneck processing time. To determine which one is more valuable to Mole Industries, consider what would happen if the company had an unlimited order quantity of each product, and could run the bottleneck operation nonstop, all day (which equates to 1,440 minutes). The operating results would be:

Product	Throughput per Minute		Total Processing Time Available		Total Throughput
Mole Hole Digger	$200	×	1,440 minutes	=	$288,000
Mole Driver Deluxe	100	×	1,440 minutes	=	144,000

Clearly, the Mole Hole Digger, with its higher throughput per minute, is much more valuable to Mole Industries than its Mole Driver Deluxe product. Consequently, the company should push sales of the Mole Hole Digger product whenever possible.

The constraint analysis model is essentially a production plan that itemizes the amount of throughput that can be generated, as well as the total amount of operating expenses and investment. In the model, we use four different products, each requiring some processing time in the bottleneck operation. The columns in the model are as follows:

- *Throughput per minute.* This is the total amount of throughput that a product generates, divided by the amount of processing time at the bottleneck operation.
- *Bottleneck usage.* This is the number of minutes of processing time required by a product at the bottleneck operation.
- *Units scheduled.* This is the number of units scheduled to be processed at the bottleneck operation.
- *Total bottleneck time.* This is the total number of minutes of processing time required by a product, multiplied by the number of units to be processed.
- *Total throughput.* This is the throughput per minute multiplied by the number of units processed at the bottleneck operation.

This grid produces a total amount of throughput to be generated if production proceeds according to plan. Below the grid of planned production, there is a subtotal of the total amount of throughput, from which the total amount of operating expenses are subtracted to arrive at the amount of profit. Finally, the total amount of investment in assets is divided into the profit to calculate the return on investment. Thus, the model provides a complete analysis of all three ways in which the results of a company can be improved – increase throughput, decrease operating expenses, or increase the return on investment. An example of the model follows:

Sample Constraint Analysis Model

Product	Throughput per Minute	Bottleneck Usage (minutes)	Units Scheduled	Total Bottleneck Time	Total Throughput
1. Hedgehog Deluxe	$80	14	1,000	14,000	$1,120,000
2. Hedgehog Mini	70	20	500	10,000	700,000
3. Hedgehog Classic	65	40	200	8,000	520,000
4. Hedgehog Digger	42	10	688	6,880	288,960
		Total bottleneck scheduled time		38,880	
		Total bottleneck time available*		38,880	
			Total throughput		$2,628,960
			Total operating expenses		2,400,000
			Profit		$228,960
			Profit percentage		8.7%
			Investment		$23,000,000
			Annualized return on investment		11.9%

* Minutes per month (30 days × 24 hours × 60 minutes × (1 – 0.10 maintenance time)

In the example, the Hedgehog Deluxe product has the largest throughput per minute, and so is scheduled to be the first priority for production. The Hedgehog Digger has the lowest throughput per minute, so it is given last priority in the production schedule. If there is less time available on the bottleneck operation, the company should reduce the number of the Hedgehog Digger product manufactured in order to maximize overall profits.

In the middle of the model, the "Total bottleneck scheduled time" row contains the total number of minutes of scheduled production. The row below it, labeled "Total bottleneck time available," represents the total estimate of time that the bottleneck should have available for production purposes during the scheduling period. Since the time scheduled and available are identical, this means that the production schedule has completely maximized the availability of the bottleneck operation.

One calculation anomaly in the model is that the profit percentage is normally calculated as profit divided by revenues. However, since revenues are not included in the model, we instead use profits divided by throughput. Since throughput is less than revenue, we are overstating the profit percentage as compared to the traditional profit percentage calculation.

Use the constraint analysis model in a before-and-after mode, to see what effect a proposed change will have on profitability or the return on investment. If the model improves as a result of a change, then implement the change. In the next few sections, we will examine how the constraint analysis model is used to arrive at several management decisions.

The Decision to Sell at a Lower Price

A common scenario is for a customer to promise a large order, but only if the company agrees to a substantial price drop. The sales department may favor such deals, because they bolster the company backlog, earn commissions, and increase market share. The trouble is that these deals also elbow out other jobs that may have higher throughput per minute. If so, the special deal drops overall throughput and may lead to a loss. The following example, which uses the basic constraint model as a baseline, illustrates the problem.

EXAMPLE

Mole Industries has received an offer from a customer to buy 2,000 units of its highly profitable Hedgehog Deluxe, but only if the company reduces the price. The new price will shrink the Deluxe's throughput per minute to $60. The analysis is:

Product	Throughput per Minute	Bottleneck Usage (minutes)	Units Scheduled	Total Bottleneck Time	Total Throughput
1. Hedgehog Deluxe	$60	14	2,000	28,000	$1,680,000
2. Hedgehog Mini	70	20	500	10,000	700,000
3. Hedgehog Classic	65	40	22	880	57,200
4. Hedgehog Digger	42	10	0	0	0
		Total bottleneck scheduled time		38,880	
		Total bottleneck time available*		38,880	
			Total throughput		$2,437,200
			Total operating expenses		2,400,000
			Profit		$37,200
			Profit percentage		1.5%
			Investment		$23,000,000
			Annualized return on investment		1.9%

* Minutes per month (30 days × 24 hours × 60 minutes × (1 − 0.10 maintenance time)

The baseline production configuration generated a profit of $228,960, while this new situation creates a profit of only $37,200. The profit decline was caused by a combination of lower throughput per minute for the Hedgehog Deluxe and the increased production capacity assigned to this lower-throughput product, which displaced other, more profitable products. Note that there was no production capacity available at all for the Hedgehog Digger product. Clearly, the company should reject the customer's offer.

The Decision to Outsource Production

One way to manage the bottleneck operation is to outsource work to keep some of the production burden away from the bottleneck. This option is always acceptable if the throughput generated by the outsourced products exceed the price charged to the company by the supplier, *and* the company can replace the throughput per minute that was taken away from the bottleneck operation. The following example, which uses the basic constraint model as a baseline, illustrates the concept.

EXAMPLE

Mole Industries receives an offer from a supplier to outsource the Hedgehog Classic to it. The supplier will even drop ship the product to customers, so the product would no longer impact Mole's production process in any way. The downside of the offer is that the supplier's price is higher than the cost at which Mole can produce the Classic internally, so the total monthly throughput attributable to the Classic would decline by $300,000, from $520,000 to $220,000. However, there is a large customer order backlog for the Hedgehog Digger, so Mole could give increased production priority to the Digger instead. The analysis is:

Product	Throughput per Minute	Bottleneck Usage (minutes)	Units Scheduled	Total Bottleneck Time	Total Throughput
1. Hedgehog Deluxe	$80	14	1,000	14,000	$1,120,000
2. Hedgehog Mini	70	20	500	10,000	700,000
3. Hedgehog Classic	65	40	200	N/A	220,000
4. Hedgehog Digger	42	10	1,488	14,880	624,960
		Total bottleneck scheduled time		38,880	
		Total bottleneck time available*		38,880	
				Total throughput	$2,664,960
				Total operating expenses	2,400,000
				Profit	$264,960
				Profit percentage	9.9%
				Investment	$23,000,000
				Annualized return on investment	13.8%

* Minutes per month (30 days × 24 hours × 60 minutes × (1 − 0.10 maintenance time)

Despite a large decline in throughput caused by the outsourcing deal, the company actually earns $36,000 more profit overall, because the Hedgehog Classic uses more of the bottleneck time per unit (40 minutes) than any other product; this allows the company to fill the

177

available bottleneck time with 800 more Hedgehog Digger products, which require the smallest amount of bottleneck time per unit (10 minutes), and which generate sufficient additional throughput to easily offset the throughput decline caused by outsourcing. Mole Industries should accept the supplier's offer to outsource.

The Capital Investment Decision

In a large production environment, there are constant requests to invest more funds in various areas in order to increase efficiencies. However, it rarely makes sense to invest in areas that do not favorably impact the bottleneck operation in some way. In particular, investments in the capacity of operations located downstream from the bottleneck operation rarely yield a return, since improving them does nothing for the overall profitability of the entire system. The issue is addressed in the following example, which uses the basic constraint model as a baseline.

EXAMPLE

The industrial engineering manager of Mole Industries examines the entire production line, and concludes that he can double the speed of the paint shop for an investment of $250,000. This operation is located at the very end of the production line, and so is located downstream from the bottleneck operation. The analysis is:

Product	Throughput per Minute	Bottleneck Usage (minutes)	Units Scheduled	Total Bottleneck Time	Total Throughput
1. Hedgehog Deluxe	$80	14	1,000	14,000	$1,120,000
2. Hedgehog Mini	70	20	500	10,000	700,000
3. Hedgehog Classic	65	40	200	8,000	520,000
4. Hedgehog Digger	42	10	688	6,880	288,960
		Total bottleneck scheduled time		38,880	
		Total bottleneck time available*		38,880	
				Total throughput	$2,628,960
				Total operating expenses	2,400,000
				Profit	$228,960
				Profit percentage	8.7%
				Investment	$23,250,000
				Annualized return on investment	11.8%

* Minutes per month (30 days × 24 hours × 60 minutes × (1 − 0.10 maintenance time)

The only item that changes in the analysis is the amount of the investment, which increases by $250,000 and results in a reduced return on investment. Improving the capacity of the paint shop has no effect on throughput, since the entire production line can still only run at the maximum pace of the bottleneck operation.

There are some types of investment that can make sense, even if they are not associated with the bottleneck operation. In particular, if an investment can reduce the cost of an operation, the investment is acceptable, as long as the return on investment percentage increases as a result of the change. The concept is illustrated in the following example.

EXAMPLE

Rather than proposing a capacity increase in the paint shop (as was the case in the last example), the industrial engineering manager of Mole Industries proposes to invest $250,000 in the paint shop, but only to add sufficient automation to reduce operating expenses by $5,000 per month. The analysis is:

Product	Throughput per Minute	Bottleneck Usage (minutes)	Units Scheduled	Total Bottleneck Time	Total Throughput
1. Hedgehog Deluxe	$80	14	1,000	14,000	$1,120,000
2. Hedgehog Mini	70	20	500	10,000	700,000
3. Hedgehog Classic	65	40	200	8,000	520,000
4. Hedgehog Digger	42	10	688	6,880	288,960
		Total bottleneck scheduled time		38,880	
		Total bottleneck time available*		38,880	
				Total throughput	$2,628,960
				Total operating expenses	2,395,000
				Profit	$233,960
				Profit percentage	8.7%
				Investment	$23,250,000
				Annualized return on investment	12.1%

* Minutes per month (30 days × 24 hours × 60 minutes × (1 – 0.10 maintenance time)

The investment creates a sufficient decline in total operating expenses to yield an increase in the annualized rate of return, to 12.1%. Consequently, this is a worthwhile investment opportunity.

The Decision to Cancel a Product

Cost accountants sometimes review all products issued by a company, carefully allocating costs to each one, to see if any are losing money. If so, management may agree to cancel them. However, when products are reviewed from the perspective of constraint analysis, they are almost never cancelled. The reason is that the basis of measurement should be throughput, which is revenues minus totally variable expenses, and since the cost of materials is really the only variable expense, there is *always* throughput. A company rarely prices its products at or below the cost of its materials, since that would result in catastrophic losses.

Since all products are likely to have throughput, the real question is not which products have the lowest throughput, but rather which ones have the highest throughput. By focusing on these high-throughput products, the cost accountant can recommend which items to bring most forcibly to the attention of customers. If the result is an increased volume of production of products having high throughput, then the low throughput products may be forced out of the production mix, simply because there is no production capacity left to manufacture them.

If a cost accountant were to follow the more traditional approach of assigning overhead to products and then deciding if they are unprofitable, the result would be the ongoing elimination of products, as overhead costs are gradually shifted to fewer and fewer remaining products, driving up the cost of each one in turn and forcing management to conclude that each one should be cancelled. The following example illustrates the concept.

EXAMPLE

Mole Industries has three versions of a trench digging tool. The company has $4,000,000 of overhead that it allocates to the three products. The company allocates the overhead based on revenue. The cost characteristics of the products are:

Product	Revenue	Variable Costs	Overhead Costs	Margin
Hedgehog Classic	$2,000,000	$1,300,000	$800,000	-$100,000
Hedgehog Mini	3,000,000	1,600,000	1,200,000	200,000
Hedgehog Deluxe	5,000,000	2,400,000	2,000,000	600,000
Totals	$10,000,000	$5,300,000	$4,000,000	$700,000

Hedgehog's president decides that, since the full cost of the Hedgehog Classic results in a loss, he should cancel that product. This results in the next table, where the same overhead is now being allocated (based on revenue) between the two remaining products.

Product	Revenue	Variable Costs	Overhead Costs	Margin
Hedgehog Mini	$3,000,000	$1,600,000	$1,500,000	-$100,000
Hedgehog Deluxe	5,000,000	2,400,000	2,500,000	100,000
Totals	$8,000,000	$4,000,000	$4,000,000	$0

Hedgehog's president now sees that the Hedgehog mini is losing money! Not knowing what else to do, he cancels that product, too. The result is shown in the next table:

Product	Revenue	Variable Costs	Overhead Costs	Margin
Hedgehog Deluxe	5,000,000	2,400,000	4,000,000	-$1,400,000
Totals	$5,000,000	$2,400,000	$4,000,000	-$1,400,000

Hedgehog's president gives up, closes down the company, and takes a cost accounting class to figure out what happened. He later learns that all three products were contributing toward the pool of overhead that needed to be paid for. As he successively stripped away each product, that left the remaining products to shoulder more of the overhead load. Eventually, the Hedgehog Deluxe was left, and it did not generate enough of a margin to pay for all of the overhead.

Comparison of Activity-Based Costing to Constraint Analysis

Another popular form of analysis is activity-based costing (ABC), which involves a detailed review of overhead costs, and the allocation of those costs. The process is described in some detail in the Activity-Based Costing chapter. How does ABC compare to constraint analysis?

The central difference between ABC and constraint analysis is that ABC does not recognize the existence of a bottleneck operation, preferring instead to focus management's attention on the reduction of overhead costs throughout a facility. Reducing costs is certainly a laudable goal, but costs can only be reduced so far. Constraint analysis, on the other hand, focuses on increasing throughput, and there is no upper limit on doing so. Since ABC does assist in achieving one of the three goals of constraint analysis (which are the improvement of throughput and return on investment, as well as cost reduction), it can be used in conjunction with constraint analysis. However, doing so can be confusing to employees, since constraint analysis essentially ignores the details of exactly what comprises overhead, while ABC dives into these details.

Summary

Constraint analysis is one of the primary tools of the cost accountant. It makes quite clear where the bottleneck operation is located, the extreme expense associated with not maximizing it, and how to manage operations to maximize profits. However, it can be a foreign concept to many managers, who have spent their careers working on local optimization issues, allocating overhead, and improving the efficiency of labor – all of which are concepts that constraint analysis teaches do not improve overall profitability.

Chapter 16
Capital Budgeting Analysis

Introduction

Capital budgeting is a series of analysis steps followed to justify the decision to purchase an asset, usually including an analysis of the costs, related benefits, and impact on capacity levels of the prospective purchase. The cost accountant may become involved in capital budgeting, especially if the fixed assets in question are intended for the production process, or if there is no financial analyst who would otherwise engage in this activity.

In this chapter, we will address a broad array of issues to consider when deciding whether to recommend the purchase of a fixed asset, including constraint analysis, the lease versus buy decision, and post-acquisition auditing.

Related Podcast Episodes: Episodes 45, 144, and 145 of the Accounting Best Practices Podcast discuss capital budgeting. They are available at: **accounting-tools.com/podcasts** or **iTunes**

Overview of Capital Budgeting

The normal capital budgeting process is for the management team to request proposals to acquire fixed assets from all parts of the company. Managers respond by filling out a standard request form, outlining what they want to buy and how it will benefit the company. The financial analyst or cost accountant then assists in reviewing these proposals to determine which are worthy of an investment. Any proposals that are accepted are included in the annual budget, and will be purchased during the next budget year. Fixed assets purchased in this manner also require a certain number of approvals, with more approvals required by increasingly senior levels of management if the sums involved are substantial.

These proposals come from all over the company, and so are likely not related to each other in any way. Also, the number of proposals usually far exceeds the amount of funding available. Consequently, management needs a method for ranking the priority of projects, with the possible result that some proposals are not accepted at all. The traditional method for doing so is net present value (NPV) analysis, which focuses on picking proposals with the largest amount of discounted cash flows.

The trouble with NPV analysis is that it does not account for how an investment might impact the profit generated by the entire system of production; instead, it tends to favor the optimization of specific work centers, which may have no particular impact on overall profitability. Also, the results of NPV are based on the future projections of cash flows, which may be wildly inaccurate. Managers may even tweak their cash flow estimates upward in order to gain project approval, when they know that actual cash flows are likely to be lower. Given these issues, we favor constraint analysis over NPV, though NPV is also discussed later in this chapter.

A better method for judging capital budget proposals is constraint analysis, which focuses on how to maximum use of the bottleneck operation. The bottleneck operation is the most constricted operation in a company; if the overall profitability of the firm is to be improved, then concentrate all attention on management of that bottleneck. This has a profound impact on capital budgeting, since a proposal should have some favorable impact on that operation in order to be approved. Additional aspects of the concept are discussed in the Constraint Analysis chapter.

There are two scenarios under which certain project proposals may avoid any kind of bottleneck or cash flow analysis. The first is a legal requirement to install an item. The prime example is environmental equipment, such as smokestack scrubbers, that are mandated by the government. In such cases, there may be some analysis to see if costs can be lowered, but the proposal *must* be accepted, so it will sidestep the normal analysis process.

The second scenario is when a company wants to mitigate a high-risk situation that could imperil the organization. In this case, the emphasis is not on profitability at all, but rather on the avoidance of a situation. If so, the mandate likely comes from top management, so there is little additional need for analysis, other than a review to ensure that the lowest-cost alternative is selected.

A final scenario is when there is a sudden need for a fixed asset, perhaps due to the catastrophic failure of existing equipment, or due to a sudden strategic shift. These purchases can happen at any time, and so usually fall outside of the capital budget's annual planning cycle. It is generally best to require more than the normal number of approvals for these items, so that management is made fully aware of the situation. Also, if there is time to do so, they are worthy of an unusually intense analysis, to see if they really must be purchased at once, or if they can be delayed until the next capital budgeting approval period arrives.

Once all items are properly approved and inserted into the annual budget, this does not end the capital budgeting process. There is a final review just prior to actually making each purchase, with appropriate approval, to ensure that the company still needs each fixed asset.

The last step in the capital budgeting process is to conduct a post-implementation review, in which the actual costs and benefits of each fixed asset are summarized and compared to the initial projections included in the original application. If the results are worse than expected, this may result in a more in-depth review, with particular attention being paid to avoiding any faulty aspects of the original proposal in future proposals.

Bottleneck Analysis

Under constraint analysis, the key concept is that an entire company acts as a single system, which generates a profit. Under this concept, capital budgeting revolves around the following logic:

1. Nearly all of the costs of the production system do not vary with individual sales; that is, nearly every cost is an operating expense; therefore,
2. It is necessary to maximize the throughput (revenues minus totally variable costs) of the *entire* system in order to pay for the operating expense; and
3. The only way to increase throughput is to maximize the throughput passing through the bottleneck operation.

Consequently, give primary consideration to those capital budgeting proposals that favorably impact the throughput passing through the bottleneck operation.

This does not mean that all other capital budgeting proposals will be rejected, since there are a multitude of possible investments that can reduce costs elsewhere in a company, and which are therefore worthy of consideration. However, throughput is more important than cost reduction, since throughput has no theoretical upper limit, whereas costs can only be reduced to zero. Given the greater ultimate impact on profits of throughput over cost reduction, any non-bottleneck proposal is simply not as important.

Net Present Value Analysis

Any capital investment involves an initial cash outflow to pay for it, followed by a mix of cash inflows in the form of revenue, or a decline in existing cash flows that are caused by expense reductions. We can lay out this information in a spreadsheet to show all expected cash flows over the useful life of an investment, and then apply a discount rate that reduces the cash flows to what they would be worth at the present date. A discount rate is the interest rate used to discount a stream of future cash flows to their present value. Depending upon the application, typical rates used as the discount rate are a firm's cost of capital or the current market rate.

This calculation is known as *net present value*. Net present value is the traditional approach to evaluating capital proposals, since it is based on a single factor – cash flows – that can be used to judge any proposal arriving from anywhere in a company.

EXAMPLE

Milford Sound, a manufacturer of audio equipment, is planning to acquire an asset that it expects will yield positive cash flows for the next five years. Its cost of capital is 10%, which it uses as the discount rate to construct the net present value of the project. The following table shows the calculation:

Year	Cash Flow	10% Discount Factor	Present Value
0	-$500,000	1.0000	-$500,000
1	+130,000	0.9091	+118,183
2	+130,000	0.8265	+107,445
3	+130,000	0.7513	+97,669
4	+130,000	0.6830	+88,790
5	+130,000	0.6209	+80,717
		Net Present Value	-$7,196

The net present value of the proposed project is negative at the 10% discount rate, so Milford should not invest in the project.

In the "10% Discount Factor" column, the factor becomes smaller for periods further in the future, because the discounted value of cash flows is reduced as they progress further from the present day. The discount factor is widely available in textbooks, or can be derived from the following formula:

$$\text{Present value of a future cash flow} = \frac{\text{Future cash flow}}{(1 + \text{Discount rate})^{\text{squared by the number of periods of discounting}}}$$

To use the formula for an example, if we forecast the receipt of $100,000 in one year, and are using a discount rate of 10 percent, the calculation is:

$$\text{Present value} = \frac{\$100,000}{(1+.10)^1}$$

Present value = $90,909

A net present value calculation that truly reflects the reality of cash flows will likely be more complex than the one shown in the preceding example. It is best to break down the analysis into a number of sub-categories, to see exactly when cash flows are occurring and with what activities they are associated. Here are the more common contents of a net present value analysis:

- *Asset purchases*. All of the expenditures associated with the purchase, delivery, installation, and testing of the asset being purchased.
- *Asset-linked expenses*. Any ongoing expenses, such as warranty agreements, property taxes, and maintenance, that are associated with the asset.
- *Contribution margin*. Any incremental cash flows resulting from sales that can be attributed to the project.
- *Depreciation effect*. The asset will be depreciated, and depreciation shelters a portion of any net income from income taxes, so note the tax reduction caused by depreciation.
- *Expense reductions*. Any incremental expense reductions caused by the project, such as automation that eliminates direct labor hours.
- *Tax credits*. If an asset purchase triggers a tax credit (such as a purchase of energy-reduction equipment), then note the credit.
- *Taxes*. Any income tax payments associated with net income expected to be derived from the asset.
- *Working capital changes*. Any net changes in inventory, accounts receivable, or accounts payable associated with the asset. Also, when the asset is eventually sold off, this may trigger a reversal of the initial working capital changes.

By itemizing the preceding factors in a net present value analysis, one can more easily review and revise individual line items.

We have given priority to bottleneck analysis over net present value as the preferred method for analyzing capital proposals, because bottleneck analysis focuses on throughput. As stated in the Constraint Analysis chapter, the key improvement factor is throughput, since there is no upper limit on the amount of throughput that can be generated, whereas there are only so many operating expenses that can be reduced. This does not mean that net present value should be eliminated as a management tool. It is still quite useful for operating expense reduction analysis, where throughput issues are not involved.

The Payback Method

The simplest and least accurate evaluation technique is the payback method. This approach is still heavily used, because it provides a very fast "back of the envelope" calculation of how soon a company will earn back its investment. This means that it provides a rough measure of how long a company will have its investment at risk before earning back the original amount expended. Thus, it is a rough measure of risk. There are two ways to calculate the payback period, which are:

1. *Simplified*. Divide the total amount of an investment by the average resulting cash flow. This approach can yield an incorrect assessment, because a proposal with cash flows skewed far into the future can yield a payback period that differs substantially from when actual payback occurs.

2. *Manual calculation.* Manually deduct the forecasted positive cash flows from the initial investment amount, from Year 1 forward, until the investment is paid back. This method is slower, but ensures a higher degree of accuracy.

EXAMPLE

Milford Sound has received a proposal from a manager, asking to spend $1,500,000 on equipment that will result in cash inflows in accordance with the following table:

Year	Cash Flow
1	+$150,000
2	+150,000
3	+200,000
4	+600,000
5	+900,000

The total cash flows over the five-year period are projected to be $2,000,000, which is an average of $400,000 per year. When divided into the $1,500,000 original investment, this results in a payback period of 3.75 years. However, the briefest perusal of the projected cash flows reveals that the flows are heavily weighted toward the far end of the time period, so the results of this calculation cannot be correct.

Instead, the cost accountant runs the calculation year by year, deducting the cash flows in each successive year from the remaining investment. The results of this calculation are:

Year	Cash Flow	Net Invested Cash
0		-$1,500,000
1	+$150,000	-1,350,000
2	+150,000	-1,200,000
3	+200,000	-1,000,000
4	+600,000	-400,000
5	+900,000	0

The table indicates that the real payback period is located somewhere between Year 4 and Year 5. There is $400,000 of investment yet to be paid back at the end of Year 4, and there is $900,000 of cash flow projected for Year 5. The cost accountant assumes the same monthly amount of cash flow in Year 5, which means that he can estimate final payback as being just short of 4.5 years.

The payback method is not overly accurate, does not provide any estimate of how profitable a project may be, and does not take account of the time value of money. Nonetheless, its extreme simplicity makes it a perennial favorite in many companies.

Accounting Rate of Return

The accounting rate of return is the ratio of an investment's average annual profits to the amount invested in it. If the outcome exceeds a threshold value, then an investment is approved. The formula for the accounting rate of return is:

$$\frac{\text{Average annual accounting profit}}{\text{Initial investment}}$$

- Where the profit is calculated as the profit related to a proposed investment using all accruals and non-cash expenses. If the project involves cost reduction instead of earning a profit, then the numerator is the amount of cost savings generated by the investment.
- Where the initial investment is calculated as the fixed asset investment plus any change in working capital caused by the investment.

The result of the calculation is expressed as a percentage. Thus, if a company projects that it will earn an average annual profit of $70,000 on an initial investment of $1,000,000, then the project has an accounting rate of return of 7%.

There are several serious problems with the accounting rate of return concept, which are:

- *Time value of money.* The measure does not factor in the time value of money. Thus, if there is currently a high market interest rate, the time value of money could completely offset any profit reported by a project - but the accounting rate of return does incorporate this factor, so it clearly overstates the profitability of proposed projects.
- *Cash flow.* The measure is derived from the accounting income of a business, rather than its cash flows. There can be a substantial difference between the two, which can result in unusual outcomes when compared to a discounted cash flow analysis.
- *Time-based risk.* There is no consideration of the increased risk in the variability of forecasts that arises over a long period of time.

In short, the accounting rate of return is not by any means a perfect method for evaluating a capital project, and so should be used (if at all) only in concert with a number of other evaluation tools. This measure would be of the most use for reviewing short-term investments where the impact of the time value of money is reduced.

Capital Budget Proposal Analysis

Reviewing a capital budget proposal does not necessarily mean passing judgment on it exactly as presented. A variety of suggestions can be attached to a proposal analysis, which management may incorporate into a revised proposal. Here are some examples:

- *Asset capacity*. Does the asset have more capacity than is actually needed under the circumstances? Is there a history of usage spikes that call for extra capacity? Depending on the answers to these questions, consider using smaller assets with less capacity. If the asset is powered, this may also lead to reductions in utility costs, installation costs, and floor space requirements.

- *Asset commoditization*. Wherever possible, avoid custom-designed machinery in favor of standard models that are readily available. By doing so, it is easier to obtain repair parts, and there may even be an aftermarket for disposing of the asset when the company no longer needs it.

- *Asset features*. Managers have a habit of wanting to buy new assets with all of the latest features. Are all of these features really needed? If an asset is being replaced, it is useful to compare the characteristics of the old and new assets, and examine any differences between the two to see if they are really needed. If the asset is the only model offered by the supplier, would the supplier be willing to strip away some features and offer it at a lower price?

- *Asset standardization*. If a company needs a particular asset in large quantities, adopt a policy of always buying from the same manufacturer, and preferably only buying the same asset every time. By doing so, the maintenance staff becomes extremely familiar with maintenance requirements, and only has to stock replacement parts for one model.

- *Bottleneck analysis*. As noted earlier in this chapter, assets that improve the amount of throughput in a production operation are usually well worth the investment, while those not impacting the bottleneck require substantially more justification, usually in the direction of reducing operating expenses.

- *Extended useful life*. A manager may be applying for an asset replacement simply because the original asset has reached the end of its recommended useful life. But is it really necessary to replace the asset? Consider conducting a formal review of these assets to see if they can still be used for some additional period of time. There may be additional maintenance costs involved, but this will almost certainly be lower than the cost of replacing the asset.

- *Facility analysis*. If a capital proposal involves the acquisition of additional facility space, consider reviewing any existing space to see if it can be compressed, thereby eliminating the need for more space. For example, shift storage items to less expensive warehouse space, shift from offices to more space-efficient cubicles, and encourage employees to work from home or on a later shift. If none of these ideas work, at least consider acquiring new facilities through a sublease, which tends to require shorter lease terms than a lease arranged with the primary landlord.

- *Monument elimination.* A company may have a large, fixed asset around which the rest of the production area is configured; this is called a monument. If there is a monument, consider adopting a policy of using a larger number of lower-capacity assets. By doing so, management can avoid the risk of having a single monument asset go out of service and stopping all production, in favor of having multiple units, among which work can be shifted if one unit fails.

The sponsors of capital proposals frequently do *not* appreciate this additional review of their proposals, since it implies that they did not consider these issues themselves. Nonetheless, the savings can be substantial, and so are well worth the aggravation of dealing with annoyed managers.

If the additional review indicates some promising alternatives that may substantially reduce the cost of a proposal, if not eliminate it entirely, it may be politically wise to route the proposed changes through the controller or chief financial officer, who may have the clout to force a serious review of the alternatives by the project sponsor.

The Outsourcing Decision

It may be possible to avoid a capital purchase entirely by outsourcing the work to which it is related. By doing so, the company may be able to eliminate all assets related to the area (rather than acquiring more assets), while the burden of maintaining a sufficient asset base now shifts to the supplier. The supplier may even buy the company's assets related to the area being outsourced. This situation is a well-established alternative for high technology manufacturing, as well as for information technology services, but is likely not viable outside of these areas.

If outsourcing is a possibility, the likely cash flows resulting from doing so will be highly favorable for the first few years, as capital expenditures vanish. However, the supplier must also earn a profit and pay for its own infrastructure, so the cost over the long term will probably not vary dramatically from what a company would have experienced if it had kept a functional area in-house. There are three exceptions that can bring about a long-term cost reduction. They are:

- *Excess capacity.* A supplier may have such a large amount of excess capacity already that it does not need to invest further for some time, thereby potentially depressing the costs that it would otherwise pass through to its customers. However, this excess capacity pool will eventually dry up, so it tends to be a short-term anomaly.
- *High volume.* There are some outsourcing situations where the supplier is handling such a massive volume of activity from multiple customers that its costs on a per-unit basis decline below the costs that a company could ever achieve on its own. This situation can yield long-term savings to a company.
- *Low costs.* A supplier may locate its facility and work force in low-cost countries or regions within countries. This can yield significant cost reductions in the short term, but as many suppliers use the same technique, it is

driving up costs in all parts of the world. Thus, this cost disparity is useful for a period of time, but is gradually declining as a long-term option.

There are risks involved in shifting functions to suppliers. First, a supplier may go out of business, leaving the company scrambling to shift work to a new supplier. Second, a supplier may gradually ramp up prices to the point where the company is substantially worse off than if it had kept the function in-house. Third, the company may have so completely purged the outsourced function from its own operations that it is now completely dependent on the supplier, and has no ability to take it back in-house. Fourth, the supplier's service level may decline to the point where it is impairing the ability of the company to operate. And finally, the company may have entered into a multi-year deal, and cannot escape from the contract if the business arrangement does not work out. These are significant issues, and must be weighed as part of the outsourcing decision.

The cautions noted here about outsourcing do not mean that it should be avoided as an option. On the contrary, a rapidly growing company that has minimal access to funds may cheerfully hand off multiple operations to suppliers in order to avoid the up-front costs associated with those operations. Outsourcing is less attractive to stable, well-established companies that have better access to capital.

In summary, outsourcing is an attractive option for rapidly growing companies that do not have sufficient cash to pay for capital expenditures, but also carries with it a variety of risks involving shifting key functions to a supplier over which a company may not have a great deal of control.

The Capital Budgeting Application Form

Most companies require managers to fill out a standardized form for all capital budgeting proposals. The type of information included in the form will vary, depending on whether the approval decision is being based on bottleneck considerations or the results of a net present value analysis. However, the header section of the form will likely be the same in all circumstances. It identifies the project, its sponsor, the date on which it was submitted, and a unique product identification number that is filled in by the recipient. A sample header is:

Sample Application Header

Project name:	50 Ton plastic injection molder		
Project sponsor:	E. R. Eddison		
Submission date:	May 28	Project number:	2011-14

If a proposal is for a legal requirement or a risk mitigation issue, it is absolved from most analysis, and will likely move to the top of the approved project list. Consequently, the form should contain a separate section for these types of projects, and involve a different set of approvers. The corporate attorney may be involved, as well as anyone involved in risk management. A sample block in the application form for legal and risk mitigation issues is:

Sample Legal and Risk Mitigation Block

		Required Approvals	
Initial cash flow:	-$250,000	All proposals	*Susan Lafferty*
Year 1 cash flow:	-10,000		Attorney
Year 2 cash flow:	-10,000		
Year 3 cash flow:	-10,000	< $100,000	*George Mason*
			Risk Officer
Describe legal or risk mitigation issue:			
Replanting of pine forest on southern property, with annual forestry review, per new zoning requirements		$100,000+	*Fred Scurry*
			President

If bottleneck considerations are the main focus of capital budgeting approvals, then include the following block of text in the application form. This block focuses on the changes in cash flow that are associated with a capital expenditure (which is a payment to acquire or upgrade an asset). The block requests an itemization of the cash flows involved in the purchase (primarily for finance planning considerations), followed by requests for information about how the investment will help the company – via an improvement in throughput, a reduction in operating costs, or an increase in the return on investment (the Constraint Analysis chapter explains these issues in more detail). In the example, note that the primary improvement used as the basis for the proposal is the improvement in throughput. This also leads to an enhancement of the return on investment. There is an increase in the total net operating cost, which represents a reduction in the positive effect of the throughput, and which is caused by the annual $8,000 maintenance cost associated with the investment.

The approvals for a bottleneck-related investment change from the ones shown previously for a legal or risk mitigation investment. In this case, a process analyst should verify the information include in the block, to ensure that the applicant's claims are correct. The supervisor in whose area of responsibility the investment falls should also sign off, thereby accepting responsibility for the outcome of the investment. A higher-level manager, or even the board of directors, should approve any really large investment proposals.

Sample Bottleneck Approval Block

			Required Approvals
Initial cash flow:	-$125,000	All proposals	*Monica Byers*
Year 1 cash flow:	-8,000		Process Analyst
Year 2 cash flow:	-8,000		
Year 3 cash flow:	-8,000	< $100,000	*Al Rogers*
			Responsible Supervisor
Net throughput change:*	+$180,000		
		$100,000+	*Fred Scurry*
Net operating cost change:*	+$8,000		President
Change in ROI:*	+0.08%		

* On an annual basis

If a bottleneck-oriented application is not employed, the following block may be useful in the application. It is based on the more traditional analysis of net present value. Also consider using this block as a supplement to the bottleneck block just noted, in case some managers prefer to work with both sets of information.

Sample Net Present Value Approval Block

Year	Cash Out (payments)	Cash In (Revenue)	Incremental Tax Effect	Totals
0	$1,000,000			-$1,000,000
1	-25,000	+$200,000	+$8,750	+183,750
2	-25,000	+400,000	-61,250	+313,750
3	-25,000	+400,000	-61,250	+313,750
4	-25,000	+400,000	-61,250	+313,750
5	-25,000	+400,000	-61,250	+313,750
Totals	-$1,125,000	+$1,800,000	-$236,250	+$438,750
			Tax Rate:	35%
			Hurdle Rate:	12%
			Net Present Value:	+$13,328

The net present value block requires the presentation of cash flows over a five-year period, as well as the net tax effect resulting from this specific transaction. The tax effect is based on $25,000 of maintenance expenses in every year shown, as well as $200,000 of annual depreciation, and a 35% incremental tax rate. Thus, in Year 2, there is $400,000 of revenue, less $225,000 of depreciation and maintenance expenses, multiplied by 35%, resulting in an incremental tax effect of $61,250.

The block goes on to state the corporate hurdle rate, which is 12% in the example. We then discount the stream of cash flows from the project at the hurdle rate of 12%, which results in a positive net present value of $13,328. Based on just the net present value analysis, this appears to be an acceptable project.

A variation on the rather involved text just shown is to shift the detailed cash flow analysis to a backup document, and only show the resulting net present value in the application form.

The text blocks shown here contain much of the key information that management should see before it decides whether to approve a capital investment. In addition, there should be a considerable amount of supporting information that precisely describes the nature of the proposed investment, as well as backup information that supports each number included in the form.

Capital Rationing

The typical organization only has a limited pool of funds available at any time for investments in fixed assets. The amount available is constrained by its ability to raise additional funds from a combination of borrowings and the sale of stock. The ability to raise funds may be tightly restricted for a number of reasons, such as:

- *Lending crisis*. There are periodic crises in the banking system, when lenders are more interested in calling existing loans than in extending new ones. In this environment, borrowed cash is essentially not available.
- *Historical results*. Even in a loose money environment, lenders may have no interest in lending money when a company has a history of inadequate financial results, since the risk of default is high.
- *Market feedback*. A company's entire industry may have fallen into disfavor with the investment community, so that the sale of stock can only be achieved at low multiples of sales or profits, which may significantly reduce the ownership percentages of existing shareholders.
- *Privately held*. A company may be owned by a small number of investors who are not interested in expanding the ownership to a new group of investors, which effectively cuts off equity as a source of funding.

Alternatively, there may be adequate funding, but the management team does not believe it has sufficient time to oversee more than a certain number of projects. Or, the owners of a business believe in maintaining a conservative debt level, and so will not take on additional debt, irrespective of the presence of tempting investment projects.

In these cases, management may have more qualified investment proposals than it can fund. If so, it must impose capital rationing, where it uses a special set of criteria to decide which proposals to accept. There are a number of ways in which to deal with this situation, which are:

- *Support strategic direction.* If management wants to re-orient the company in a specific direction, it can invest the bulk of available funds in this area, irrespective of the net present value or internal rate of return indicated for individual investment proposals. This places a focus on long-term outcomes, but tends to ignore high-return short-term projects.
- *Use highest outcomes.* If discounted cash flow analysis is being used, select those proposals having the highest net present value or internal rate of return. This approach results in "cherry picking" a selection of projects that yield the best return on investment, but which may not be coordinated from a strategic perspective. The discount rate can be increased in order to determine which investment proposals still have a positive net present value.
- *Bottleneck focus.* As noted in the Constraint Analysis chapter, management invests heavily in those parts of the business that support the functioning of the bottleneck operation, and de-emphasize all other investments.

The situation can become more complicated when outlays for certain projects will continue for several years, and capital rationing is ongoing through that period. In this case, an early investment can block later investments from being made because it is absorbing a large part of the available cash.

If management can reasonably predict the absolute amount of cash that will be available for investment in each of the next few years, it can be useful to feed this information back through the organization. Doing so may reorient the managers who usually submit investment proposals, so that they do not waste time creating proposals for marginal investments that will almost certainly not be approved, given the funding constraint.

Capital Budgeting with Minimal Cash

What if a company has very little money to spend on capital investments? If so, the capital budgeting choices may be entirely different. The primary target is to obtain the maximum return on investment as fast as possible, while spending a minimum amount of cash. Here are some options:

- *Repairs.* Evaluate the extent to which the lives of existing equipment can be prolonged, and see if there is old, unused equipment that can be brought back to workable condition with a modest investment in repairs. The cost of these repairs should be limited to a level well below the cost of investing in new equipment. The result may be equipment that is not overly efficient, but this is acceptable as long as the amount of funds invested is low.
- *Operating hours.* See if it is possible to extend the operating hours of the existing equipment. It may be much less expensive to have a few people work overtime or on an additional shift than to buy new equipment. The

result could be equipment that runs for all three shifts, though be aware that the cost of maintenance will increase when usage levels go up.

- *Outsource*. It may save cash to outsource work to a third party, even if the cost is higher on a per-unit basis than producing in-house. To keep options open for bringing work back to the company in the future, only sign short-term agreements to outsource work.
- *Buy used equipment*. Place a major emphasis on purchasing used equipment. The market prices of used equipment can be so much less than for new equipment that it may be worthwhile to institute a rule that new equipment can only be acquired with the prior approval of senior management. However, consider the availability of spare parts before acquiring older equipment. If parts are in short supply, it may be inordinately expensive to repair the equipment.
- *Lease assets*. Be sure to institute a lease versus buy analysis (see the Lease versus Buy Decision section). A lease may carry a relatively high implicit interest rate, but has the particular advantage of deferring the payment of cash to later periods.
- *Cash inflow analysis*. When cash is in short supply, only invest in equipment that will generate an immediate return. This means equipment that can produce verifiable cash flows within a few weeks is much better than equipment that is only intended to provide spare capacity, and which may not be needed immediately. Also, do not acquire equipment for which the associated cash inflows are speculative.

In short, being in survival mode changes the orientation of the capital budgeting process to one where the intent is to get by with what is available, scrounge for used equipment, and only invest when the offsetting cash inflows are certain. With the orientation on day-to-day survival, there is no long-term analysis of return on investment. Instead, this is a rare case where the much-maligned payback method (as described earlier) could be a useful tool, since its focus is on the amount of time required to pay back the initial investment.

There are some issues with the recommendations noted here. First, older equipment is likely to be less efficient, and may require additional maintenance time. Also, the result could be a clutter of equipment that does not work together very well. These points are acceptable in the short term, but should be addressed over the long term, assuming the company has emerged from its cash-poor situation and can afford better equipment.

The Post Installation Review

It is very important to conduct a post installation review of any capital expenditure project, to see if the initial expectations for it were realized. If not, the results of this review can be used to modify the capital budgeting process to include better information.

Another reason for having a post installation review is that it provides a control over those managers who fill out the initial capital budgeting proposals. If they know there is no post installation review, they can wildly overstate the projected results of their projects with impunity, just to have them approved. Of course, this control is only useful if it is conducted relatively soon after a project is completed. Otherwise, the responsible manager may have moved on in his career, and can no longer be tied back to the results of his work.

It is even better to begin a post installation review while a project is still being implemented, and especially when the implementation period is expected to be long. This initial review gives senior management a good idea of whether the cost of a project is staying close to its initial expectations. If not, management may need to authorize more vigorous management of the project, scale it back, or even cancel it outright.

If the post implementation review results in the suspicion that a project proposal was unduly optimistic, this brings up the question of how to deal with the responsible manager. At a minimum, the proposal reviews can flag any future proposals by this reviewer as suspect, and worthy of especially close attention. Another option is to tie long-term compensation to the results of these projects. A third possibility is to include the results of these project reviews in personnel reviews, which may lead to a reduction in employee compensation. A really catastrophic result may even be grounds for the termination of the responsible party.

EXAMPLE

Milford Sound has just completed a one-year project to increase the amount of production capacity at its speaker production work center. The original capital budgeting proposal was for an initial expenditure of $290,000, resulting in additional annual throughput of $100,000 per year. The actual result is somewhat different. The cost accountant's report includes the following text:

> **Findings:** The proposal only contained the purchase price of the equipment. However, since the machinery was delivered from Germany, Milford also incurred $22,000 of freight charges and $3,000 in customs fees. Further, the project required the installation of a new concrete pad, a breaker box, and electrical wiring that cost an additional $10,000. Finally, the equipment proved to be difficult to configure, and required $20,000 of consulting fees from the manufacturer, as well as $5,000 for the materials scrapped during testing. Thus, the actual cost of the project was $350,000.

> Subsequent operation of the equipment reveals that it cannot operate without an average of 20% downtime for maintenance, as opposed to the 5% downtime that was advertised by the manufacturer. This reduces throughput by 15%, which equates to a drop of $15,000 in throughput per year, to $85,000.

> **Recommendations:** To incorporate a more comprehensive set of instructions into the capital budgeting proposal process to account for transportation, setup, and testing costs. Also, given the wide difference between the performance claims of the

manufacturer and actual results, to hire a consultant to see if the problem is caused by our installation of the equipment; if not, we recommend not buying from this supplier in the future.

The Lease versus Buy Decision

Once the asset acquisition decision has been made, management still needs to decide if it should buy the asset outright, or lease it. In a leasing situation, a lessor buys the asset and then allows the lessee to use it in exchange for a monthly fee. Depending on the terms of the lease, it may be treated in one of two ways:

- *Capital lease*. The lessee records the leased asset on its books as a fixed asset and depreciates it, while recording interest expense separately.
- *Operating lease*. The lessor records the leased asset on its books as a fixed asset and depreciates it, while the lessee simply records a lease payment.

The decision to use a lease may be based on management's unwillingness to use its line of credit or other available sources of financing to buy an asset. Leases can be easier to obtain that a line of credit, since the lease agreement always designates the asset as collateral. Collateral is an asset that a borrower has pledged as security for a loan. The lender has the legal right to seize and sell the asset if the borrower is unable to pay back the loan by an agreed date.

There are a multitude of factors that a lessor includes in the formulation of the monthly rate that it charges, such as the down payment, the residual value of the asset at the end of the lease, and the interest rate, which makes it difficult to break out and examine each element of the lease. Instead, it is much easier to create separate net present value tables for the lease and buy alternatives, and then compare the results of the two tables to see which is the better alternative.

EXAMPLE

Milford Sound is contemplating the purchase of an asset for $500,000. It can buy the asset outright, or do so with a lease. Its cost of capital is 8%, and its incremental income tax rate is 35%. The following two tables show the net present values of both options.

Buy Option

Year	Depreciation	Income Tax Savings (35%)	Discount Factor (8%)	Net Present Value
0				-$500,000
1	$100,000	$35,000	0.9259	32,407
2	100,000	35,000	0.8573	30,006
3	100,000	35,000	0.7938	27,783
4	100,000	35,000	0.7350	25,725
5	100,000	35,000	0.6806	23,821
Totals	$500,000	$175,000		$360,258

Lease Option

Year	Pretax Lease Payments	Income Tax Savings (35%)	After-Tax Lease Cost	Discount Factor (8%)	Net Present Value
1	$135,000	47,250	$87,750	0.9259	$81,248
2	135,000	47,250	87,750	0.8573	75,228
3	135,000	47,250	87,750	0.7938	69,656
4	135,000	47,250	87,750	0.7350	64,496
5	135,000	47,250	87,750	0.6806	59,723
Totals	$675,000	$236,250	$438,750		$350,351

Thus, the net purchase cost of the buy option is $360,258, while the net purchase cost of the lease option is $350,351. The lease option involves the lowest cash outflow for Milford, and so is the better option.

Summary

This chapter addressed a variety of issues to consider when deciding whether to recommend the purchase of a fixed asset. We put less emphasis on net present value analysis, which has been the primary capital budgeting tool in industry for years, because it does not take into consideration the impact on throughput of a company's bottleneck operation. The best capital budgeting analysis process is to give top priority to project proposals that have a strong favorable impact on throughput, and then use net present value to evaluate the impact of any remaining projects on cost reduction.

Chapter 17
Cost Collection Systems

Introduction

Cost accounting involves a variety of analyses that require information not contained in the classic source of accounting information – the general ledger. The general ledger is the master set of accounts that summarize all financial transactions in a business. Though the general ledger is a source of information, the cost accountant needs a great deal of additional information from other sources, such as the exact contents of products, the amount of labor used to provide a service, the capacity utilization of equipment, and so forth. To provide effective advice to management, the accountant needs cost-effective methods for collecting this broad array of information, while also ensuring its accuracy. This chapter describes the characteristics of a variety of data collection systems.

Before we enter into a discussion of the merits of individual data collection systems, we first address the problem of data entry accuracy, which can seriously impact the quality of information that is available for analysis.

Data Entry Accuracy

If any data is manually keyed into a database, there is a high probability that a noticeable proportion of the information entered will be wrong, no matter how qualified the data entry person may be. The best way to avoid this data entry error problem is to not use manual entry at all. Here are several examples of automated systems:

- *Bar coding.* A bar code label contains a standardized block of information that an employee or a machine can scan with a laser scanner. The scan automatically transfers the information encoded in the bar code to a computer system, thereby avoiding the risk of data entry error.
- *Document imaging.* A computer can scan documents, extract their contents, and store the results in a database. There is a risk of incorrect content extraction, but more sophisticated systems are quite accurate.
- *Electronic data interchange (EDI).* Electronic data interchange is the electronic transfer of business transactions between companies, using a standardized set of electronic forms. The data entry system can accept EDI transactions from business partners, which can be imported automatically into the cost accounting database. Since this information has presumably already been reviewed and corrected by the business parties, it should have a higher accuracy rate than manually entered data.
- *Radio frequency identification (RFID).* A radio frequency identification tag contains encoded information that it transmits by radio signal. A properly

configured receiver collects this information and transfers it to a computer system.

Of the forms of automated data entry just noted, bar coding is by far the best established and most commonly used. RFID is much newer technology and so far is only used by a small number of companies. Document imaging is well-established, but its cost and conversion requirements have not resulted in broad acceptance. All three are explained in greater detail in the following sections.

Data Entry with Bar Codes

Bar coding is especially useful for applications that require very high levels of data accuracy for transactions that occur in large volumes. It involves encoding a string of either numeric or alphanumeric data in a bar code; when scanned, a computer accesses the file containing the information in the bar code, and calls up the information linked to the bar coded string, such as a product description and price. A two-dimensional bar code contains a complete set of information, and so requires no link to a computer database to extract additional information. For example, a single two-dimensional bar code can include not only a product's part number, but also the related production date, batch number, unit of measure, and quantity.

Bar coding receives very heavy usage in the warehouse and production areas, where bar codes track inventory items as they move in and out of various storage locations and through the manufacturing process. It is also common to affix bar code labels to fixed assets, for use in periodic fixed asset audits. Another application is to paste bar codes onto employee badges, which they can then swipe through computerized time clocks to track their hours worked.

EXAMPLE

Hammer Industries has a large work force that produces exercise equipment for commercial gyms. The cost accountant asks the production manager to have the production staff write down their hours worked on each production job for the month of March, so that he can complete an activity-based costing project involving labor usage.

The identification number of each job is a string of 12 random numbers and letters. The production staff writes down the job numbers on a tracking sheet, along with their hours worked, and submits the sheets to a data entry person who re-enters the information into a cost accounting database. The results are completely unusable, because the 12-digit codes were frequently written down incorrectly by the production staff, and then incorrectly entered by the data entry person.

The cost accountant commissions a programming project to create a data entry screen that the production staff can use at their work stations. The project also involves bar coding all of the job numbers, and placing a bar code scanner at each work station. Employees now scan the job numbers, and enter their hours worked with a keypad. There is no longer a data entry person, since the production staff is entering their information directly into the database.

The result is much more accurate data. The cost accountant receives permission to use the new system in May, and successfully collects the information that he needs.

Different types of bar codes are used in different situations. The most common bar coding formats are:

- *Code 39*. Contains alphanumeric characters, and is used most prominently in manufacturing.
- *Interleaved 2 of 5*. Contains only numeric characters, and is used most prominently in the warehousing and automotive sectors.
- *Universal Product Code (UPC)*. Contains only numeric characters, and is used heavily in the retailing industry.

Two-dimensional bar codes contain information that is either "stacked" (two linear bar codes laid one over the other) or "matrix," which is laid out in a pattern of cells. Two-dimensional codes can be extremely small, and so are ideal for use in small products, such as hand-held electronics. Two-dimensional codes are designed to be highly redundant, so that it is still possible to extract a complete set of information from a damaged bar code.

Bar codes can be printed by a third party in high-resolution format and delivered to a company for application to various documents or products. It is also possible to purchase bar code printing software, and then print the bar codes from a local computer and printer. Bar codes must be printed with high resolution, or the data encoded into them cannot be scanned. Consequently, if they are printed on-site, only use a laser printer or high-quality ink jet printer to do so. If a bar code is being attached to a fixed object for repeated scans over time (as would be the case with a location bar code in the warehouse), test how many layers of tape or laminate can be laid over the bar code before a scanner can no longer interpret its contents. Otherwise, employees may spend a great deal of time installing a large number of sturdy laminated bar codes, only to find that scanners do not detect them.

Once the bar codes are in place, the following options are available for scanning them, listed in order of most common usage:

- *Hand-held scanner with direct computer link*. This scanner is attached to a local computer or terminal and is used by employees to scan documents and products. This scanner is heavily used in a retail check-out area. The scanner includes a motor that makes many rapid laser scans across a bar code, there-by improving the odds of success in reading it.
- *Hand-held scanner with radio link*. This scanner has the same functionality as a hand-held scanner with a direct computer link, except that it can be used in a mobile capacity. This usually means that the scanner is still within a facility, such as in the warehouse or production areas, where the scanners can not only upload scans to a local server in real time, but also accept information back. These scanners contain portable power units, radio equipment, and considerable shock mounting, and so are more expensive than other scanner models.

- *Stationary scanner*. This scanner is designed for an automated materials handling environment, where materials are moved past the scanner. The scanner usually has multiple motorized laser scans, which examine materials from all possible angles. If it cannot obtain a scan, it automatically directs the item being examined through a shunting gate, so that it can be manually inspected. This is an expensive solution.
- *Light pen*. This scanner contains a single fixed laser beam, which results in a much lower level of scanning success. Conversely, it is by far the least expensive scanning alternative available. It is older technology, and is being supplanted by the other scanners already mentioned.

If two-dimensional bar codes will be used, then imaging technology is used instead of laser scanners. Imagers require special lighting and label materials to operate properly.

The main issue preventing bar coding from even more widespread distribution is that it requires a moderate amount of preparation to create individual bar codes. This makes it difficult to incorporate the labels into short-duration processes.

Data Entry with Radio Frequency Identification (RFID)

RFID tags are most useful for applications where location information is collected about an object as it moves through a facility; doing so by hand is cost-prohibitive and highly subject to error, whereas a radio collection device situated at a travel bottleneck can easily collect this information with perfect accuracy from objects as they pass by it. RFID technology does not require line-of-sight access to a tag, which is an improvement over bar codes. Also, since there is no manual data entry, the overall velocity of a process can be greatly increased.

EXAMPLE

Hammer Industries has recently eliminated the majority of its receiving functions, in favor of having suppliers deliver components directly to its production lines. The trouble is that suppliers are complaining that Hammer is short-paying them for goods delivered. To verify their deliveries, Hammer installs stationary scanners at the end of each production line that automatically count all completed finished goods, and uses backflushing to determine the amounts of raw materials that must have been used to complete those goods.

This new system provides evidence for the amounts paid to suppliers, though it does not account for any leakage from the production system, as may be caused by raw materials removed due to scrap, spoilage, or rework.

The preceding example noted the use of backflushing. This involves counting finished goods and then breaking down the components of those finished goods, based on bills of material, to determine what raw materials were used in their manufacture. This is a way to record the transfer of raw materials to finished goods after production has taken place.

There are two types of RFID tags. *Passive tags* are the most common, and contain no power source. Instead, they draw power from a reader, though they can only do this at very short distances. These tags are attached to whatever object is being tracked. Readers are positioned wherever management wants to collect information, and they emit an electromagnetic field that activates tags as they pass by. The tags then transmit information to the reader. The advantage of passive tags is their extremely low cost, so they can be used in many applications, such as inventory control and theft prevention.

Active tags contain a power source, and so are able to transmit information to readers located much further away. Given their higher cost, active tags have found limited application, usually for the tracking of fixed assets (or not-so-fixed assets, such as rail cars).

Document Imaging

A well-established company has probably accumulated a large amount of paperwork that describes any number of transactions over the preceding years. This may involve a large amount of storage space, and represents a great deal of search time if anyone wants to locate a specific document. It is possible to eliminate virtually all of this paperwork by converting it to a digital image and storing it on a server. By doing so, the information becomes searchable through an index, cannot be lost, can be accessed by multiple people at the same time, and eliminates travel time to and from the document storage area. Clearly, there are many advantages to using document imaging.

The basic conversion process with a document imaging system is to use a digital scanner to convert a document to a digital image, identify it with an index code, and store it in a server. Users then access the document imaging system through their computers. The primary search tool is the index code that was originally used to identify the document, but it is also possible to search the PDF formats into which many of the documents were converted. Another option is to use image recognition software to convert the documents into more readable text.

The cost accountant uses a document imaging system to research source documents in a variety of areas, such as:

- Employee time cards
- Purchase orders
- Purchase requisitions
- Receiving logs
- Supplier invoices

All of these documents contain information that may be needed for a variety of cost analyses. To understand how best to store these documents for later research purposes, the accountant must understand the drill down system employed by most accounting systems. The typical accounting research begins in the general ledger, where all accounting transactions are stored by small businesses, and where summary-level transaction information is stored by larger businesses. The researcher then accesses the specific transaction needed, either within the general ledger or by drilling down to a subsidiary ledger, and then views a digitized document that is attached to that transaction. To make this drill down search work properly, a company needs to link digital documents to accounting transactions, which can be quite labor intensive. On the other hand, it makes research incredibly easy. To see if this type of digital document storage makes sense, evaluate the number of searches that are likely to occur for a specific type of document, and whether the cost of scanning and linking those documents to the accounting system will make searches more cost-effective.

EXAMPLE

Hammer Industries operates in a market where material costs are constantly fluctuating, so management decides to alter the standard costs in its item master file every three months, to keep them as close to actual costs as possible. The cost accountant is asked to research these cost changes and coordinate the standard cost updates. The trouble is that the accounting system only records total costs billed by suppliers, not the unit costs charged for each line item within each supplier invoice. Thus, to collect the unit cost information for commodities, he needs to access the original supplier invoices. Currently, this means looking up invoices in the accounting department's filing cabinets and pending payment files.

This appears to be a good application for document imaging, since there is a continuing need for access to a specific document type. He presents the case that he needs to access 250 supplier invoices every three months, which is 1,000 invoices over a one-year period. He can spend 50% of his time each year finding invoices, copying out information from them, and returning them to their storage locations, versus 20% of his time on pure cost research if he can drill down to the documents in the accounting system. His fully burdened cost is $75,000 per year. Thus, the cost of locating the supplier invoices is $22,500 ($75,000 annual cost × 30%).

The accounts payable manager calculates that incorporating a document scan into the accounts payable process will add 30% of the time of a payables clerk, whose annual fully burdened cost is $35,000. Thus, the cost of digitizing the needed information is $10,500 ($35,000 annual cost × 30%).

The controller decides to proceed with the project, since it frees up 30% of the cost accountant's time for other projects, and it digitizes information that may also be useful for other employee research projects, as well. The project does not directly save any money, since the cost accountant is still going to be paid a salary, irrespective of the tasks that he is working on.

As just noted in the example, it can make more sense to very selectively determine which documents are most likely to be accessed on an ongoing basis and in high volume, and just use document imaging on those documents. If *all* transaction-related documents in a company are to be digitized, the cost of doing so may be too great in comparison to the benefits to be gained. A good option is to adopt document imaging for a small pilot project, and then roll it out to additional areas if there is a definitive need for it. The likely result will not be a full implementation of document imaging, but it will be available where it is most needed.

The reason for a selective implementation is the cost of a comprehensive installation. Document imaging for a large company can easily cost more than $1 million just for the computer hardware and software, but if small systems are installed for very select purposes, the cost may only be a few thousand dollars. Hardware costs can be substantial if there are tens or hundreds of thousands of documents to be stored, but storage costs are always declining, so this issue will be of less importance over time. The real problem is the cost of scanning and indexing labor, which can call into question the need to digitize historical documents that are rarely accessed – in brief, the total cost of scanning labor is much higher than the total cost of research labor saved, which makes document imaging a more defensible project if historical documents are left alone and efforts are concentrated on scanning documents on a go-forward basis.

Special Considerations for Labor Tracking

The tracking of labor costs presents a special problem for the cost accountant, because labor can be quite a small proportion of total company costs, but is frequently the most expensive type of cost to track, because each employee may work on a variety of different activities or jobs that may be relevant to a costing study. Thus, a key decision is whether it is worthwhile to incur the cost of a full labor tracking study, or to ignore this costing element entirely. Here are several additional considerations:

- *Company profitability.* If the company competes in an industry with razor-thin margins, it may be necessary to track *everything* in order to monitor costs, and that includes labor.
- *Type of labor.* If there are a large number of employees who bill their time directly to customers (such as consultants and attorneys), there must be a labor tracking system in order to create billings.
- *Asset base.* If the asset base that a company uses to generate sales is large (such as an oil refinery), the prime driver of profitability is really the ability to generate sufficient sales to pay for that large pool of overhead; if revenues are too low, the business will lose money, irrespective of the efficiency of its employees. Thus, a large asset base equates to less need for labor tracking.

If the situation absolutely requires the use of labor tracking, install the least complicated and least expensive system that intrudes upon employees the least – think minimalist when setting up a labor tracking system. Here are several possible alternatives that have different costs, input requirements, and accuracy levels:

1. *Track by exception.* If employees work on the same tasks every day, there is no need to track the fact that nothing is changing. Instead, only ask employees to report on changes in their normal routines. The cost accountant then

assumes that employees work a standard day on the same tasks, unless notified otherwise. This approach works well in an environment where there is a high proportion of administrative employees.

2. *Time cards*. Employees fill out time cards that are approved by their supervisors (for overtime authorizations) and forwarded to a data entry person who enters the information into the payroll system. From the cost accountant's perspective, time cards are only relevant if they also contain activities or jobs that employees worked on. These documents interfere with employees a great deal, and tend to be inaccurate.

3. *Phone entry*. Many smart phones include data entry templates for time keeping. This is extremely useful for employees who are billing their time to customers, and who are away from the office (such as consultants).

4. *Internet data entry*. There are many commercial off-the-shelf applications available that allow employees to access a website and enter their time worked. The company pays a monthly fee for access to this service, which usually allows a download of information into the company's computer system. This approach avoids having to create an in-house software application that requires ongoing maintenance. However, if Internet access goes down, employee access to the system stops.

5. *Computer time clock*. There are a variety of time clocks available that connect to a computer. Employees swipe badges through a reader to record their time, and can enter additional cost accounting information on a keypad. These devices can be very expensive if rolled out in large numbers, but reduce employee timekeeping activities, and create very accurate cost information. They also introduce a number of controls over when employees are allowed to clock in and out, and the costing information that they can enter. Finally, they eliminate any manual rekeying of data, which improves accuracy levels.

Another consideration is the type of labor-related information to be collected. Here are the types of information, and the issues related to each one:

1. *Name*. The employee name is needed if cost information is being compiled, since the payroll system will use the employee name to derive each person's pay rate. If cost information is not being collected, such as when a labor routing is being verified, this information is not needed.

2. *Date*. The date is mostly needed to compile payroll information, and so may not be needed for other types of cost studies.

3. *Time worked*. This is the primary information item needed for almost all labor cost studies, usually combined with one or more of the following items.

4. *Job worked*. The identification number on which time is applied is key for recording information in a job costing system (see the Job Costing chapter). However, this may also increase the amount of record keeping by an order of magnitude. For example, an employee who only records his hours worked

per shift will record his hours once a day, but if he works on ten jobs during that time, he is now recording the time and job ten times during the day.

5. *Task worked.* A task is a subset of a job. There may be many tasks within a job, so the level of recordkeeping may become overwhelming if employees are involved in many tasks. Consequently, keep the number of task codes to be tracked to a minimum.

6. *Activity worked.* This information is usually compiled for an activity-based costing project (see the Activity-Based Costing chapter). It is very detailed, and is best compiled on a project basis, rather than continually, since recording it intrudes considerably on employee time.

In short, the amount of labor required to record employee time expands as more in-depth information is collected. Simply collecting hours per day for each employee requires a single record, while recording tasks worked within a job could yield several dozen entries per day for each employee. The latter situation wastes a great deal of employee time, so only collect labor cost information at the most minimal level possible. Ideally, labor cost collection on an ongoing basis should be as close to unnoticeable as possible for employees; if really in-depth information is needed, try to collect it only on a project basis, so that the level of intrusiveness is only for a short period of time.

EXAMPLE

Hammer Industries has a facility in San Jose that manufactures a high-end line of customized gym equipment for home use. Customers can have equipment modified to suit their specific heights and frame sizes. During a study to compare of the costs to operate each of its facilities, the controller discovers that the San Jose facility has an unusually unproductive direct labor force. He sends the cost accountant, Mr. Dunworthy, to investigate.

Mr. Dunworthy conducts a study to see what activities the employees are engaged in during a typical day. He notes that each product stays in one work center until it is moved to the paint shop at the end of the production process. The employees, who are specialists, move between the work centers to work on multiple products in a typical day. One item of note is their elaborate timekeeping system. Since the products are customized, the facility controller wants to track the cost accumulated by each product, so that the company can appropriately price various forms of customization and still be assured of making a profit. Consequently, the employees are required to track the amount of time spent on each job, as well as the work done on each product.

A sample timesheet is:

Name: Arnie Hilpers			
Date: August 19			
Time In	Time Out	Job No.	Task
8:00	8:50	05109	Standard pulley install
8:51	9:25	05092	Standard pulley install
9:26	10:10	05173	Standard pulley install
10:11	11:30	05201	Custom pulley wiring
11:31	12:30	Lunch Break	N/A
12:31	1:50	05089	Standard pulley install
1:51	2:40	05100	Standard pulley install
2:41	3:18	05150	Custom pulley wiring
3:19	5:00	05176	Standard pulley install

Mr. Dunworthy notes that, of the eight jobs that Arnie Hilpers worked on during the day in question, only two of the jobs involve custom work. The other six jobs all involve standard installations. A further perusal of time sheets indicates that this proportion of custom work is typical.

There are numerous costs associated with this timekeeping system, such as employee time to fill out the forms, data entry time to record the timesheets in the cost accounting database, and yet more time to track down and correct errors. The primary cost is the time needed by employees to fill out their timesheets, which Mr. Dunworthy estimates to be ten minutes per day. At a fully burdened cost of $21.00 per hour, this means the 100 direct labor employees cost $350 per day to record their time ($1/6^{th}$ hour × $21.00 × 100 employees). Over the facility's standard 250-day work year, this amounts to $87,500. Also, one-half of an accounting clerk's time is needed to record these timesheets in the cost accounting system, which costs another $12,500 per year. Thus, the timesheet system is costing the facility $100,000 per year.

This is clearly an expensive system, and the only way to justify it is by locating an offsetting amount of benefits from its use. Accordingly, Mr. Dunworthy requests a copy of the variance reports for each job, to see how far off the actual cost of the jobs are from the costs calculated by the company's quoting system. The reports show the following distribution:

Number of Jobs	Variance From Quote	Dollar Variance
5	Under more than 10%	-$8,417
12	Under 2% to 10%	-5,417
82	Within 2%	4,917
19	Over 2% to 10%	19,119
4	Over more than 10%	29,053
122		$39,255

The distribution shows that the quoting is quite accurate, with only a small number of jobs requiring a significant amount of additional labor. Even if the quoting system were absolutely accurate, it would only eliminate a total variance of $39,255, which is far less than the total timekeeping cost of $100,000.

Mr. Dunworthy recommends that the quoting system be spot-checked on an annual basis to see if the costs it uses are still accurate, rather than using the current, overly-detailed time reporting system. The facility subsequently converts to computerized time clocks that only track hours per day for each employee.

The Duration of Cost Collection

The duration of cost collection has a major impact on what type of collection system the cost accountant should use. There are a great many cost-related projects that are only needed for a single report, or perhaps a time-series analysis that will only last for a few months. In these situations, it is probably quite cost-effective to use manual data collection on a sample basis, since the information is only to be collected once, or just a few times. Conversely, if management believes there is value in collecting cost information over the long term, eliminate manual data collection in favor of much more industrial applications that use automation to reduce costs to the greatest extent possible.

There are two sub-issues within the general topic of cost collection duration that are of concern. They are:

- *Project inertia.* Some cost accounting projects take on a life of their own, so that what was supposed to be a one-month project becomes a multi-year endeavor through sheer inertia – no one took the time to stop the project. Thus, the issue is not whether the company should expend funds on an au-tomated data collection system, but rather whether the project for which the data is being collected should be shut down.
- *Declining results.* Management may have authorized ongoing data collec-tion, because it found real value in the ongoing monitoring of a specific item, such as employee overtime. However, it is quite rare to experience continuing cost reductions by collecting cost information over a very long period of time. Instead, there are usually large favorable results clustered

near the beginning of a project, after which improvements decline rapidly. At some point, the cost of data collection is probably higher than the supposed benefits. At this point, it makes more sense to eliminate the data collection activity entirely, and substitute a periodic audit to see if performance results are backsliding from their previous levels.

In short, place an emphasis on avoiding long-term data collection wherever possible. In most cases, a brief period of data collection is all that is needed, and only on a sample basis. Over the long term, a simple audit is usually sufficient to detect problems. Only install highly automated data collection systems where there is a strong need to maintain comprehensive monitoring of transactions. The main driver in this decision is the duration of cost collection.

The Chart of Accounts

The chart of accounts is a listing of all the accounts used in the general ledger. The account numbering system is used by the accounting software to aggregate information into an entity's financial statements. The accountant may elect to store some of the costing information in general ledger accounts, in which case an account code structure and accounts are needed to best suit the situation.

The Account Code Structure

When creating a chart of accounts for cost accounting purposes, the first issue to consider is the account code structure. At the lowest level, a three-digit code could be used, which is commonly employed when management only wants to track specific types of expenses. An example is:

Account Number	Account Description
400	Benefits expense
410	Rent expense
420	Utilities expense
430	Wage expense

The ten-digit gaps in the account numbers in the preceding example set aside enough room to add additional accounts later on, as needed.

The next level of complexity is to track transactions at the departmental level. Doing so allows for the creation of reports that aggregate costs by individual department, which is invaluable for any company structured with multiple departments. The chart of accounts requires at least an additional two digits to identify departments, while also tracking the three-digit expenses already noted. An example is:

Account Number	Department	Account Description
30-400	Production	Benefits expense
30-410	Production	Rent expense
30-420	Production	Utilities expense
30-430	Production	Wage expense
40-400	Sales	Benefits expense
40-410	Sales	Rent expense
40-420	Sales	Utilities expense
40-430	Sales	Wage expense

The preceding example shows that we have doubled the number of accounts in order to record information separately for two departments. The same approach can be used if there are multiple company locations, with departments contained within each one. This chart of accounts requires at least two more digits to identify the locations, while also tracking the departments and expenses already noted. For example:

Account Number	Location	Department	Account Description
10-30-400	San Jose	Production	Benefits expense
10-30-410	San Jose	Production	Rent expense
10-30-420	San Jose	Production	Utilities expense
10-30-430	San Jose	Production	Wage expense
10-40-400	San Jose	Sales	Benefits expense
10-40-410	San Jose	Sales	Rent expense
10-40-420	San Jose	Sales	Utilities expense
10-40-430	San Jose	Sales	Wage expense

The longer account code structures are certainly capable of compartmentalizing a great deal of financial information, but they are also more difficult to keypunch into the accounting system, which results in more transaction errors. Consequently, choosing the correct account code structure involves a balance of segregating the information that a company really needs in order to operate, while keeping the account code structure simple enough to be usable. For most companies having a single location, the XX-XXX coding structure for departments and accounts is recommended; it is simple, and segregates information at an adequate level.

The Account Code Format

The commentary thus far about the chart of accounts has been at a general level, and may not pertain directly to the cost accountant's work. However, the following points about the account code format directly relate to storing cost accounting information:

- *Work centers.* It may be necessary to accumulate cost information at the work center level, and usually within the production department. If so, there needs to be a gap in the department account numbering between the production department code and the next department's code. By doing so, codes can be inserted for each work center within the production department. The contents of these work centers then roll up into the production department when the accounting system aggregates information for the financial statements. A sample coding structure for these work centers is:

Account Code	Department Description
XX-30-XXX	Production
XX-31-XXX	Cooker line
XX-32-XXX	Extrusion line
XX-33-XXX	Wrapper line
XX-34-XXX	Bagging
XX-35-XXX	Packaging
XX-40-XXX	Sales

- *Fixed and variable costs.* If reports will be generated that differentiate between fixed and variable costs, it may be necessary to create accounts that identify them as such, which is easy enough – just state whether they are fixed or variable in the account description field. However, if information for a single expense will be separated into its fixed and variable components, keep in mind that the accounts payable employees who enter this information from supplier invoices will have a hard time figuring out which accounts to use. Thus, splitting the same expense into fixed and variable components is not recommended. Instead, do this on a project basis, and do not attempt to store the information in the general ledger.
- *Government reporting.* If a company sells to a government entity, there is a good chance that the government will require extremely detailed cost tracking on an individual project basis. If so, create these accounts within the main accounting system, but be aware that there will eventually be many accounts. If the company plans to do a great deal of such business over the

long term, consider buying specialized government accounting software that has the capability to deal with these coding requirements.

It is also entirely possible that there is no need to store cost information in general ledger accounts. The general ledger is designed for the storage of financial information over long periods of time, so if cost information is to be accumulated for a short project, it would be better to do so either manually or in a separate database. Otherwise, the chart of accounts will contain a large number of accounts that were only used for a short time and then abandoned.

Accounts for the Cost Accountant

The cost accountant routinely uses a specific set of accounts to store information that is useful for his reports. Here are the accounts, subdivided into accounts that appear in the balance sheet and in the income statement:

Balance sheet accounts:

- *Raw materials inventory*. This account stores the cost of all purchased components and other materials. A vast number of transactions flow through this account, so there may be a temptation to create a number of sub-accounts. If so, confine them to commodity-level accounts, to restrict the number of sub-accounts. Otherwise, the accounts payable staff will have a hard time deciding where to record transactions.
- *Work-in-process inventory*. This account is used in all accounting textbooks to differentiate (as the name implies) inventory items that are still in the production process. However, if the production process is a simple one, there may be so little inventory in the production area that it is not worth differentiating this inventory from raw materials. Also, if the use of this account can be skipped, inventory movement transactions go straight from the raw materials inventory to the finished goods inventory, without any need for an entire additional set of transactions shifting inventory into and out of work-in-process inventory.
- *Finished goods inventory*. As was the case with the raw materials inventory account, a large number of transactions flow through this account. However, try to avoid creating sub-accounts to track individual products, since the number of accounts may be overwhelming. Instead, only create sub-accounts for general categories of finished goods, such as consignment inventory.

Income statement accounts:

- *Revenue*. There may be a need to separately report on the revenues of individual products, and perhaps even at the level of individual geographical regions. If so, it is acceptable to create a large number of accounts for all products, but keep them in a subsidiary ledger. A subsidiary ledger is a ledger containing a detailed sub-set of transactions. The total of the transactions in the subsidiary ledger roll up into the general ledger. Another option is to only create separate accounts for the highest-volume products, and cluster all other sales into a Miscellaneous Product Sales account.

- *Cost of quality.* If a business tracks its cost of quality, it likely accumulates the related costs in a number of accounts, and then compiles the information in a spreadsheet to arrive at its total cost of quality (see the Cost of Quality chapter). An alternative is to create sub-accounts for all of the various costs of quality, and have them roll up into a Cost of Quality account.
- *Direct materials cost.* This is the largest component in the cost of goods sold for most companies. Given its size, it may be necessary to create sub-accounts for such items as supplies or certain commodities.
- *Inventory count variance.* If an organization engages in physical inventory counts, either as large month-end events or ongoing cycle counting (which involves a small number of daily inventory counts), there will be differences between the amounts counted and the amounts recorded in the inventory records. This variance is useful for determining the accuracy of the company's inventory records.
- *Material scrap.* There is some amount of scrap in almost any manufacturing process, but if management wants to drive it down, or if there are instances of abnormal scrap, track it separately. If management wants to focus solely on abnormal scrap, consider only tracking this information in a separate account, and record normal scrap within the cost of goods sold account.
- *Overhead.* Overhead costs are not usually compiled into a single account; instead, there are many overhead accounts, each of which is used to accumulate a specific type of cost (such as supplies, rent, or utilities).
- *Overtime.* If there is significant overtime caused by unusual conditions, such as rush jobs, or by increasing capacity without adding an additional shift, consider tracking the cost separately. If the exact causes of overtime can be pinpointed, management may make changes to cut back on a significant cost.
- *Rework.* If there is a substantial amount of rework involved in a production process, consider breaking out the expense. However, since many manufacturing processes may be involved in rework, collecting the information may be more expensive than the benefit from the resulting information.
- *Rush freight.* There is usually a freight expense account associated with either deliveries to the company or deliveries to customers; but there may also be a significant cost associated with rush deliveries (either in or out) that are caused by poor processes. If this appears to be a large problem, track just the cost of rush freight separately.

There are also a number of accounts that can be used to track variances in a standard costing system. See the Standard Costing chapter for more information.

The accounts described here may be too many for some companies and too few for others; the precise configuration of accounts depends on how a company operates its business, the size of the costs that will be stored in each account, and whether the information is needed on a continual basis, or only occasionally. As always, it is best to keep the number of accounts at a minimum, only adding new accounts when there is a clear need for the associated information.

Backflushing

A traditional cost accounting system collects and records information about the movement of inventory at each step of the flow of goods. This means that a transaction is recorded when goods are received, moved to the production floor, and sent in finished form to the warehouse. This can result in a massive number of transactions, and a correspondingly large number of potential data entry errors. Some organizations have sidestepped all of this transaction volume by instead using backflushing.

Backflushing is the concept of waiting until the manufacture of a product has been completed, and then using a single transaction to record all of the related issuances of inventory from stock that were required to create the product. This approach does not follow the traditional recordation of information as inventory moves through a business. Instead, the completion of goods triggers a single entry that flushes the costs of goods out of raw materials (hence the name of this method) and moves them into finished goods. Thus, backflushing is not a separate cost collection system, but rather a way to eliminate the collection of information.

Backflushing is entirely automated, with a computer handling all transactions. The backflushing formula is:

$$\text{Number of units produced} \times \text{Unit count listed in the bill of materials for each component}$$
$$= \text{Pick total}$$

Backflushing is a theoretically elegant solution to the complexities of cost collection systems, but it is difficult to implement. Backflushing is subject to the following problems:

- *Accurate production count.* The number of finished goods produced is the multiplier in the back flush equation, so an incorrect count will relieve an incorrect amount of components and raw materials from stock.
- *Accurate bill of materials.* The bill of materials contains a complete itemization of the components and raw materials used to construct a product. If the items in the bill are inaccurate, the back flush equation will relieve an incorrect amount of components and raw materials from stock.
- *Accurate scrap reporting.* There will inevitably be unusual amounts of scrap or rework in a production process that are not anticipated in a bill of materials. If these items are not separately deleted from inventory, they will remain in the inventory records, since the backflush equation does not account for them.
- *Rapid production.* Backflushing does not remove items from inventory until after a product has been completed, so the inventory records will remain

incomplete until such time as the backflushing occurs. Thus, a very rapid production cycle time is the best way to keep this interval as short as possible. Under a backflushing system, there is no recorded amount of work-in-process inventory.

Backflushing is not suitable for long production processes, since it takes too long for the inventory records to be reduced after the eventual completion of products. It is also not suitable for the production of customized products, since this would require the creation of a unique bill of materials for each item produced. Further, backflushing does not strictly adhere to the accounting standards, since it makes no provision for the recordation of work-in-process – instead, inventory is assumed to shift directly from raw materials to finished goods.

Other Sources of Cost Information

The discussion thus far has been about the cost accountant collecting his own cost information and storing it either in accounts in the accounting database, or in separate spreadsheets for project-level analyses. There are a number of other locations in a company where additional cost-related information may already be collected. The accountant should be aware of these additional sources of information:

- *Contracts*. The legal department may summarize all outstanding contracts in a database that describes the key dates and terms of each contract, as well as the dates when any pricing changes take effect. This information is especially useful for budgeting when purchase costs are scheduled to change.
- *Engineering*. The engineering department maintains drawings of all products, as well as their bills of material. Use this information to estimate where common parts can be used across multiple designs, as well as to assist in a target costing project (see the Target Costing chapter). The department may also maintain a project tracking system, which is useful for determining when milestone review dates are scheduled for new products.
- *Maintenance*. The maintenance department should have a database that tracks the maintenance intervals of all manufacturing equipment, as well as the cost of any repairs and maintenance. This is useful for evaluating when a machine is due for replacement.
- *Materials management*. The database operated by the materials management department is the "mother lode" for the cost accountant, since it contains a vast amount of information pertaining to cost issues, such as the tracking of inventory, scrap, rework, and production. Some information from the system will likely find its way into almost any cost accounting analysis.
- *Payroll*. The payroll department usually maintains a comprehensive listing of pay rates by employee, overtime payments, shift differentials (which is the incremental payment per hour that is paid in exchange for that person working a late shift), payroll taxes, and so on. This information is very useful for determining the full cost of labor.

A company may have installed an enterprise resources planning (ERP) system, which is a single, massive computer system that integrates all of a company's information needs. If so, most or all of the above systems may be accessible within various modules of the ERP system.

It is not at all uncommon for the cost accountant to begin a research project in the accounting system, and then drill down through various levels of information until he must switch to a system maintained by another department, and continue his research on the other system.

It is also possible that a company has not shifted information into any electronic database at all. It may have concluded that some items of information are so rarely accessed that it is not cost-effective to convert them into a database, or that the information is too complex for employees to easily enter into the computer system. Here are some of the documents that it may be necessary to research on paper:

- *Bill of materials*. This is an itemization of the contents of a product. It is increasingly included in electronic databases, but expect to see it on electronic spreadsheets in companies that only have a few products. It is very useful for compiling the cost of a product.

- *Job summaries*. This is a detailed accounting of all costs incurred on a job, including the materials and labor. This information is needed to investigate why the cost of a job was higher or lower than expected. Though commonly stored in a database in larger companies, this information may be tracked manually in smaller ones.

- *Labor routings*. This lists the amount of labor needed to manufacture a product, itemized by work center. It represents the standard cost of labor for a product, so it is used as a baseline for tracking down labor variances.

- *Machine maintenance summary*. This is a historical record of what maintenance activities were performed on each machine, the maintenance time required, and the labor and materials used during these maintenance operations. It may also include notes about impending breakdowns. This information is useful for compiling costs by machine (see the Activity-Based Costing chapter), as well as for predicting when to replace a machine.

- *Rework sheet*. This is a form that is begun by the quality assurance staff when they remove a product from the production process for rework, and to which the production staff adds notations regarding the rework activities performed to bring the product up to a sellable condition. The sheet is very useful for compiling the cost of rework. This is one of the least automated forms.

- *Scrap notification*. This is a form that the production staff updates whenever they remove scrap from the production process, and is a good indicator of the scale of scrap levels. There is considerable inconsistency in how well employees fill out this form, so it tends to be incomplete.

- *Time cards*. This is a form on which employees list their hours worked, and possibly the jobs or other activities that they have worked on. This is extremely useful for tracking down labor cost variances, or the total labor cost of various activities.

Of the documents noted here, machine maintenance summaries, rework sheets, and scrap notifications are the ones most rarely included in a computer database, so expect to deal with paper-based information when researching these topics.

Summary

The subject of cost collection systems is an important one for the cost accountant, because there are many types of collection options from which to choose, some types of data are more expensive than others to collect, and there are a broad range of cost-benefit situations associated with each option. The situation is further complicated by whether there is a need to collect data for just a short-term project, or whether a more robust, long-term cost collection system is required. There are some situations where it is more cost-effective to record information on paper, rather than in a computer database.

The chart of accounts should only contain accounts in which cost information will be stored for many accounting periods. Otherwise, separately track the information in an electronic spreadsheet for individual projects. By doing so, the general ledger is not cluttered with an inordinate number of accounts that are only briefly used.

Chapter 18
Cost Variability

Introduction

Some costs may appear to be fixed, but *all* costs are variable outside of certain limits. Since all costs vary, it is useful to understand their behavior in order to construct proper analyses. This chapter explores the variety of situations in which costs vary, with particular attention to whether labor costs are really variable, how purchased component costs vary with volume, whether costs actually vary at the batch level, and how costs vary over time.

Related Podcast Episode: Episode 117 of the Accounting Best Practices Podcast discusses cost variability. It is available at: **accountingtools.com/podcasts** or **iTunes**

Mixed Costs

A mixed cost is a cost that contains both a fixed component and a variable component. As the level of usage of a mixed cost item increases, the fixed component of the cost will not change, while the variable component will increase. The formula for this relationship is:

$$Y = a + bx$$

The components of the formula are:

Y = Total cost
a = Total fixed cost
b = Variable cost per unit of activity
x = Number of units of activity

For example, if a company owns a building, the total cost of that building in a year is a mixed cost. The depreciation associated with the asset is a fixed cost, since it does not vary from year to year, while the utilities expense will vary depending upon the company's usage of the building. The fixed cost of the building is $100,000 per year, while the variable cost of utilities is $250 per occupant. If the building contains 100 occupants, the mixed cost calculation is:

$125,000 Total cost = $100,000 Fixed cost + ($250/occupant × 100 occupants)

EXAMPLE

Blitz Communications has a broadband contract with the local cable company, which it pays $500 per month for the first 500 gigabytes of usage per month, after which the price increases by $1 per gigabyte used. The following table shows the mixed cost nature of the situation, where there is a baseline fixed cost, above which the cost increases at the same pace as usage:

Gigabyte Usage	Variable Cost	Fixed Cost	Total Cost
500	$0	$500	$500
600	100	500	600
700	200	500	700
800	300	500	800
900	400	500	900

Mixed costs are common, since many departments have a certain amount of baseline fixed costs in order to support any activities at all, and also incur variable costs to provide varying quantities of service above the baseline level of support. Thus, the cost structure of an entire department can be said to be a mixed cost.

A common question that the cost accountant deals with is how much a product costs. The quickest route to an answer is to extract the cost from a product's bill of materials. Here is an example of a typical bill of materials (for a desk phone):

Component	Quantity	Cost/Each	Total Cost
Base	1	$2.50	$2.50
Keypad	1	0.45	0.45
Microphone	1	0.65	0.65
Cord	1	0.80	0.80
Shell	1	3.75	3.75
Speaker	1	1.15	1.15
Overhead	--	4.20	4.20
			$13.50

The sample bill of materials has a total cost of $13.50, and the accountant may be tempted to answer any inquiries with that number. However, the bill is essentially a mixed cost, because the first six components are completely variable, while the seventh item (overhead) is fixed.

How fixed is the overhead cost listed in the bill of materials? Let us suppose that the overhead is comprised of costs related to the production line on which the phone is built, the costs traceable to the production line are $42,000 per month, and the line manufactures 1,000 phones per month. If the production line manufactures one less unit per month, it will still incur $42,000 of costs. Thus, over the indicated time span, the overhead cost assigned to the phone is entirely fixed.

Because of the mixed nature of the costs ascribed to the phone, it would be better to inform users that the totally variable cost of the phone is $9.30, and that there is an additional fixed overhead cost of $4.20 per unit. If the user of this information needs it to develop a price for a one-time pricing situation, it is much more valuable to know about the variable cost component, and develop a price based on it, rather than on the full cost of the product.

Separating out mixed costs is only one of the issues we should consider when addressing cost variability. In particular, the cost of overhead shown in the preceding example can be broken down further, as we will see in the next section.

Labor-Based Fixed Costs

The cost of labor used to manufacture goods is described as "direct labor," but in fact it behaves less like a variable cost and more like a fixed cost. The true test of a variable cost is whether it changes in direct proportion to the underlying activity (such as the production of one incremental unit). Direct labor rarely behaves in this fashion, and usually only to the extent of any piece rate bonus payments made, which is a relatively rare form of payment. Piece rate pay is when an employee is paid a specific amount for each unit of production completed.

In a normal production environment, approximately the same number of direct labor employees are working every day, even if the amount of production varies somewhat. The number of workers will certainty shift over time as the production manager adjusts to the vagaries of the production schedule, but these changes are usually over a longer period than the cycle time needed to manufacture a product. Thus, there is no direct link between the production of a single unit and the labor used to create it.

Managers strongly prefer to avoid laying off production employees, even in the face of declining production. Here are several reasons why they prefer to avoid layoffs:

1. *Legal restrictions.* Some countries impose restrictions on large layoffs, requiring a notification period and sometimes large severance payments.
2. *Skills.* Employees usually have significant skill sets, and a company would have to train new employees later, when production ramps up again.
3. *Unemployment taxes.* The unemployment tax that companies pay will increase if they lay off a large number of employees.
4. *Unions.* There may be a collective bargaining agreement that restricts the company's ability to lay off workers, and which may also make it reluctant to hire more employees.

Thus, direct labor is really a fixed cost when considered in relation to the cost of a single unit of production.

Let's return to the bill of materials for the desk phone. A bill usually includes a line item for the cost of direct labor, so we will show it again with that item added:

Component	Unit Type	Quantity	Cost/Each	Total Cost
Base	Each	1	$2.50	$2.50
Keypad	Each	1	0.45	0.45
Microphone	Each	1	0.65	0.65
Cord	Each	1	0.80	0.80
Shell	Each	1	3.75	3.75
Speaker	Each	1	1.15	1.15
Direct labor	Hour	0.25	15.00	3.75
Overhead	--	--	4.20	4.20
				$17.25

The bill of materials now contains two fixed costs, which are direct labor and overhead. These two costs together comprise 46% of the total cost of the product in the example, which is quite substantial. Given this cost structure, it would be best to respond to any inquiries about the cost of the phone with a clear differentiation of the two types of costs. For short-term pricing decisions in particular, management needs to know that the variable cost of the phone is only $9.30 and not the full cost of $17.25.

Costs Based on Purchase Quantities

The cost of many purchased components vary considerably, based on the quantities in which they are purchased. For example, if a widget is bought in a standard supplier's economy pack of 100 units, the supplier charges $5.00 per unit. However, if a smaller quantity is needed, which requires the supplier to break its normal packaging and ship the widget in a custom-sized shipping container, the price increases to $15.00. Further, if purchases can be made in massive quantities, such as a truckload, the supplier can reduce the price further, to $3.50 per unit. Thus, the cost of a purchased component can vary substantially, depending upon the quantities in which it is purchased.

EXAMPLE

Blitz Communications is considering developing a new desktop phone. The marketing department estimates that there is a 25% chance that the phone will sell 20,000 units or less, a 60% chance that it will sell between 20,000 and 50,000 units, and a 15% chance that it will sell more than 50,000 units. The phone is to be constructed almost entirely from purchased parts, with final assembly at the Blitz factory. The cost accountant's cost analysis is:

Component	(25% Probability) 20,000 Units or Less	(60% Probability) 20,001 – 50,000 Units	(15% Probability) 50,000+ Units
Price/Unit	$25.00	$25.00	$25.00
Base	3.00	2.50	2.00
Keypad	0.54	0.45	0.36
Microphone	0.78	0.65	0.52
Cord	0.96	0.80	0.64
Shell	4.50	3.75	3.00
Speaker	1.38	1.15	0.92
Direct labor	3.75	3.75	3.75
Overhead	8.00	4.20	2.00
Cost Total	$22.91	$17.25	$13.19
Profit	$2.09	$7.75	$11.81
Profit %	8%	31%	47%

The analysis uses the 20,001 to 50,000 unit range as the baseline. If product sales fall below the 20,001 unit level, the analysis shows that purchased component costs will increase by 20%, and that costs will decrease by 20% if the product sells more than 50,000 units. Further, the amount of fixed overhead costs must be spread over fewer units if the product sells 20,000 units or less, with the reverse effect if it sells more than 50,000 units.

The analysis reveals the problem that management faces; there is a one in four chance that the profit of the product will severely underperform, with a lower probability of outsized profits. Consequently, management needs to decide if it should take the risk of releasing the product into the market, or of setting a lower price to attract more sales, or of reengineering the product to reduce its cost.

Costs Based on Production Batch Sizing

If a company manufactures its own products, it should be aware of how costs vary with the size of production batches.

The historical view of the cost of a production batch is that there is a very significant cost associated with setting up a new production run, and that this cost must be allocated to the components or products created during that production run. For example, it takes $10,000 of staff time to re-set several machines to produce a different product, as well as $2,000 of spoilage from initial faulty test runs of the production line; 2,000 units are run through the production line. Therefore, the $12,000 of setup costs should be allocated to the 2,000 units at an allocation rate of $6 per unit. This basis of allocation is strongly supported under the activity-based costing concept.

But is this allocation warranted? The $10,000 of staff time used in the example was probably for salaried positions that would not have been laid off if the batch setup never occurred – they would just work on something else or be underutilized. Employees experienced in machine setups are a valuable resource, and are rarely laid off. Therefore, is there really a direct link between the effort expended to set up machines for a production batch? No. The only situation where a cost allocation would be warranted is when the setup team is paid a bonus when it completes a setup; in this situation, the cost of the bonus could be allocated to the batch, because the bonus would not have been incurred if the setup had not been completed.

However, the cost of spoilage *is* associated with a specific batch, because that cost would not have been incurred if the batch had not been set up. To continue with the same example, we should allocate the $2,000 of spoilage over the 2,000 units produced, which results in an allocation rate of $1 per unit.

Thus, costs can be linked to the presence of a production batch, but only to the extent that the costs would not have occurred if the batch had never been produced.

Cost Based on Step Costs

Costs can vary whenever they reach a step cost boundary. For example, a production manager finds that his facility can produce a maximum of 3,000 widgets per week if he uses one shift, but that he needs to start a second shift in order to meet any additional demand. When he adds on the shift, the company will have to incur certain additional fixed costs, such as the salary of a supervisor for that shift.

When a company exceeds a step cost boundary and incurs a new step cost, how does this impact the cost of an individual unit of production? For incremental costing decisions, it does nothing at all, since the variable cost of producing a single unit has not changed. It has, however, increased the total overhead cost of the production system, as well as (presumably) the ability of the system to produce more units. The only way to see if a step cost has improved or reduced the ability of a production system to produce a profit is to subject it to constraint analysis, which we deal with in the Constraint Analysis chapter.

For the purposes of the cost variability topic of this chapter, the main consideration for the cost accountant is to point out to management the existence of any impending step costs, their amount, and how they impact the production system. When management becomes aware of an impending step cost, it needs to decide if it has a long-term need for the additional production capacity that the step cost represents, or whether it makes more sense to avoid the step cost by either turning away additional business or outsourcing it.

Time-Based Costs

All costs are variable over the long term. If a company is leasing a warehouse for ten years, the cost of that warehouse is fixed for ten years, but is variable over a period of ten years and one day, when management can elect to not renew the lease.

Further, the company could possibly sub-lease the warehouse, which makes it a variable expense within a few days. It is useful to keep in mind that there are ways to modify or eliminate supposedly immovable costs, either through the passage of time or more innovative solutions.

Some fixed costs are more immovable than others, or at least a company may have more incentive to retain some fixed costs than others. Here is a subdivision of costs that provide a different perspective on the situation, presented in order from the easiest to the most difficult to avoid:

- *Sunk costs*. A sunk cost is a cost that a company has incurred, and which it can no longer recover by any means. Do not consider a sunk cost when making the decision to continue investing in an ongoing project, since the cost cannot be recovered. However, many managers continue investing in projects because of the sheer size of the amounts already invested in the past. They do not want to "lose the investment" by curtailing a project that is proving to not be profitable, so they continue pouring more cash into it. Thus, these costs have already been incurred, but there is a tendency to build upon them with more expenditures in the future.
- *Discretionary costs*. A discretionary cost is a cost or capital expenditure that can be curtailed or even eliminated in the short term without having an immediate impact on short-term profitability. However, a prolonged period of reduction in these costs can have such impacts as reducing the quality of a company's product pipeline, reducing awareness by customers, and increasing machine downtime. Examples of discretionary costs are advertising, equipment maintenance, and research and development.
- *Committed costs*. A committed cost is an investment that a company has already made and cannot recover by any means, as well as obligations already made that the business cannot get out of. For example, if a company buys a machine for $40,000 and also issues a purchase order to pay for a maintenance contract for $2,000 in each of the next three years, all $46,000 is a committed cost, because the company has already bought the machine, and has a legal obligation to pay for the maintenance.

Of the costs noted here, sunk costs have already been incurred and do not need to be incurred again, so one can make a (relatively) easy decision to not let them impact future expenditure decisions. Discretionary costs can be avoided, but the negative impact of doing so tends to build up over time. Finally, committed costs are the most difficult to avoid prior to their normal termination dates.

Most fixed costs that are considered to be fixed in the short term fall into one of these categories. All three are related in some way to the passage of time – sunk costs have already occurred, discretionary costs tend to become more important over time, and committed costs can be avoided once a certain period of time has passed. It is important to realize which category a fixed cost falls into, to more easily determine its true level of variability over time.

Experience-Based Costs

If a company is in a situation where it may ramp up to much larger production volumes, the experience curve will likely take effect. The experience curve is the concept that an organization requires less time or cost to produce a product as the production volume increases. The concept is usually stated as a percentage improvement for every doubling of production volume.

The experience curve works because organizations become more efficient at very high production volumes, partially because the company continually develops new production techniques and procedures, and partially because it can afford to install more expensive automation. Even if the experience curve percentage holds through increasing volumes of production, the cost reductions gradually decline as a percentage of total costs, simply because the total amount of costs from which the percentage is derived also decline.

EXAMPLE

Blitz Communications has begun selling a new office phone model, and initial indications are that it is being received well in the marketplace. Corporate management is wondering if they should reduce the price to spur sales, and asks the cost accountant to create an experience curve analysis of its likely cost at certain volume levels, based on the company's prior experience with other models.

The cost accountant conducts a review of the issue over the past few years, and concludes that the company has a 6% experience curve. He develops the following table of how the experience curve will alter the cost of the product:

Production Volume	Experience Curve %	Cost Per Unit	Incremental Cost Reduction
5,000	6%	$25.00	--
10,000	6%	23.50	$1.50
20,000	6%	22.09	1.41
40,000	6%	20.76	1.33
80,000	6%	19.52	1.24
160,000	6%	18.35	1.17

Management examines the table and concludes that the telephone has the potential to sell in annual volumes of 80,000 units. The product is currently priced at $40, which yields a profit of 37.5%. Management lowers the price to $31, which yields almost the same profit at the $19.52 cost level predicted at an annual unit volume of 80,000.

The example shows that cost reductions caused by the experience curve can be substantial. Consequently, if the subject of a cost analysis may be impacted by the experience curve, be sure to include it in the analysis over the anticipated range of production volumes.

The experience curve effect tends to be less substantial if the production of the item in question is sporadic, since employees need to relearn production processes. The effect is more dramatic if a company continually manufactures a product, since employees can lock in and build upon their prior experience with the product.

The experience curve may be a particularly important cost accounting concept if a company intends to capture large amounts of market share through low pricing. These organizations use the experience curve to make assumptions about how their costs will be lower at higher volume levels, and set their prices based on having production volumes that they have not yet achieved. This results in short-term losses at the initially lower production volumes, and then gradually improving profits as the company ramps up its targeted production volume.

EXAMPLE

Blitz Communications decides to adopt the $31 price point that was described in the preceding example. It is selling 5,000 units of the telephone model when it adopts this price point, and gradually increases its sales over two years until it reaches the target volume of 80,000 units per year. The experience curve estimates derived in the last example prove to be correct, with resulting profits shown in the following table.

Sales Volume	Price Per Unit	Cost Per Unit	Profit Per Unit	Profit Percentage
5,000	$31.00	$25.00	$6.00	19.4%
10,000	31.00	23.50	7.50	24.2%
20,000	31.00	22.09	8.91	28.7%
40,000	31.00	20.76	10.24	33.0%
80,000	31.00	19.52	11.48	37.0%

The table reveals that, because of the cost reductions brought about by the experience curve, Blitz approximately doubles its profit percentage on the new telephone by increasing its production volumes by 16x over the two-year period.

The experience curve can be a powerful tool for an aggressive management team, but competitive responses must also be factored in. Other companies do not take a loss of market share lightly, and so will either lower their product prices as well, or roll out new products that compete more closely with the company's offerings. Consequently, it can be quite difficult to achieve the sales volumes and associated profit improvements shown in the last example. In reality, a company would have to drop its prices further to fend off competitors, and it would also be less likely to reach its targeted sales levels.

Incorporating Cost Variability into Cost Reports

This chapter has shown that precise costs can be difficult to pin down, since they are only fixed within certain ranges. Outside of those ranges, costs can vary wildly. Consequently, when reporting on cost information to management, it is very helpful to include in the report the ranges within which the cost information is valid. Better yet, show the costs that would arise in the adjacent ranges, especially if there is a chance that actual results may fall outside of the target range.

EXAMPLE

Blitz Communications is interested in selling one of its telephones in several other countries through distributor agreements. By doing so, it can increase the production volume of the phone from 25,000 units per year to 100,000. There is a risk that sales will not be that high, since the telephone must pass certification requirements in all of the target countries. Blitz is also exploring further distributor agreements for sales in additional countries. Blitz management assigns a probability of 25% to sales being approximately 50,000 units per year, 50% for sales being 100,000 units, and 25% that sales will reach 200,000 units. The production at the 50,000 through 100,000 unit levels can be accommodated by an existing production line, which will produce this telephone exclusively. Ramping up to 200,000 units will require construction of a new production line. The wholesale price of the product will be $50. The company estimates that the benefits from its experience curve are 6%.

Management asks the cost accountant for an analysis of what the telephone costs will be. He constructs an analysis for all three scenarios, as follows:

	(25% Probability) 50,000 Units	(50% Probability) 100,000 Units	(25% Probability) 200,000 Units
Price per unit	$50.00	$50.00	$50.00
Components	28.00	25.00	22.00
Labor and overhead	8.00	6.00	8.00
Experience factor*	-0.48	-0.70	-1.35
Cost subtotal	35.52	30.30	28.65
Profit	$14.48	$19.70	$21.35
Profit %	29%	39%	43%

* Applied only to the labor and overhead cost.

The component cost of the phone is by far its largest cost component, and this cost declines as production volumes increase, due to volume purchase discounts. The entire overhead and labor cost of the production line is applicable to this analysis, since the line is reserved for production of this specific telephone. The cost of labor and overhead per unit declines to $6.00 at the 100,000 unit level, since these costs are being spread across the maximum number of units that the line can support. The labor and overhead cost increases to $8.00 per unit at the 200,000 unit level, because the cost of a new production line has been added.

In addition, Blitz needs to add sales, administrative, and legal staff to handle the distributors in the other countries. The costs are directly related to this telephone product, since Blitz is setting up the distributors solely to handle it. These additional costs start at $400,000 for the initial 50,000 units of production, double at the 100,000 unit level, and double again at the 200,000 unit level. These additional costs are shown in the following table, along with an analysis of the profits that can be generated at the various volume levels.

	(25% Probability) 50,000 Units	(50% Probability) 100,000 Units	(25% Probability) 200,000 Units
Gross margin per unit	$14.48	$19.70	$21.35
Units sold	50,000	100,000	200,000
Total gross margin	$724,000	$1,970,000	$4,270,000
Administration costs	400,000	800,000	1,600,000
Profit	$324,000	$1,170,000	$2,670,000

The analysis reveals that this is an extremely worthwhile endeavor, where the projected reduction in the purchase prices of components drive considerable profit improvements at the highest volume levels. Based on this information, management decides on an all-out effort to increase international sales of the product.

Giving management the extra information noted in the preceding exhibit is extremely helpful, but it also requires a great deal of extra cost accounting time to complete. Consequently, it is not necessary to include the extra range of information if the cost analysis is a routine one where actual results are likely to fall within the specified range. The accountant can save the effort of constructing a more comprehensive analysis for those situations where there is a broad range of possible outcomes, and the monetary effects on the company from those outcomes can be severe.

The cost accountant cannot be expected to know about the uses to which a cost analysis will be put, so it helps to ask a few probing questions about analysis requests, such as:

Questions	Comments
How do you plan to use this information?	General question to get an overview of the topic.
What production volumes are expected?	Determine the probability that the most likely and high/low volumes will be reached.
What time period does this cover?	If the project covers a short time period, the accountant can probably use direct costs, but will need to include full costs for a longer-term situation. If the time period is lengthy, this may also trigger contractually-mandated changes in cost as of specific future dates.
Will this change throughput?	If the project impacts the bottleneck operation, be sure to note the impact on throughput in the report.
Will this change operating expenses?	See if there will be any specific cost reductions or increases. In particular, inquire about any step costs that may be triggered.

The answers to these questions will assist in determining the scope of the topic, in order to build cost variability into the report.

Summary

This chapter has presented a variety of issues that the cost accountant needs to be aware of when determining the cost of a product, service or activity. In short, costs will vary outside of a limited range, so be sure of all assumptions before completing a cost analysis. There may be a reasonable chance that the actual result will fall outside of the range for which cost information is being provided; if so, include estimates of what might happen to costs in the less probable areas, so that management will have a comprehensive understanding of the most likely range of outcomes.

A related subject is constraint analysis, which holds that a company is a single production system, and that the only issue that matters is maximizing the throughput (sales minus totally variable costs) passing through the bottleneck operation. This concept is addressed in the Constraint Analysis chapter. Being aware of the two concepts of cost variability and constraint analysis allows the accountant to have an excellent understanding of how a company creates a profit, and which actions or events will change that profit.

Chapter 19
Cost of Quality

Introduction

A key sales advantage for any company is to provide products to their customers with a noticeably higher level of quality than those offered by competitors, especially if this difference can yield a higher price. In addition, by putting in the systems needed to assure higher quality, a company will find that it is actually *less* expensive to do business, since a number of administrative, warranty, and rework costs are reduced. This chapter explores the types of quality, and how to track and report on the costs impacted by quality.

Types of Quality

What is product quality? A customer perceives a product as having a high level of quality if it conforms to his expectations. Thus, high quality is really just making sure that a product does what a customer expects it to do.

EXAMPLE

Rapunzel Hair Products has designed a comb made of titanium, and markets it as a light weight product for the frequent traveler. Not only is the comb made of titanium, but it is also stamped with the world-famous RHR logo, and has a special low-friction coating that keeps hair tangles from being trapped in the comb. It sells for $20, and costs $16 to manufacture. The margin is unacceptably low, so the product manager is searching for ways to reduce the cost.

He surveys comb owners, and finds that their perception of quality is not that the comb is made of titanium, but simply that it is light weight. After some research, the product manager finds that titanium is twice as strong as aluminum, but is 60% heavier than that metal. Product testing reveals that aluminum is sufficiently strong to prevent bending. Aluminum is also ten times less expensive than titanium.

Consequently, Rapunzel changes the composition of the comb to an all aluminum version that it can produce (with some extra heat tempering steps) for just $4. Since the weight of the product has declined, customers perceive the comb to have a higher quality level than the titanium version.

Based on this definition, quality is *not* having the highest possible standards for creating the ultimate product. Thus, if management insists on creating a mahogany interior for a car's glove box when the customer only wants it to be big enough to store maps, then it has just gone to considerable expense to create something that a customer does not define as being of high quality.

This view of quality means that a company can eliminate any costs that customers have no quality perceptions about. The cost reduction can impact a great many areas. For example, it may be perfectly acceptable to use lower-quality or thinner materials, or to allow blemishes in areas where customers cannot see them, or to allow production at a lower tolerance level than is currently the case (which eliminates some rework costs).

There are two types of quality that a company should be concerned about, one of which originates in the engineering department, while the other is the responsibility of the entire organization. They are:

- *Quality of design.* This is the ability of a company to design a product that conforms to the quality expectations of a customer. In other words, the quality that customers expect is designed into the product. This type of quality requires a considerable amount of interpretation of what engineers think customers want, and how these wishes are integrated into the final product design. If quality is not designed into the basic structure of a product, there is no way to improve the quality situation later, short of replacing the product with a new version.
- *Quality of conformance.* This is the ability of a company to produce a product that conforms to the original product design. This type of quality is not just the responsibility of the production department; the purchasing staff has to acquire the correct materials, the shipping department must deliver it without damage, and the marketing department must communicate the attributes of the product that matter most to customers.

EXAMPLE

Rapunzel Hair Products wants to create a hair straightener for women who travel frequently. A survey of such travelers reveals that their views of quality for such a product encompass light weight, the ability to operate at different voltages, a variable temperature setting, and a power cord that will not break or pull away from the unit.

Of these four quality issues, three are entirely design issues – the engineering staff must design for low weight, a variable voltage capability, and a variable temperature setting. Only one of the quality issues is entirely a quality of conformance issue, which is the power cord. The purchasing department must obtain a sufficiently robust power cord to ensure that it will not break.

The quality of conformance does have a secondary role in ensuring the quality of this product, however. The purchasing staff must be sure to acquire power transformers and temperature rheostats that will continue to work properly for a long period of rough handling.

Costs Impacted by Quality

There are several types of costs that are impacted by the quality of a product. They are:

- *Prevention costs*. These are costs incurred to avoid product failures. These costs include production procedure development, staff training, product testing, preventive maintenance on the machinery used to create products, and supplier qualification assessments.
- *Appraisal costs*. These are the costs of inspection needed to reduce the risk of sending defective products to customers. These costs include supplier component testing, quality control product testing, process analysis, and the cost of any testing equipment.
- *Internal failure costs*. These are the costs associated with defective products that are uncovered prior to delivery to customers. These costs include re-work of the defective products, additional testing of the reworked products, scrap, purchasing replacement parts, and the lost profit on products that must be sold as seconds.
- *External failure costs*. These are the costs associated with defective products that are uncovered subsequent to delivery to customers. These costs include lost revenue from customers who will not buy from the company again, the processing of returned goods, administering warranty claims, field service costs, liability lawsuits, and possibly even a comprehensive product recall.

It is more cost-effective to pay for cost improvements in-house, rather than waiting for customers to discover defects. The primary reason is that customers are much less likely to buy from the company again if they discover defects, which can make external failure costs more expensive than all of the other costs combined.

Reporting on the Cost of Quality

It is cost-prohibitive to create a cost of quality tracking system that is absolutely comprehensive. Such a system would require a massive amount of data collection, and may very well offset any benefits to be gained from the system. Instead, eliminate any costs that are inordinately difficult to measure, assess what the resources are for measuring the remaining costs, and finally discuss with management which specific types of quality-related costs they wish to monitor. The result will likely be a cost collection system that varies over time, redirecting its focus to different costs as management gradually tackles and improves upon each one.

One way to aggregate cost of quality information is to create new accounts for them in the chart of accounts (see the Cost Collection Systems chapter). However, it may be difficult for the accounting staff to discern which costs to assign to these accounts, so in many cases it may make more sense to track the costs on a project basis only; by doing so, one can undertake a small collection effort and store the information in an electronic spreadsheet. Afterwards, if the results of the project indicate that there can be long-term cost reductions to be gained from continual cost collection efforts, it may be worth investigating the use of general ledger accounts in which to store this information.

Once the cost of quality information has been collected, format it into a report structure that presents the maximum amount of actionable information to management. The following example uses a format that aggregates costs into the four types of quality costs already described – prevention, appraisal, internal failure, and external failure. This format not only shows management where most of its quality costs lie (clearly in the external failure cost area), but also the sub-categories of expenses from which these costs are originating. This report format tells management roughly where to look if it wants to reduce its cost of quality.

EXAMPLE

The president of Rapunzel Hair Products commissions a cost of quality analysis to determine where the company incurred the bulk of its quality-related costs over the past three-month period. Her intent is to use the results of this study to focus more closely on reducing costs in the areas where most costs are incurred. The results are:

Cost Type / Cost Line Item	Cost Line Item Results	Summary Totals
Prevention Cost Category		
Production procedure development	$6,500	
Staff training	5,000	
Product testing	2,000	
Preventive maintenance	12,000	
Supplier qualification assessments	19,000	
		$44,500
Appraisal Cost Category		
Supplier component testing	$4,200	
Quality control product testing	5,000	
Process analysis	7,100	
Testing equipment	3,000	
		$19,300
Internal Failure Cost Category		
Rework of defective products	$23,000	
Testing of reworked products	3,800	
Purchasing replacement parts	1,900	
Lost profit on products sold as seconds	25,000	
		$53,700

Cost Type / Cost Line Item	Cost Line Item Results	Summary Totals
External Failure Cost Category		
Processing of returned goods	$61,000	
Administering warranty claims	23,000	
Field service costs	5,900	
		$89,900
Total		$207,400

The report reveals that internal and external failure costs comprise 69% of the company's $207,400 total cost of quality, with the processing of returned goods being by far the largest cost incurred.

This report can also be converted into a percentage of sales format, which is useful if sales are varying a great deal over the reporting timeline. The cost of quality varies with sales volume, so if sales are fluctuating, only a percentage of sales format will show if a cost of quality reduction campaign is really working.

The preceding cost of quality report tells management what types of general quality costs a company is incurring, but it does nothing to inform them about where specific quality problems are arising. Locating such information requires detailed investigative work by the cost accountant. It may be necessary to conduct a separate root cause analysis for each problem encountered, such as the one in the following example. This report tells management what is causing a quality cost, and the proportion of total incidents. They use this report to take immediate action steps. Thus, the report in the preceding example is needed to give them a general view of where quality costs occur, and the root cause analysis to create a cost reduction action.

EXAMPLE

The president of Rapunzel Hair products reviews the cost of quality report, and decides that the rework of defective products (which costs $23,000) is the most troubling. She asks the cost accountant to delve further into this specific area, and create a root cause analysis report.

He investigates the situation, targeting the reasons why products become defective. He finds that there is roughly a 50/50 split between problems arising from purchased goods and from goods manufactured in Rapunzel's own facilities. From this analysis, he investigates further and then generates the following report:

Proportion of Incidents	Root Cause	Recommendation
Purchased Goods Issues		
39%	Performance specifications were incorrect	Tighten the tolerances on purchased product specifications (may result in cost increase)
32%	Damaged in Rapunzel warehouse	Change putaway and picking procedures. Also require suppliers to ship in more robust packaging
18%	Supplier quality too low	Institute supplier certification system and prepare to change suppliers
11%	Other issues not investigated	
100%		
Manufactured Goods Issues		
41%	Inferior quality raw materials	Purchase higher grade resin (may result in cost increase)
29%	Scratches incurred during internal moves	Replace move containers with padded versions
13%	Machine tolerances incorrect	Revise machine setup procedures
17%	Other issues not investigated	
100%		

The report indicates that there will be a cost associated with several of the proposed fixes, which will require a management decision. Another major cause of problems is the packaging and handling of products, which will likely require further analysis to determine precise causes.

The preceding report gives management detailed information that it can act on, or which at least takes it well down the path of finding the root cause of a quality problem.

Summary

The cost of quality is spread throughout a company – there are related costs everywhere, including administration, engineering, production, and customer service. Since the cost of quality is so pervasive, it is clearly an excellent source of potential profits. If management can improve product and service quality, then related costs decline throughout the organization.

Given the massive potential impact on profits, one should be well aware of the types of quality-related costs, make an attempt at constructing at least a rudimentary cost of quality data collection and reporting system, and make periodic efforts to educate management about how quality impacts profits. If management takes action, an organization could experience a significant profit boost.

Glossary

A

Absorption costing. A methodology under which all fixed and variable manufacturing costs are assigned to products, while all non-manufacturing costs are charged to expense in the current period.

Activity driver. The most significant cause of an activity. An example of an activity driver is the number of customer orders, which is used to allocate order entry costs to individual customers. A defensible activity driver is one where there is a strong causal relationship between the cost pool and the activity. Thus, if the activity does not occur, the cost in the related cost pool is not incurred.

Allocation base. The basis upon which an entity allocates its overhead costs. It takes the form of a quantity, such as machine hours used, kilowatt hours consumed, or square footage occupied. The allocation base should be a cause, or driver, of the cost being allocated. A good indicator that an allocation base is appropriate is when changes in the allocation base roughly correspond to changes in the actual cost. Thus, if machine usage declines, so too should the actual cost incurred to operate the machine.

B

Backflushing. The counting of finished goods and then breaking down the components of those finished goods, based on bills of material, to determine what raw materials were used in their manufacture. This is a way to record the transfer of raw materials to finished goods after production has taken place.

Bill of materials. The record of materials used to construct a product. It can include raw materials, sub-assemblies, and supplies. It is used to calculate the cost of a product, as well as to order parts from suppliers.

C

Capacity. The maximum sustainable rate of output that an operation can achieve.

Capital budgeting. A series of analysis steps followed to justify the decision to purchase an asset, usually including an analysis of the costs, related benefits, and impact on capacity levels of the prospective purchase.

Capital expenditure. A payment to acquire or upgrade an asset. It is recorded as an asset and depreciated it over its useful life, rather than charging it immediately to expense.

Causal relationship. A situation where one event is brought about by another. Thus, an activity causes specific changes elsewhere.

Collateral. An asset that a borrower has pledged as security for a loan. The lender has the legal right to seize and sell the asset if the borrower is unable to pay back the loan by an agreed date.

Contribution margin. A product's price minus its variable costs, resulting in the incremental profit earned for each unit sold.

Cost. The expenditure required to create and sell products and services, or to acquire assets. When sold or consumed, a cost is charged to expense. Thus, if a firm pays $10,000 for parts that it will eventually assemble into a product, the $10,000 is part of the cost of the product, but this amount is not charged to expense until the product has been sold.

Cost object. Any item for which costs are being separately measured. Examples of cost objects are products, services, departments, machining operations, processes, suppliers, customers, distribution channels, and geographic regions.

Cost pool. A grouping of individual costs, typically by department or service center. Cost allocations are then made from the cost pool. For example, the cost of a maintenance department is accumulated in a cost pool and then allocated to those departments using its services.

Cycle counting. The process of counting a small proportion of the total inventory on a daily basis, and not only correcting any errors found, but also investigating the underlying reasons why the errors occurred. Cycle counts can address all types of inventory uniformly, or counts can be skewed to address higher-value or higher-usage items more frequently.

D

Direct cost. A cost that can be clearly associated with specific activities or products. Examples of direct costs are direct materials and direct labor.

Discount rate. The interest rate used to discount a stream of future cash flows to their present value. Depending upon the application, typical rates used as the discount rate are a firm's cost of capital or the current market rate.

E

Electronic data interchange. The electronic transfer of business transactions between companies, using a standardized set of electronic forms.

F

Fair value hedge. A hedge of the exposure to changes in the fair value of an asset or liability that are attributable to a specific risk.

Full cost. The aggregation of all costs associated with a product or other item, so that one can see the total cost of all materials, labor, and overhead that relate to that item.

G

General ledger. The master set of accounts that summarize all financial transactions in a business. There may also be a subsidiary set of more detailed ledgers that summarize into the general ledger.

Gross margin. Revenues less the cost of goods sold. The gross margin reveals the amount that an entity earns from the sale of its products and services, before the deduction of any selling and administrative expenses.

H

Horizontal analysis. The comparison of the trend line of historical financial information over a series of reporting periods. It can be used to spot unusual spikes or dips in the reported results in the income statement, balance sheet, and statement of cash flows.

I

Incremental cost. The extra cost associated with manufacturing one additional unit of production.

Item master. A record that lists the name, description, unit of measure, weight, dimensions, ordering quantity, and other key information for a component part.

J

Joint cost. A cost which benefits more than one product, and for which it may not be possible to separate its contribution to each product.

K

Kaizen costing. The process of continual cost reduction that occurs after a product design has been completed and is now in production. Cost reduction techniques can include working with suppliers to reduce the costs in their processes, or implementing less costly re-designs of the product, or reducing waste costs.

L

Labor routing. A document showing the work steps required to complete the manufacture of a product, and includes the time required for each work step.

M

Manufacturing overhead. All of the costs of a manufacturing facility, other than those costs that are directly traceable to products. It is also known as factory overhead.

Materials review board (MRB). A group that is responsible for periodically reviewing the inventory and deciding whether any items should be designated as obsolete and disposed of. The MRB is composed of representatives from every department having any interaction with inventory issues – accounting, engineering, logistics, and production.

O

Overhead. Those costs required to run a business, but which cannot be directly attributed to any specific business activity, product, or service. Thus, overhead costs do not directly lead to the generation of profits. Overhead is still necessary, since it provides critical support for the generation of profit-making activities.

Overhead absorbed. Manufacturing overhead that has been applied to products or other cost objects. Overhead is *overabsorbed* when the amount allocated to a product or other cost object is higher than the actual amount of overhead, while the amount is *underabsorbed* when the amount allocated is lower than the actual amount of overhead.

Overhead allocation. Those costs that cannot be directly attributed to the costs of production or of services provided. Allocation of overhead is the process of assigning overhead costs to products or services based on some relevant measure of activity.

P

Period cost. A cost that is charged to expense in the period in which it is incurred, because the cost was consumed during that period.

Perpetual inventory system. A system that allows an organization to continually update its inventory records to account for additions to and subtractions from inventory for such activities as received inventory items, goods picked from stock, and items picked from inventory for use in the production process. This results in an accurate ending inventory balance at all times.

Piece rate pay. When an employee is paid a specific amount for each unit of production completed.

Piece rate plan. A compensation system under which employees are paid for the specific number of units produced. It is frequently combined with a base-level wage, so the base-level wage is a fixed cost to the employer, and the piece rate plan is a variable cost.

R

Relevant cost. A cost that relates to a specific management decision, and which will change in the future as a result of that decision.

S

Shift differential. The incremental payment per hour that is paid to an employee in exchange for that person working a late shift.

Spoilage. The production of goods that cannot be sold at normal prices, due to damage. Normal spoilage is the amount of damage that naturally arises during a production process, while abnormal spoilage exceeds the normal or expected rate of spoilage.

Step cost. A fixed cost that does not change within a specific range of utilization levels. Once utilization shifts outside of that range, additional costs must be incurred (for increased utilization levels) or can be eliminated (for decreased utilization levels).

Subsidiary ledger. A ledger containing all of a detailed sub-set of transactions. The total of the transactions in the subsidiary ledger roll up into the general ledger. For example, a subsidiary ledger may contain all accounts receivable, accounts payable, or fixed asset transactions.

Sunk cost. An expenditure made in a prior period, which will not be affected by any current or future decisions.

T

Target costing. The analysis of a proposed new product to determine in advance how much it should cost, and to monitor subsequent design work to see if the product can be produced for the target cost, while still generating a reasonable profit at a predetermined price point.

Throughput. Revenue minus totally variable expenses. For a product, throughput is generally considered to be its selling price minus the cost of its materials.

V

Variable cost. A cost that varies in relation to changes in production volume. Direct materials are a variable cost. Direct labor may not be a variable cost if labor is not added to or subtracted from the production process as production volumes change. Overhead is not a variable cost.

W

Work-in-process inventory. Inventory that has been partially converted through the production process, but for which additional work must be completed before it can be recorded as finished goods inventory.

Working capital. The amount of an entity's current assets minus its current liabilities, which is considered to be a prime measure of its liquidity. The key components of working capital are cash, accounts receivable, inventory, and accounts payable.

Index

244

Made in the USA
San Bernardino, CA
29 January 2017